Pro iPhone Development with SwiftUI

Design and Manage Top-Quality Apps

Fourth Edition

Wallace Wang

Apress®

Pro iPhone Development with SwiftUI: Design and Manage Top-Quality Apps

Wallace Wang
San Diego, CA, USA

ISBN-13 (pbk): 978-1-4842-9543-4 ISBN-13 (electronic): 978-1-4842-9544-1
https://doi.org/10.1007/978-1-4842-9544-1

Managing Director, Apress Media LLC: Welmoed Spahr
Acquisitions Editor: Miriam Haidara
Development Editor: James Markham
Coordinating Editor: Jessica Vakili

Distributed to the book trade worldwide by Springer Science+Business Media New York, 1 NY Plaza, New York, NY 10004. Phone 1-800-SPRINGER, fax (201) 348-4505, e-mail orders-ny@springer-sbm.com, or visit www.springeronline.com. Apress Media, LLC is a California LLC and the sole member (owner) is Springer Science + Business Media Finance Inc (SSBM Finance Inc). SSBM Finance Inc is a **Delaware** corporation.

For information on translations, please e-mail booktranslations@springernature.com; for reprint, paperback, or audio rights, please e-mail bookpermissions@springernature.com.

Apress titles may be purchased in bulk for academic, corporate, or promotional use. eBook versions and licenses are also available for most titles. For more information, reference our Print and eBook Bulk Sales web page at http://www.apress.com/bulk-sales.

Any source code or other supplementary material referenced by the author in this book is available to readers on the Github repository: https://github.com/Apress/Pro-iPhone-Development-with-SwiftUI. For more detailed information, please visit http://www.apress.com/source-code.

Printed on acid-free paper

Table of Contents

About the Author

Wallace Wang is a former Windows enthusiast who took one look at Vista and realized that the future of computing belonged to the Mac. He's written more than 40 computer books, including *Microsoft Office for Dummies*, *Beginning Programming for Dummies*, *Steal This Computer Book*, *Beginning ARKit for iPhone and iPad*, and *Beginning iPhone Development with SwiftUI*. He also wrote a book on game design called *The Structure of Game Design*, which explains how to create all types of games including board, card, and video games. In addition to programming the Mac and iPhone/iPad, he also performs stand-up comedy, having appeared on A&E's *An Evening at the Improv* and having performed in Las Vegas at the Riviera Comedy Club at the Riviera Hotel and Casino. When he's not writing computer books or performing stand-up comedy, he enjoys blogging about screenwriting at his site, The 15 Minute Movie Method (https://15minutemoviemethod.com), where he shares screenwriting tips with other aspiring screenwriters who all share the goal of breaking into Hollywood.

About the Technical Reviewer

Massimo Nardone has more than 22 years of experience in security, web and mobile development, cloud, and IT architecture. His true IT passions are security and Android.

He has been programming and teaching how to program with Android, Perl, PHP, Java, VB, Python, C/C++, and MySQL for more than 20 years.

Massimo also holds a master of science degree in computing science from the University of Salerno, Italy.

He has worked as a project manager, software engineer, research engineer, chief security architect, information security manager, PCI/SCADA auditor, and senior lead IT security/cloud/SCADA architect for many years.

His technical skills include security, Android, cloud, Java, MySQL, Drupal, Cobol, Perl, web and mobile development, MongoDB, D3, Joomla, Couchbase, C/C++, WebGL, Python, Pro Rails, Django CMS, Jekyll, Scratch, etc.

He currently works as Chief Information Security Officer (CISO) for Cargotec Oyj.

He worked as visiting lecturer and supervisor for exercises at the Networking Laboratory of the Helsinki University of Technology (Aalto University). He holds four international patents (PKI, SIP, SAML, and Proxy areas).

CHAPTER 1

Organizing Code

Programs are rewritten and modified far more often than they are ever created. That means most of the time developers must change and modify existing code either written by someone else or written by you sometime in the past. Since you may be writing code that you or someone else will eventually modify in the future, you should organize your code to make it easy to understand.

While every developer has their own programming style and no two programmers will write the exact same code, programming involves writing code that works and writing code that's easy to read.

Writing code that works is hard. Unfortunately, once developers get their code to work, they rarely clean it up and optimize it. The end result is a confusing mix of code that works but isn't easy to understand. To modify that code, someone has to decipher how it works and then rewrite that code to make it cleaner to read while still working as well as the original code. Since this takes time and doesn't add any new features, it's often ignored.

Since few developers want to take time to clean up their code after they get it to work, it's best to get in the habit of writing clear, understandable code right from the start. That involves several tasks:

- Writing code in a consistent and understandable style

- Making the logic of your code clear so anyone reading it later can easily understand how it works

- Organizing code to make it easy to modify later

When writing code, focus on clarity and readability. It's possible to write code that works but is hard to understand. That makes modifying that code difficult. Many times, it can be easier to rewrite code from scratch rather than waste time trying to figure out how it works.

© Wallace Wang 2023
W. Wang, *Pro iPhone Development with SwiftUI*, https://doi.org/10.1007/978-1-4842-9544-1_1

Swift lets you choose any name for variables and constants. However, it's a good idea to use descriptive names to help you understand what type of data that variable or constant can hold. Consider the following variable names:

```
var x: Int = 8
var dgie83: Double = 13.48
var FLdkjep: String = "Right"
```

While valid, these names don't make it clear what type of data they hold. A far better solution is to use descriptive names like this:

```
var age: Int = 8
var weight: Double = 13.48
var direction: String = "Right"
```

Single word variable names can be fine, but you may want to use multiple words to make a variable or constant name even more descriptive. When combining multiple words to form a variable or constant name, Swift programmers commonly use camelCase, which uses lowercase letters for the first word and an uppercase letter for the first letter of each succeeding word like this:

```
var ageOfPet: Int = 8
var weightInKilograms: Double = 13.48
var directionToTurn: String = "Right"
```

Just as variable and constant names can be too short, they can also be too long. Ideally, use descriptive names that get their meaning across using as few words and characters as possible.

When declaring variables or constants, you can optionally define the data type they hold by adding a prefix or suffix that identifies the type of data they contain such as

```
var strName : String
var intAge : Int
var dblSalary : Double

var nameStr : String
var ageInt : Int
var salaryDbl : Double
```

Note   The idea of adding data type prefixes to variable and constant names is known as Hungarian Notation, which was invented by Charles Simonyi, who worked at Xerox PARC and Microsoft.

The ultimate goal is to write self-documenting code that makes it easy for anyone to understand at first glance. One huge trap that programmers often make is assuming they'll be able to understand their own code months or even years later. Yet even after a few weeks, your own code can seem confusing because you're no longer familiar with your assumptions and logic that you had when you wrote the code originally.

If you can't even understand your own code months or even weeks later, imagine how difficult other programmers will find your code when they have to modify it in your absence. Good code doesn't just work, but it's easy for other programmers to understand how it works and what it does as well.

When developing your own programming style, strive for consistency and organization. Consistency means you use the same convention for writing code whether it's naming variables with prefixes or suffixes that identify the data type or indenting code the same way to highlight specific steps.

Organization means using spacing and storing related code together such as putting variables and functions in the same location consistently. This can group chunks of code in specific places to make code easier to understand as shown in Figure 1-1.

```
import SwiftUI

struct ContentView: View {

    @State private var choiceArray = [Int]()
    @State private var randomNumber = 0
    @State private var message = ""
    @State private var arrayLength = 100
    @State private var maxNumber: Double = 100

    var body: some View {
        VStack {
            Slider(value: $maxNumber, in: 1...100)
            Text("Max value = \(Int(maxNumber))")
                .padding()
            Button(action: {
                choiceArray.removeAll()
                for _ in 0...arrayLength - 1 {
                    randomNumber = Int.random(in:
                        1...Int(maxNumber))
                    choiceArray.append(randomNumber)
                    message = "\(choiceArray)"
                }
            }) {
                Text("Create array")
            }
            TextEditor(text: $message)
        }
    }
}

struct ContentView_Previews: PreviewProvider {
    static var previews: some View {
        ContentView()
    }
}
```

Figure 1-1. *Grouping related code together makes it easy to know where to look for certain information*

The specific placement of code is arbitrary, but what's important is that you organize code in a consistent and predictable manner so it's easy to find. The clearer your code, the easier it will be to fix and modify it later.

Using the //MARK: Comment

Besides physically grouping related items together such as functions and variables, you can also make searching for groups of related code easier by using the //MARK: comment. By placing a //MARK: comment, followed by descriptive text, you can make it easy to jump from one section of code to another through Xcode's pull-down menu as shown in Figure 1-2.

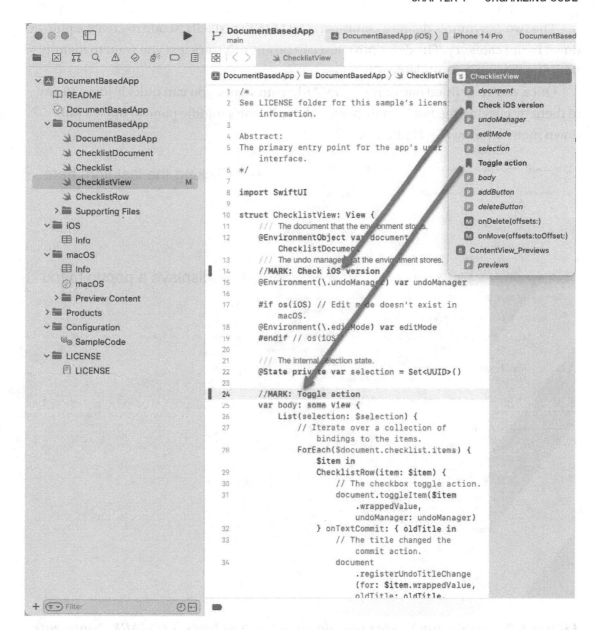

Figure 1-2. *The //MARK: comment creates categories in Xcode's pull-down menus*

The structure of the //MARK: comment looks like this:

```
// MARK: Descriptive text
```

The two // symbols define a comment. The MARK: text tells Xcode to create a pull-down menu category. The descriptive text can be any arbitrary text you want to identify the code that appears underneath.

Once you've defined one or more //MARK: comments, you can quickly jump to any of them by clicking the last item displayed above Xcode's middle pane to open a pull-down menu as shown in Figure 1-3.

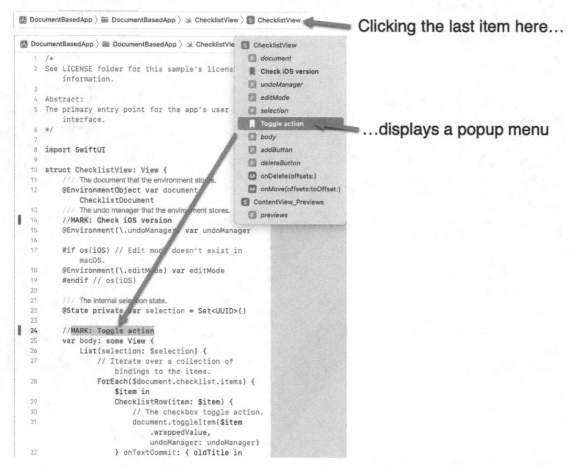

Figure 1-3. *Displaying Xcode's pull-down menu that lists all //MARK: comments*

Use the //MARK: comment generously throughout each .swift file. This will make it easy to jump to different parts of your code to modify or study later.

Using Files and Folders

Theoretically, you could create a single file and cram it full of code. While this would work, it's likely to be troublesome to read and modify. A far better solution is to divide your project into multiple files and store those multiple files in separate folders in Xcode's Navigator pane.

Separate files and folders exist solely for your benefit to organize your project. Xcode ignores all folders and treats separate files as if they were all stored in a single file. When creating separate files, the two most common types of files to create are shown in Figure 1-4:

- SwiftUI View
- Swift File

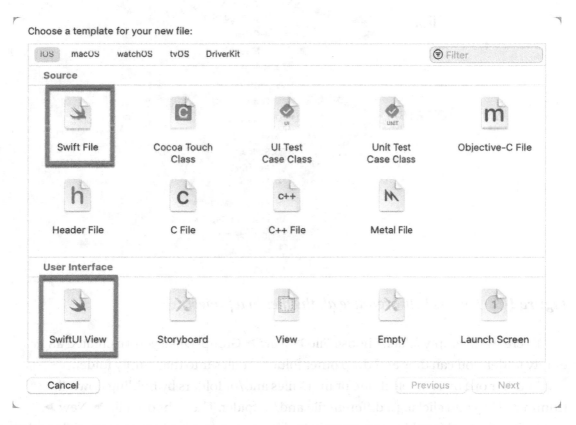

Figure 1-4. *The two most common types of .swift files in a project*

SwiftUI View files define user interfaces that appear on an iOS screen.

The Swift File option creates a blank .swift file for storing and isolating code such as defining a list of variables, data structures, or classes.

The more .swift files you add to a project, the harder it can be to find any particular file. To help organize all the files that make up a project, Xcode lets you create folders. By using folders, you can selectively hide or display the contents of a folder as shown in Figure 1-5.

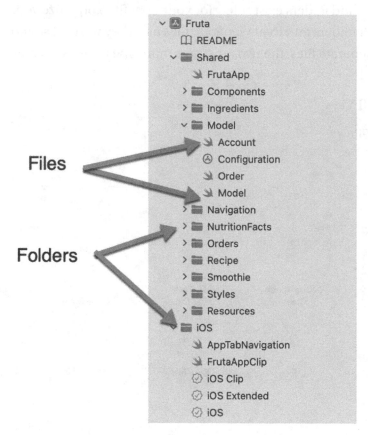

Figure 1-5. *Folders help organize all the files in a project*

To create an empty folder, choose File ➤ New ➤ Group. Once you've created an empty folder, you can drag and drop other folders or files into that empty folder.

Another option is to select one or more files and/or folders by holding down the Command key and clicking a different file and/or folder. Then choose File ➤ New ➤ Group from Selection. This creates a new folder and automatically stores your selected items into that new folder.

You can also right-click in the Navigator pane to display a popup menu with the New Group or New Group from Selection commands as shown in Figure 1-6.

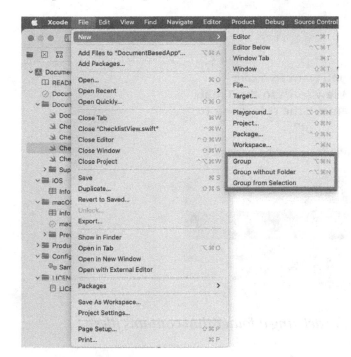

File pull-down menu

Right-click popup menu

Figure 1-6. *Menu commands to create a new folder*

Note   If the Group or Group from Selection commands are grayed out, click a file to select it before choosing the File ➤ New ➤ Group or File ➤ New ➤ Group from Selection command.

Once you've created a folder, you can always delete that folder afterward. To delete a folder, follow these steps:

1. Click the folder you want to delete in the Navigator pane.

2. Choose Edit ➤ Delete, or right-click the folder, and when a popup menu appears, choose Delete. If the folder is not empty, Xcode displays a dialog to ask if you want to remove references to any stored files in that folder or just delete them all as shown in Figure 1-7.

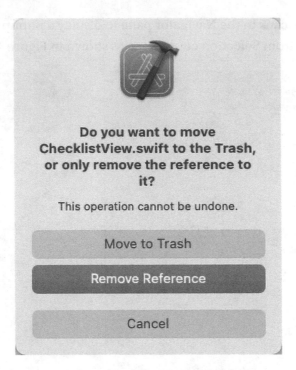

Do you want to move ChecklistView.swift to the Trash, or only remove the reference to it?

This operation cannot be undone.

Move to Trash

Remove Reference

Cancel

Figure 1-7. *Xcode alerts you if you're deleting a folder that contains files*

Note   Deleting a folder also deletes its contents, which can include other folders and files.

---

3. Click the Move to Trash button to delete the files completely (or click Remove References to keep the file and disconnect the file from your project but without deleting it).

Use Code Snippets

Remembering the exact syntax to create switch statements or for loops in Swift can be troublesome. As a shortcut, Xcode offers code snippets, which let you insert generic code in your Swift files that you can customize afterward. This lets you focus on the purpose of your code without worrying about the specifics of how Swift implements a particular way of writing branching or looping statements. In addition, code snippets help you write consistent code that's formatted the same way.

To use code snippets, follow these steps:

1. Click in the Swift file where you want to type code.

2. Click the Library icon. A window appears.

3. Click the Snippets icon to display code snippets as shown in Figure 1-8.

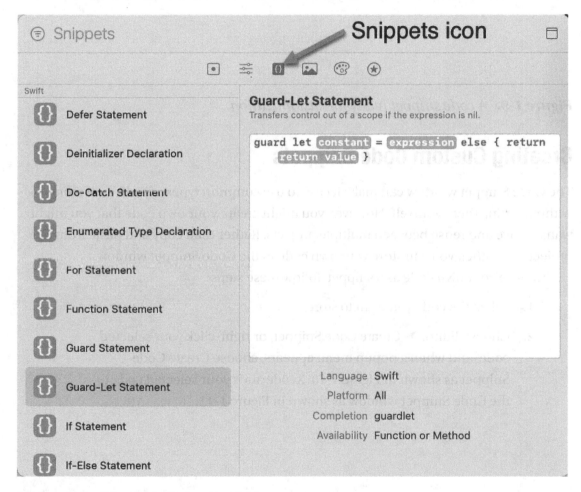

Figure 1-8. *The Code Snippet window*

4. Scroll through the Code Snippet window and click a snippet you want to use. Xcode displays a brief description of that code snippet.

5. Drag a snippet from the Code Snippet window and drop it in your Swift file. Xcode displays your snippet with placeholders for customizing the code with your own data as shown in Figure 1-9.

```
do {
    try throwing expression
} catch pattern {
    statements
}
```

Figure 1-9. *A code snippet ready for customization*

Creating Custom Code Snippets

The Code Snippet window can make it easy to use common types of Swift statements without typing them yourself. However, you might create your own code that you might want to save and reuse between multiple projects. Rather than copy and paste from one project to another, you can store your own code in the Code Snippet window.

To store your own code as a snippet, follow these steps:

1. Select the code you want to store.

2. Choose Editor ➤ Create Code Snippet, or right-click your selected code, and when a popup menu appears, choose Create Code Snippet as shown in Figure 1-10. Xcode adds your selected code to the Code Snippet window as shown in Figure 1-11.

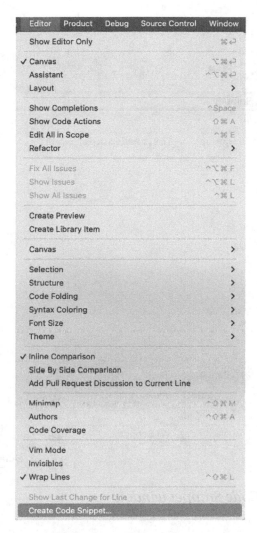
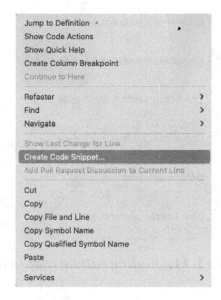

Editor pull-down menu   Right-click popup menu

Figure 1-10. *The Create Code Snippet command for adding your own code to the Code Snippet library*

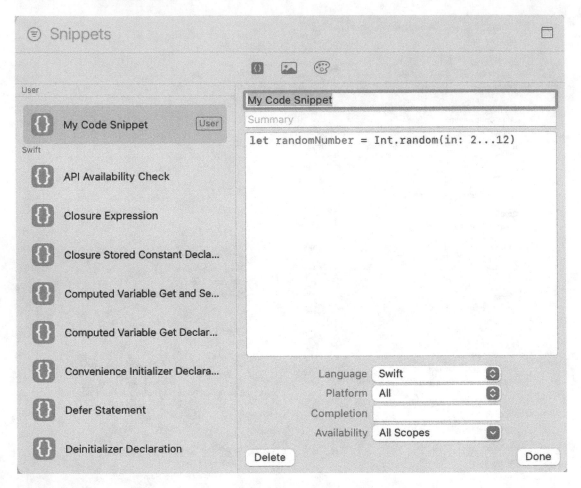

Figure 1-11. *Adding custom code to the Code Snippet window*

3. Click in the text field and type a descriptive name for your code snippet. You may also want to edit your code or modify other options as well such as typing a description of the code in the Summary text field.

4. Click Done. From now on, you'll be able to use your custom code snippet in any Xcode project.

Editing and Deleting Custom Code Snippets

After adding one or more code snippets, you may want to delete them. You can only delete any code snippets you added to Xcode; you can never delete any of Xcode's default code snippets. To delete a user-defined code snippet from the Code Snippet window, follow these steps:

1. Click a Swift file in the Navigator pane.

2. Click the Library icon to open the library window.

3. Click the Snippets icon.

4. Click the code snippet you want to edit or delete.

5. Click the Edit button. Now you can modify the code, and when you're finished, click Done. (Or click the Delete button. When Xcode asks if you really want to delete the code snippet, click Delete.)

Use View Modifiers

When designing user interfaces in SwiftUI, you typically create a view (such as Text) and then apply modifiers. If you tend to use the same modifiers over and over again, you can duplicate these modifiers for multiple views. However, duplicating modifiers can take up space and make code harder to read as shown in the following:

```
Text ("This is the first line")
    .font(.title)
    .foregroundColor(.yellow)
    .background(Color.blue)
    .cornerRadius(6)
    .padding()
Text ("Second line here")
    .font(.title)
    .foregroundColor(.yellow)
    .background(Color.blue)
    .cornerRadius(6)
    .padding()
```

Besides taking up space with duplicate code, another problem is if you want to change one or more modifiers such as changing the font size or the background color. With duplicate modifiers, you need to modify every copy, increasing the chance you'll miss one or more copies.

A better solution is to store commonly used groups of modifiers together in a separate structure defined as a ViewModifier. Then you can apply this ViewModifier structure to multiple views. Now if you need to change these modifiers, you can change them in one place rather than in multiple places throughout your code.

In the preceding example, it makes sense to store the modifiers within a ViewModifier structure like this:

```
struct MyStyle: ViewModifier {
    func body(content: Content) -> some View {
        content
            .font(.title)
            .foregroundColor(.yellow)
            .background(Color.blue)
            .cornerRadius(6)
            .padding()
    }
}
```

This ViewModifier structure encloses all the modifiers, which can then be applied to any view by using .modifier followed by the name of your structure like this:

```
struct ContentView: View {
    var body: some View {
        VStack {
            Text ("This is the first line")
                .modifier(MyStyle())
            Text ("Second line here")
                .modifier(MyStyle())
        }
    }
}
```

```
struct MyStyle: ViewModifier {
    func body(content: Content) -> some View {
        content
            .font(.title)
            .foregroundColor(.yellow)
            .background(Color.blue)
            .cornerRadius(6)
            .padding()
    }
}
```

Just as functions let you isolate and reuse code, so can ViewModifiers let you isolate and reuse modifiers for different views.

Understanding Version Control Systems

When you're just creating simple projects to learn Swift and SwiftUI, you probably don't need to worry about saving your projects later. However, once you start creating long-term projects for yourself or others, that's when you need to think about version control systems.

The idea behind a version control system is to keep track of the changes you make to your source code. The biggest problem with programming is that almost nothing ever works right the first time. That means once you create a working project, modifying that project means turning your working project into a nonworking project.

To avoid this problem, programmers make copies of their source code. That way, if they make changes that fail to work, they can revert back to their last working version and start over again. Even for solo developers, this method can quickly spiral out of control if you keep making separate copies of your source code and lose track which copy is the most recent, working version.

Even worse, you could accidentally make changes to two different copies of the same file. Now you'll have the headache of identifying the differences in each file and merging them together into a single file. Now if multiple people work on the same program, keeping track of changes can become unwieldy as people make changes to different copies of the same program.

To solve this problem, developers rely on version control systems such as Git. Version control systems offer several advantages:

- Store all source code in one place

- Track changes to the source code

- Allow you to revert back to previous versions of the source code

- Allow multiple people to work on the same files, create separate branches of the same project, and merge their changes together

Storing source code in one place ensures that everyone can access the latest version of the project. Version control systems store source code on a server that allows any team member to access from anywhere in the world.

Once people edit source code, the version control system can track each person's changes. This allows everyone to see who made what changes on what date. Then people can selectively reverse any changes (if they don't work) or continue editing the source code with their own changes.

Most importantly, version control systems allow two or more people to work on the same file simultaneously for greater efficiency. Then they can merge their changes back into the main project. Although there are dozens of version control systems available, Xcode offers built-in support for Git, one of the more popular version control systems.

Note   Learning Git, or any version control system, takes time and requires a separate book (or two) on its own.

To see how Xcode offers built-in support for Git, follow these steps:

1. Choose Xcode ➤ Settings. A dialog appears.

2. Click the Source Control icon.

3. Click the General tab and you can see all the options available as shown in Figure 1-12. The most important option is to select the Enable Source Control check box.

Figure 1-12. *The Source Control dialog*

4. Click in the Default Branch Name text field and type a name. The most common branch name for years has been "master," but many programmers have switched to calling their branch name "main" instead.

5. Click the Git tab as shown in Figure 1-13.

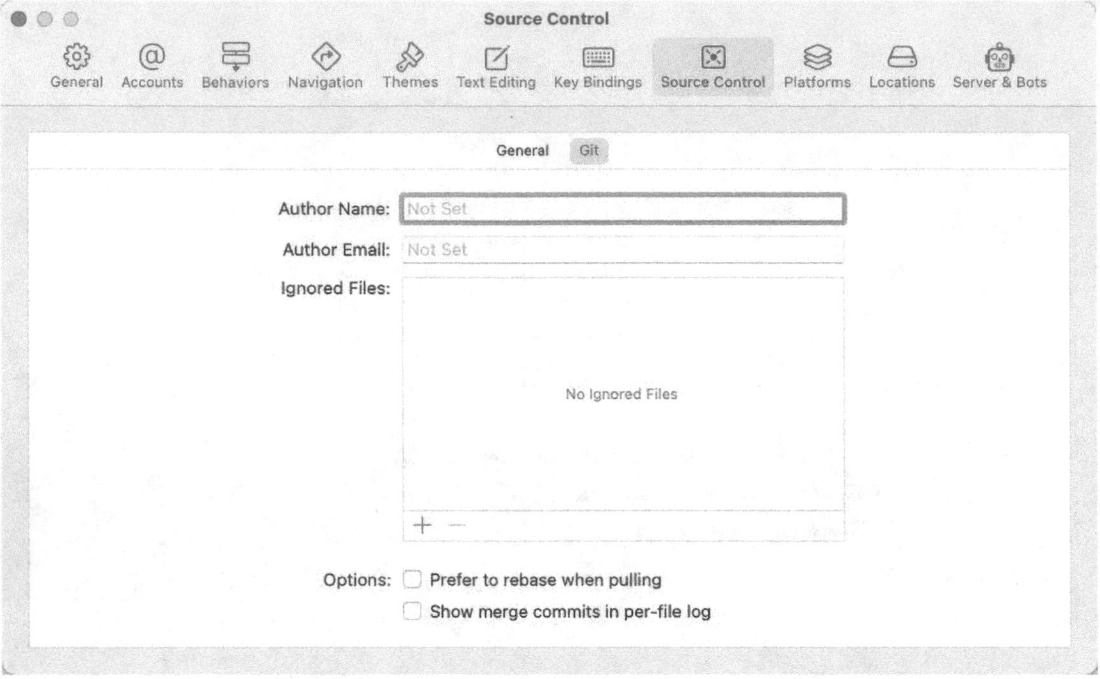

Figure 1-13. *The Git tab on the Source Control dialog*

6. Click in the Author Name text field and type your name.

7. Click in the Author Email text field and type your email address. Your name and email address will track your changes and allow others to contact you if they have questions about your code.

The preceding steps simply allow Xcode to use Git, but you'll still need to create a repository either locally (on your own computer) or remotely (on a server on the Internet such as GitHub or GitLab).

To connect to a remote repository, you'll need to set up an account on that repository and then tell Xcode how to connect to that remote repository by following these steps:

1. Choose Xcode ➤ Settings. An Accounts dialog appears.

2. Click the + icon in the bottom-left corner to open a dialog that lets you choose a remote repository as shown in Figure 1-14.

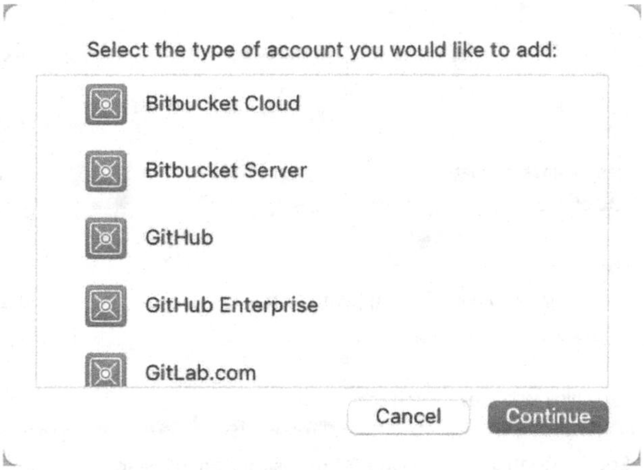

Select the type of account you would like to add:

⊠	Bitbucket Cloud
⊠	Bitbucket Server
⊠	GitHub
⊠	GitHub Enterprise
⊠	GitLab.com

Cancel   Continue

Figure 1-14. *Connecting to a remote repository*

Note   For more information on connecting to remote repositories, read Apple's official documentation: `https://developer.apple.com/documentation/ xcode/configuring-your-xcode-project-to-use-source-control`.

When you're creating a new Xcode project, you must give your project a name. When Xcode displays a dialog to let you choose where to store your project, select the Create Git repository on my Mac check box as shown in Figure 1-15.

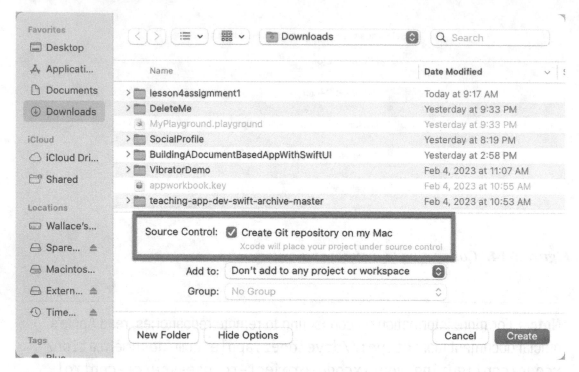

Figure 1-15. *Creating a new Xcode project with a Git repository*

If you've already created a project, you can add a Git repository by following these steps:

1. Make sure your Xcode project is open.

2. Choose Source Control ➤ New Git Repository as shown in Figure 1-16. A dialog appears as shown in Figure 1-17.

Figure 1-16. *Creating a new Git repository for an existing Xcode project*

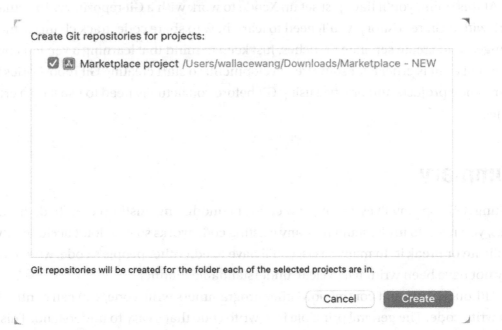

Figure 1-17. *Creating a local Git repository*

3. Click Create.

4. Click the Show Source Control Navigator icon in the Navigator pane and click Repositories. Xcode shows you your local repository for your current project as shown in Figure 1-18.

Figure 1-18. *Viewing a local Git repository within Xcode*

At this point, you'll have just set up Xcode to work with a Git repository. To actually work with a Git repository, you'll need to learn how to share code, track changes, merge changes, and create separate branches. Just keep in mind that learning a version control system like Git is crucial for software development, so start creating Git repositories for your Xcode projects and practice using Git before you actually need to use it on a critical project.

Summary

Writing iOS apps involves writing new code and modifying existing code. To do both tasks, you need to understand how any existing code works so you don't accidentally duplicate or break it. In many cases, you'll have to edit other people's code, which may or may not have been written in a clear, understandable manner.

Although you can't control how other programmers write code, you can control how you write code. The general principle is to write code that's easy to understand. This can involve adding comments (especially //MARK: comments to make it easy to jump to specific parts of your code). You should also use descriptive variable names and organize the related code in logical groups. You can do that by storing different parts of your code together. You can also organize code by storing code in separate files that you can group in folders.

To ensure you write common Swift statements in a consistent manner, you can use code snippets to insert the basic Swift code for you. Then you just have to customize it with your own data. For more flexibility, store your own code in the Code Snippet window. That way, you can reuse your own code between multiple projects in Xcode.

Organizing code is never necessary, but since most programs are modified multiple times, proper organization ahead of time can make modifying code much easier. Always assume that someone else will modify your code and make it easy on that person for the future, especially because that person could be you.

For large projects, always use some form of version control such as Git to help you track changes and collaborate with others. Version control is optional but highly recommended for all projects that you cannot afford to lose.

CHAPTER 2

Debugging Code

In the professional world of software, you'll actually spend more time modifying existing programs than you ever will creating new ones. When writing new programs or editing existing ones, it doesn't matter how much experience or education you might have because even the best programmers can make mistakes. In fact, you can expect that you will make mistakes no matter how careful you may be. Once you accept this inevitable fact of programming, you need to learn how to find and fix your mistakes.

In the world of computers, mistakes are commonly called "bugs," which gets its name from an early computer that used physical switches to work. One day, the computer failed, and when technicians opened the computer, they found that a moth had been crushed within a switch, preventing the switch from closing. From that point on, programming errors have been called bugs, and fixing computer problems has been known as debugging.

Three common types of computer bugs are

- Syntax errors – Occurs when you misspell something such as a keyword, variable name, function name, or class name or use a symbol incorrectly

- Logic errors – Occurs when you use commands correctly, but the logic of your code doesn't do what you intended

- Runtime errors – Occurs when a program encounters unexpected situations such as the user entering invalid data or when another program somehow interferes with your program unexpectedly

Syntax errors are the easiest to find and fix because they're merely misspellings of variable names that you created or misspelling of Swift commands that Xcode can help you identify. If you type a Swift keyword such as "var" or "let," Xcode displays that keyword in magenta (or whatever color you specify for displaying keywords in the Xcode editor).

27

W. Wang, *Pro iPhone Development with SwiftUI*, https://doi.org/10.1007/978-1-4842-9544-1_2

Now if you type a Swift keyword and it doesn't appear in its usual identifying color, then you know you probably typed it wrong somehow. By coloring your code, Xcode's editor helps you visually identify common misspellings or typos.

Besides using color, the Xcode editor provides a second way to help you avoid mistakes when you need to type the name of a method or class. As soon as Xcode recognizes that you might be typing a known item, it displays a popup menu of possible options. Now instead of typing the entire command yourself, you can simply select a choice in the popup menu and press the TAB or ENTER key to let Xcode type your chosen command correctly as shown in Figure 2-1.

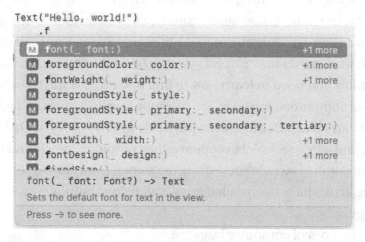

Figure 2-1. *Xcode displays a menu of possible commands you might want to use*

Syntax errors often keep your program from running at all. When a syntax error keeps your program from running, Xcode can usually identify the line (or the nearby area) of your program where the misspelled commands appears so you can fix it as shown in Figure 2-2.

```
struct ContentView: View {
    var body: some View {
        VStack {
            Image(systemName: "globe")
                .imageScale(.large)
                .foregroundColor(.accentColor)
            Text("Hello, world!" + cat)          ⊗ Cannot find 'cat' in scope
        }
        .padding()
    }
}
```

Figure 2-2. *Syntax errors often keep a program from running, which allows Xcode to identify the syntax error*

Logic errors are much harder to find and detect than syntax errors. Logic errors occur when you use Swift code correctly, but it doesn't do what you want it to do. Since your code is actually valid, Xcode has no way of knowing that it's not working the way you intended. As a result, logic errors can be difficult to debug because you think you wrote your code correctly but you (obviously) did not.

How do you find a mistake in code that you thought you wrote correctly? Finding your mistake can often involve starting from the beginning of your program and exhaustively searching each line all the way until the end. (Of course, there are faster ways than searching your entire program, line by line, which you'll learn about later in this chapter.)

Finally, the hardest errors to find and debug are runtime errors. Syntax errors usually keep your program from running, so if your program actually runs, you can assume that you have eliminated most, if not all, syntax errors in your code.

Logic errors can be tougher to find, but they're predictable. For example, if your program asks the user for a password but fails to give the user access even though the user types a correct password, you know you have a logic error. Each time you run your program, you can reliably predict when the logic error will occur.

Runtime errors are more insidious because they don't always occur predictably. For example, your app may run perfectly well on an iPhone, but the moment you run the same app on an iPad (or vice versa), the app fails. That's because conditions between two different iOS devices will never be exactly the same.

The problem is that unexpected, outside circumstances can affect an app's behavior such as another app taking up too much memory or one device might be running a different version of iOS than another device. Because runtime errors can't always be duplicated, they can be frustrating to find and even harder to fix since you can't always examine every possible condition your app might face when running on different iOS devices. Some apps can work perfectly – except if the user accidentally presses two keys at the same time. Other apps work just fine – until the user happens to save a file at the exact moment that another app tries to receive data over a WiFi connection.

Usually, you can eliminate most syntax errors and find and fix most logic errors. However, it may not be possible to find and completely eliminate all runtime errors in a program. The best way to avoid spending time hunting for bugs is to strive to write code and test it carefully to make sure it's as error-free as possible.

Note   One odd debugging technique is called Rubber Duck Debugging
(`https://en.wikipedia.org/wiki/Rubber_duck_debugging`). The idea
is that whenever your code fails to work, explain the problem to a rubber duck (a
pet, a friend, or any inanimate object you wish to use instead of a rubber duck). By
articulating the problem out loud, you can often spot your mistakes and see how to
correct the problem.

Simple Debugging Techniques

When your app isn't working, you often have no idea what could be wrong. While you
could tediously examine your code from beginning to end, it's often faster to simply
guess where the mistake might be.

Once you have a rough idea what part of your app might be causing the problem, you
have two choices. First, you can delete the suspicious code and run your app again. If the
problem magically goes away, then you'll know that the code you deleted was likely the
culprit.

However, if your app still doesn't work, you have to retype your deleted code back
into your program. A simpler solution might be to cut and paste code out of Xcode and
store it in a text editor such as the TextEdit program that comes with every Macintosh,
but this can be tedious.

That's why a second solution is to just temporarily hide code that you suspect might
be causing a problem. Then if the problem persists, you can simply unhide that code
and make it visible again. To do this in Xcode, you just need to turn your code into
comments.

Remember, comments are text that Xcode completely ignores. You can create
comments in three ways:

- Add the // symbols at the beginning of each line that you want to
  convert into a comment. This method lets you convert a single line
  into a comment.

- Add the /* symbols at the beginning of code and add the */ at the end
  of code you want to convert into a comment. This method lets you
  convert one or more lines into a comment.

- Select the lines of code you want to turn into a comment and choose Editor ➤ Structure ➤ Comment Selection (or press Command + /). This method lets you convert one or more lines into a comment by placing the // symbols at the beginning of each line of code you selected.

Note   Xcode color-codes comments in green (or whatever color you may have defined to identify comments). After creating a comment, make sure Xcode color-codes it properly to ensure you have created a comment. If Xcode fails to recognize your comments, it will treat your text as a valid Swift command, which will likely keep your code from running properly.

By turning code into comments, you essentially hide that code from Xcode. Now if you want to turn that comment back into code again, you just remove the // or /* and */ symbols that define your commented out code.

If you commented out code by choosing Editor ➤ Structure ➤ Comment Selection (or pressing Command + /), just repeat the command again to convert that commented code back to working code once more.

Besides turning your code into comments to temporarily hide it, a second simple debugging technique is to use the print command. The idea is to put the print command in your code to print out the values of a variable wherever you think your code may be making a mistake.

By doing this, you can see what values one or more variables may contain. Putting multiple print commands throughout your program gives you a chance to make sure your program is running correctly.

To see how using the print command along with commenting out code can work to help you debug a program, follow these steps:

1. Create a new iOS App project, make sure it uses SwiftUI, and give it a descriptive name (such as DebugApp).

2. Click the ContentView file in the Navigator pane. The Editor pane displays the contents of the ContentView file.

3. Edit the code as follows:

```swift
import SwiftUI

struct ContentView: View {
    @State var message = "Temperature in Celsius: "
    let temp = 100.0
    var body: some View {
        VStack {
            Text(message + "\(temp)")
            Text("Temperature in Fahrenheit: \(C2F(tempC: temp))")
        }
    }

    func C2F (tempC : Double) -> Double {
        var tempF : Double
        tempF = tempC + 32 * 9/5
        return tempF
    }

}

struct ContentView_Previews: PreviewProvider {
    static var previews: some View {
        ContentView()

    }
}
```

Notice that the Canvas pane displays the following:

Temperature in Celsius: 100.0
Temperature in Fahrenheit: 157.6

If you know anything about temperatures in Fahrenheit and Celsius, you know that the boiling point in Celsius is 100 degrees and the boiling point in Fahrenheit is 212 degrees. Yet our temperature conversion program calculates that 100 degrees Celsius is equal to 157.6 degrees in Fahrenheit, which means the Fahrenheit temperature should be 212 rather than 157.6.

Note   When testing code, start out with answers that you already know, such as knowing that 100 degrees Celsius must equal 212 degrees Fahrenheit. If the code fails to give you the answer you already know, the code must be incorrect.

Obviously, 100 degrees Celsius cannot be equal to 157.6 degrees Fahrenheit, so let's use the print command and comments to help debug the problem.

1. Make sure the DebugApp project is loaded in Xcode.

2. Click the ViewController.swift file in the Navigator pane and edit the C2F function as follows:

```swift
func C2F (tempC : Double) -> Double {
    var tempF : Double
    tempF = tempC + 32 //* 9/5
    return tempF
}
```

This comment will let us check if the tempC parameter is properly coming into the C2F function and getting stored in the tempF variable.

3. Add a "print (tempC)" command above the return statement as follows:

```swift
func C2F (tempC : Double) -> Double {
    var tempF : Double
    tempF = tempC + 32 //* 9/5
    print (tempF)
    return tempF
}
```

Note   The print command only works in the Simulator and will not work when running on the app using Live Preview in the Canvas pane. The print command displays text in the Debug Area of the Xcode window.

---

4. Click the Run button or choose Product ➤ Run. The Simulator window appears showing a blank screen.

5. Choose Simulator ➤ Quit Simulator. Notice that the Debug Area at the bottom of the middle Xcode pane displays the following text:

132.0

By commenting out the calculation part of the code and using the "print (tempF)" command, we can see that the C2F function is storing 100.0 correctly in the tempC variable and adding 32 to this value before storing it in the tempF variable. Because we commented out the calculation part of the code, we can assume that the error must be in our commented out code.

Although the formula might look correct, the error occurs because of the way Swift (and most programming languages) calculate formulas. First, they start from left to right. Second, they calculate certain operations such as multiplication before addition.

The error occurs because our conversion formula first multiplies 32 by 9 (288) and then divides the result (288) by 5 to get 57.6. Finally, it adds 57.6 to 100.0 to get the incorrect result of 157.6. What it should really be doing is multiplying 9/5 by the temperature in Celsius and then adding 32 to the result.

6. Modify the C2F function as follows:

```
func C2F (tempC : Double) -> Double {
    var tempF : Double
    tempF = tempC * (9/5) + 32
    return tempF
}
```

Notice that the program now correctly converts 100 degrees Celsius to 212 degrees Fahrenheit. For simple debugging, turning code temporarily into comments and using the print command can work, but it's fairly clumsy to keep adding and removing comment symbols and print commands. A much better solution is to use breakpoints and variable watching, which essentially duplicates using comments and print commands.

Using the Xcode Debugger

While comments and the print command can help you isolate problems in your code, they can be clumsy to use. The print command can be especially tedious since you have to type it into your code and then remember to remove it later when you're ready to ship your app.

Although leaving one or more print commands buried in your program won't likely hurt your program's performance, it's poor programming practice to leave code in your program that no longer serves any purpose.

As an alternative to typing the print command throughout your program, Xcode offers a more convenient alternative using the Xcode debugger. The debugger gives you two ways to hunt out and identify bugs in your program:

- Breakpoints

- Variable watching

Note   Breakpoints and variable watching only work in the Simulator and will not work when running on the app using the Live icon in the Canvas pane.

Using Breakpoints

Breakpoints let you identify a specific line in your code where you want your program to stop. Once your program stops, you can step through your code, line by line. As you do so, you can also peek at the contents of one or more variables to check if the variables are holding the right values.

For example, if your program converts Celsius to Fahrenheit, but somehow converts 100 degrees Celsius into –41259 degrees Fahrenheit, you know your code isn't working right. By inserting breakpoints in your code and examining the values of your variables at each breakpoint, you can identify where your code calculates its values. The moment you spot the line where it miscalculates a value, you know the exact area of your program that you need to fix.

You can set a breakpoint by doing one of the following:

- Clicking to the left of the code where you want to set the breakpoint

- Moving the cursor to a line where you want to set the breakpoint and pressing Command + \

- Choosing Debug ➤ Breakpoints ➤ Add Breakpoint at Current Line

Xcode displays breakpoints as blue arrows in the left margin as shown in Figure 2-3.

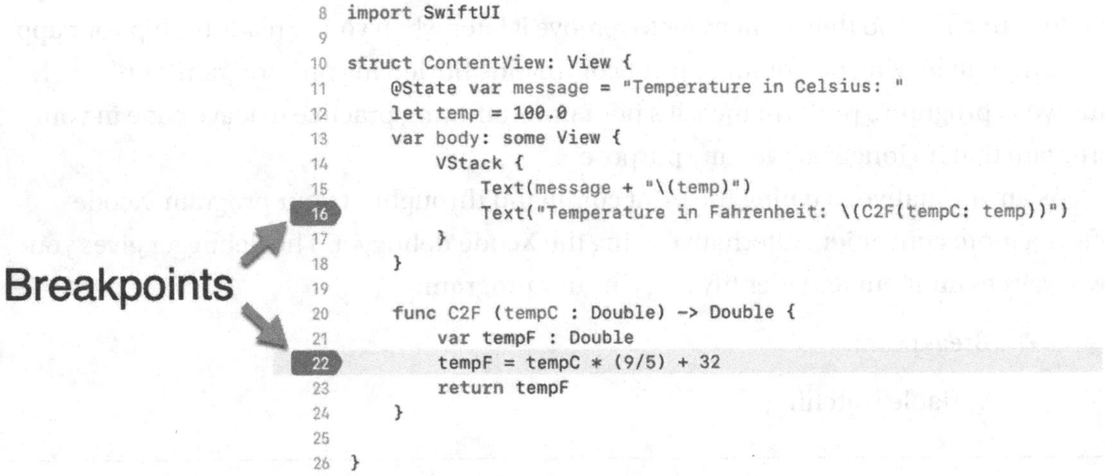

```
8   import SwiftUI
9
10  struct ContentView: View {
11      @State var message = "Temperature in Celsius: "
12      let temp = 100.0
13      var body: some View {
14          VStack {
15              Text(message + "\(temp)")
16              Text("Temperature in Fahrenheit: \(C2F(tempC: temp))")
17          }
18      }
19
20      func C2F (tempC : Double) -> Double {
21          var tempF : Double
22          tempF = tempC * (9/5) + 32
23          return tempF
24      }
25
26  }
```

Breakpoints

Figure 2-3. Breakpoints appear in the left margin

Stepping Through Code

Once a breakpoint has stopped your program from running, you can step through your code line by line using the Step command. Xcode offers a variety of different Step commands, but the three most common are

- Step Over

- Step Into

- Step Out

The Step Over command examines the next line of code, treating function or method calls as a single line of code.

The Step Into command works exactly like the Step Over command until it highlights a function or method call. Then it jumps to the first line of code in that function or method.

The Step Out command is used to prematurely exit out of a function or method that you entered using the Step Into command. The Step Out command returns to the line of code where a function or method was called.

All three Step commands are used after a program temporarily stops at a breakpoint. By using a Step command, you can examine your code, line by line, and see how values stored in different variables may change.

Such variable watching lets you examine the contents of one or more variables to verify if it's holding the correct data. The moment you spot a variable holding incorrect data, you can zero in on the line of code that's creating that error.

The best part about breakpoints is that you can easily add and remove them since they don't modify your code at all, unlike comments and multiple print commands. Xcode can remove all breakpoints automatically, so you don't have to hunt through your code to remove them one by one.

To see how to use breakpoints, step commands, and variable watching, follow these steps:

1. Make sure the DebugApp project is loaded in Xcode.

2. Click the ContentView file in the Navigator pane and modify the C2F function as follows:

```
func C2F (tempC : Double) -> Double {
    var tempF : Double
    tempF = tempC + 32 * 9/5
    return tempF
}
```

3. Move the cursor on the following line:

```
Text("Temperature in Fahrenheit: \(C2F(tempC: temp))")
```

4. Choose Debug ➤ Breakpoints ➤ Add Breakpoint at Current Line. Xcode displays a breakpoint as a blue arrow.

5. Click the Run button or choose Product ➤ Run. The Simulator window appears showing a blank screen. Notice that Xcode highlights the line where the breakpoint appears.

6. Choose Debug ➤ Step Into (or press F7). Xcode jumps from the breakpoint into the function C2F. The information in the left-hand side of the Debug Area displays the current values that your program is using as shown in Figure 2-4.

```
 8  import SwiftUI
 9
10  struct ContentView: View {
11      @State var message = "Temperature in Celsius: "
12      let temp = 100.0
13      var body: some View {
14          VStack {
15              Text(message + "\(temp)")
16              Text("Temperature in Fahrenheit: \(C2F(tempC: temp))")    =  Thread 1...
17          }
18      }
19
20      func C2F (tempC : Double) -> Double {
21          var tempF : Double
22          tempF = tempC + 32 * 9/5
23          return tempF
24      }
25
26  }
27
28  struct ContentView_Previews: PreviewProvider {
29      static var previews: some View {
30          ContentView()
31      }
32  }
33
```

■ � DebugApp ⟩ ⬤ Thread 1 ⟩ ⬛ 0 closure #1 in ContentView.body.getter

```
∨ Ⓐ self (DebugApp.ContentView)                          2023-02-07 14:36:10.788996-
  ∨ _message (SwiftUI.State<String>)                        configuration dictionar
    > _value = (String) "Temperature in Celsius: "        2023-02-07 14:36:10.789079-
    > _location (SwiftUI.AnyLocation<String>?)               configuration dictionar
  temp = (Double) 100                                     (lldb)
```

Auto ⌄   ⊚   ⓘ   ⊜ Filter   All Output ⌄

Figure 2-4. *By watching how variables change, you can see how each line of code affects each variable*

7. Choose Debug ➤ Step Over (or press F6) several more times until the Simulator displays the two temperatures in both Celsius and Fahrenheit.

8. Choose Simulator ➤ Quit Simulator to return back to Xcode.

9. Choose Debug ➤ Deactivate Breakpoints. Xcode dims the breakpoint. Xcode will ignore deactivated breakpoints.

10. Click the Run button or choose Product ➤ Run. The Simulator window appears showing a blank screen. Notice that since you deactivated breakpoints, Xcode runs the entire program without stopping at any of the breakpoints.

11. Choose Simulator ➤ Quit Simulator to return back to Xcode.

12. Choose Debug ➤ Activate Breakpoints. Notice that Xcode no longer dims the breakpoint arrow in the left margin any more.

13. Move the mouse pointer over the breakpoint and drag to the left or right.

14. Release the left mouse button. Xcode deletes the breakpoint.

Managing Breakpoints

There's no limit to the number of breakpoints you can put in a program, so feel free to place as many as you need to help you track down errors. Of course, if you place breakpoints in a program, you may lose track of how many breakpoints you've set and where they might be set. To help you manage your breakpoints, Xcode offers a Breakpoint Navigator.

You can open the Breakpoint Navigator in one of three ways:

• Choose View ➤ Navigators ➤ Breakpoints.

• Press Command + 8.

• Click the Show Breakpoint Navigator icon in the Navigator pane.

The Breakpoint Navigator lists all the breakpoints set in your program and identifies the files the breakpoints are in and the line number of each breakpoint as shown in Figure 2-5.

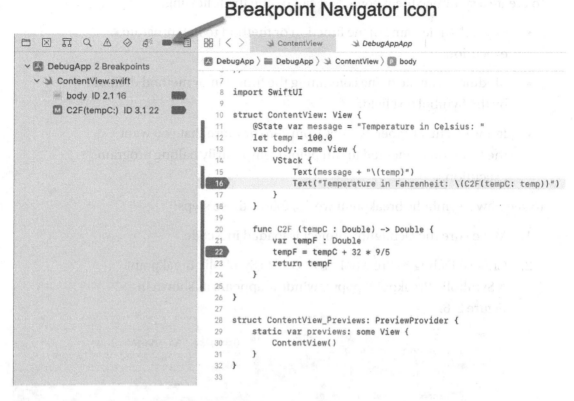

Figure 2-5. *The Breakpoint Navigator identifies all your breakpoints*

Using Symbolic Breakpoints

When you create a breakpoint, you must place it on the line where you want your program's execution to temporarily stop. However, this often means guessing where the problem might be and then using the various step commands to examine your code line by line.

To avoid this problem, Xcode offers a symbolic breakpoint. A symbolic breakpoint stops program execution only when a specific function or method runs. In case you don't want your program's execution to stop every time a particular function or method runs, you can tell Xcode to ignore it a certain number of times such as ten. That means the function or method will run up to ten times, and then on the eleventh time it's called, the symbolic breakpoint will temporarily halt execution, so you can step through your code line by line.

To create a symbolic breakpoint, you can define the following:

- Symbol – The name of the function or method to halt program execution.

- Module – The file name containing the function or method defined by the Symbol text field.

- Ignore – The number of times from zero or more that you want the function or method to run before temporarily halting program execution.

To see how a symbolic breakpoint works, follow these steps:

1. Make sure the DebugApp project is loaded in Xcode.

2. Choose Debug ➤ Breakpoints ➤ Create Symbolic Breakpoint. A Symbolic Breakpoint popup window appears as shown in Figure 2-6.

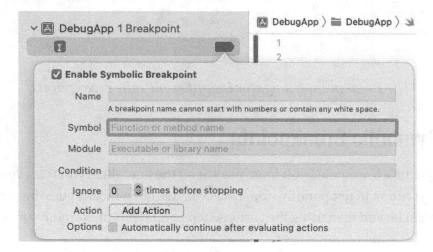

Figure 2-6. *The Symbolic Breakpoint popup window lets you define a breakpoint*

3. Click in the Symbol text field and type C2F, which is the name of the function or method you want to examine.

4. (Optional) If the function or method name you specified in the Symbol text field is used in other files, click in the Module text field and type a file name. This file name will limit the symbolic breakpoint only to that function or method in that particular file. Since the C2F function is only used once, you can leave the Module text field empty.

5. (Optional) Click in the Ignore text field and type a number to specify how many times to ignore a function or method being called before halting program execution. In this case, leave zero in the Ignore text field.

6. Click anywhere away from the Symbolic Breakpoint popup window to make it disappear.

7. Click the Run button or choose Product ➤ Run. The Simulator window appears showing a blank screen. The C2F symbolic breakpoint causes the program to temporarily halt execution on the first line of code in the C2F function that calculates a result as shown in Figure 2-7.

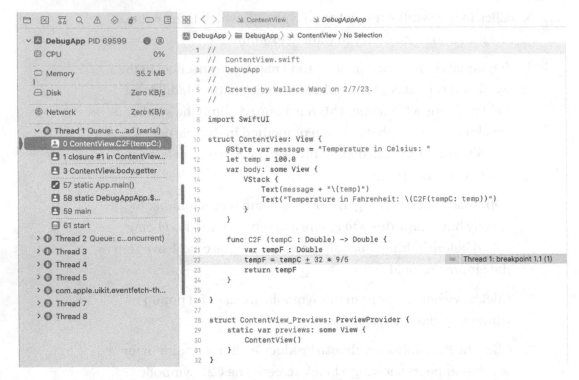

Figure 2-7. *The symbolic breakpoint halts program execution in the C2F function defined by the Symbol text field*

8. Choose Product ➤ Stop, or click the Stop button, to make your program stop running.

9. Choose View ➤ Navigators ➤ Breakpoints. The Breakpoint Navigator pane appears.

10. Right-click the C2F breakpoint in the Breakpoint Navigator pane, and when a popup menu appears, choose Delete Breakpoint. There should be no breakpoints displayed in the Breakpoint Navigator pane.

Note   Another way to set a breakpoint without specifying a specific line of code is to create an Exception breakpoint. Normally, if your program crashes, Xcode displays a bunch of cryptic error messages, and you have no idea what caused the error. If you set an Exception breakpoint, Xcode can identify the line of code that created the crash so you can fix it.

Using Conditional Breakpoints

Breakpoints normally stop program execution at a specific line every time. However, you may want to stop program execution on a particular line only if a certain condition holds true, such as if a variable exceeds a certain value, which can signal when something has gone wrong.

To see how a conditional breakpoint works, follow these steps:

1. Make sure the DebugApp project is loaded in Xcode.

2. Place a breakpoint on the following line by clicking in the left margin or moving the cursor in the line and pressing Command + \ or choosing Debug ➤ Breakpoints ➤ Add Breakpoint at Current Line:

   ```
   tempF = tempC + 32 * 9/5
   ```

3. Choose View ➤ Navigators ➤ Breakpoints, or click the Breakpoint Navigator icon. The Breakpoint Navigator pane appears, showing the breakpoint you just created.

4. Right-click the breakpoint in the Breakpoint Navigator pane and choose Edit Breakpoint. A popup window appears.

5. Click in the Condition text field, type tempC > 20 as shown in Figure 2-8.

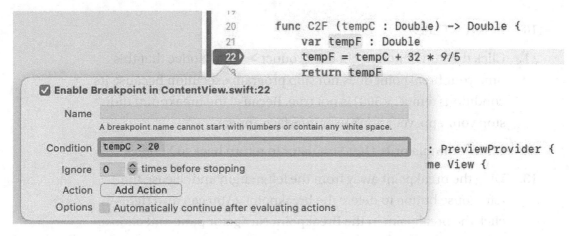

Figure 2-8. *Creating a conditional breakpoint*

6. Click the Run button or choose Product ➤ Run. Xcode highlights your breakpoint to temporarily stop program execution, which means that the condition tempC > 20 must be true.

7. Choose Product ➤ Stop, or click the Stop button, to make your program stop running and return back to Xcode.

8. Choose View ➤ Navigators ➤ Breakpoints, right-click the breakpoint you created, and choose Edit Breakpoint. The popup window appears.

9. Click in the Condition text field and edit the text so it reads tempC > 500 as shown in Figure 2-9.

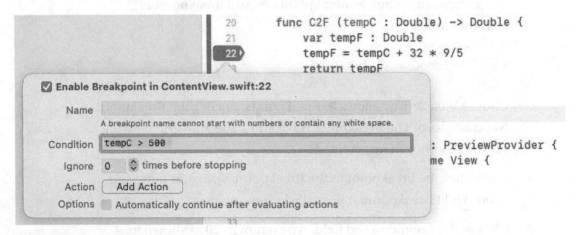

Figure 2-9. *Editing a conditional breakpoint*

10. Press ENTER.

11. Click the Run button or choose Product ➤ Run. Notice that this time your breakpoint does not stop program execution because its condition (tempC > 500) is not true. Because the breakpoint didn't stop your app, your app's user interface appears.

12. Choose Simulator ➤ Quit Simulator to return back to Xcode.

13. Drag the breakpoint away from the left margin and release the left mouse button to delete the breakpoint. (You can also right-click the breakpoint in the Breakpoint Navigator pane and choose Delete Breakpoint.)

Summary

Errors or bugs are unavoidable in any app. While syntax errors are easy to find and fix, logic errors can be tougher to find because you thought your code would create one type of result but it winds up creating a different result. Now you're left trying to figure out what you did wrong when you thought you were doing everything right. Even harder errors to track down are runtime errors that occur seemingly at random because of unknown conditions that affect an app.

To help you track down and eliminate most bugs, you can use the print command along with comments, but for most robust debugging, you should use Xcode's built-in debugger. With the debugger, you can set breakpoints in your code and watch how values get stored in one or more variables.

A conditional breakpoint only stops program execution when a certain condition occurs. A symbolic breakpoint only stops program execution when a specific function or method gets called. Once a breakpoint stops a program, you can continue examining your code line by line using various step commands. The Step Into command lets you view code stored inside a function or method, while the Step Out command lets you prematurely exit out of a function or method and jump back to the function or method call.

By using breakpoints and step commands, you can exhaustively examine how your program works, line by line, to eliminate as many errors as possible. The fewer errors your app contains, the happier your users will be.

CHAPTER 3

Understanding Closures

Reading a single sentence isn't difficult for most people, but when you combine thousands of sentences together, reading a long mass of text can be cumbersome. That's why people divide large amounts of text into parts such as paragraphs and chapters. Programming is no different.

Rather than write code as one large mass of text, programmers typically divide a large program into smaller functions where each function performs a single task. Not only do functions help make a large program easier to understand, but functions also act like building blocks that you can reuse in other programs.

You should already be familiar with the standard way to create a function by using the func keyword followed by a descriptive name, parameter list, and a block of code such as

```
func descriptiveName() {
    // Code here
}
```

To run a function, you have to call it by name such as

```
descriptiveName()
```

If a function returns a value, you can assign a function to represent a value such as

```
var x = descriptiveName()
```

To use functions, you need to follow a two-step process:

1. Create a function.
2. Call that function.

© Wallace Wang 2023
W. Wang, *Pro iPhone Development with SwiftUI*, https://doi.org/10.1007/978-1-4842-9544-1_3

Another way to write a function is as a closure. Closures simply give you another way to write functions that let you create and call them in a single step. Functions store code in a separate location, which makes it cumbersome to see how that code works. Closures store code right where it's being used, so it's easier to see how it works.

By using closures as a different way to write functions, you can write more concise code (with the drawback of being harder to read and understand). Closures can be written in several different ways. When you create a function, you need to use the func keyword followed by a descriptive name, a parameter list, and code that calculates a result such as

```
func multiplyBy2 (x: Int) -> Int {
    return x * 2
}
```

One way to rewrite this function as a closure involves dropping the func keyword and the function name, then enclose the rest of the code in curly brackets like this:

```
let y = {(x: Int) -> Int in return x * 2}
```

A second way to write a closure is to eliminate the parameter list altogether like this:

```
let z = {x in return x * 2}
```

Still another shortcut is to eliminate the return keyword altogether like this:

```
let w = {x in x * 2}
```

An even more condensed version of a closure simply displays the return calculation by eliminating any variables and replacing them with placeholders that identify different parameters such as

```
let v = {$0 * 2}
```

To see how to use closures, follow these steps:

1. Choose File ➤ New ➤ Playground and create an iOS Blank playground.

2. Name it **ClosurePlayground**.

3. Type the following:

```
print ("func multiplyBy2 (x: Int) -> Int {")
func multiplyBy2 (x: Int) -> Int {
    return x * 2
}

print(multiplyBy2(x: 4))
print(multiplyBy2(x: 17))

print("{(x: Int) -> Int in return x * 2}")
let y = {(x: Int) -> Int in return x * 2}
print (y(4))
print (y(17))
print("{x in return x * 2}")
let z = {x in return x * 2}
print (z(4))
print (z(17))

print("{x in x * 2}")
let w = {x in x * 2}
print (w(4))
print (w(17))

print("{$0 * 2}")
let v = {$0 * 2}
print(v(4))
print(v(17))
```

4. Click the Run button. The debug area displays the following:

```
func multiplyBy2 (x: Int) -> Int {
8
34
{(x: Int) -> Int in return x * 2}
8
34
{x in return x * 2}
8
```

```
34
{x in x * 2}
8
34
{$0 * 2}
8
34
```

Notice how all versions of the closure work exactly the same as the function declaration. The only difference is how concise each written closure appears. By understanding the different ways closures can be written, you can recognize them in code written by other people.

Create a closure in whatever style you wish that makes most sense to you. For simplicity, many programmers use the concise version that uses $0 as a placeholder for the first passed parameter, $1 for the second passed parameter, $2 for the third passed parameter, and so on.

Closures with Multiple Parameters

When declaring a function, you need to explicitly define the data type of each parameter such as

```
func addNumbers (x: Int, y: Int) -> Int {
    return x + y
}
```

When using closures, you need to enclose all parameters inside parentheses. In many cases, you do not need to define the data type of each parameter since Swift can infer that value based on the data type of the return value. For example, if the return value data type is an integer, Swift infers that the passed parameters must be integers as well such as

```
{(x, y) -> Int in return x + y}
```

However, if there is any ambiguity, you must explicitly define the data types of your parameters such as

```
{(x: Int, y: Int) in return x + y}
{(x: Int, y: Int) in x + y}
{$0 as Int + $1 as Int}
```

Notice that the top two examples define the integer data type with a colon and the Int keyword, while the last example defines the integer data type with the "as" and Int keywords.

Modify your ClosurePlayground file as follows and click the Run button:

```
print ("func addNumbers (x: Int, y: Int) -> Int ")
func addNumbers (x: Int, y: Int) -> Int {
    return x + y
}
print(addNumbers(x: 4, y: 5))
print(addNumbers(x: 17, y: 9))

print("{(x, y) -> Int in return x + y}")
let y = {(x, y) -> Int in return x + y}
print (y(4, 5))
print (y(17, 9))

print("{(x: Int, y: Int) in return x + y}")
let z = {(x: Int, y: Int) in return x + y}
print (z(4, 5))
print (z(17, 9))

print("{(x: Int, y: Int) in x + y}")
let w = {(x: Int, y: Int) in x + y}
print (w(4, 5))
print (w(17, 9))

print("{$0 as Int + $1 as Int}")
let v = {$0 as Int + $1 as Int}
print(v(4, 5))
print(v(17, 9))
```

Understanding Value Capturing

When you declare variables and constants within a function, they can only be accessed inside that function. However, when you declare a variable or constant outside of a function, that function can access that value as shown in Figure 3-1.

```
let randomValue = 2
                                        Value capturing
func addNumbers (x: Int, y: Int) -> Int {
    let wildCard = 4
    let sum = x + y + wildCard + randomValue
    return sum
}
```

Figure 3-1. *A function can access variables inside and above a function*

In Figure 3-1, the "randomValue" constant is declared outside of the function, but the function can still access its value. However, the "wildcard" constant is declared inside the function, so it can only be accessed inside that function and nowhere else.

Since "wildcard" is declared inside the function, we cannot access that value outside that function as shown in Figure 3-2.

```
func addNumbers (x: Int, y: Int) -> Int {
    let wildCard = 4
    let sum = x + y + wildCard + randomValue
    return sum
}

print(wildCard)                                    ⊘ Use of unresolved identifier 'wildCard'
```

Figure 3-2. *Values declared inside a function cannot be accessed outside that function*

Because closures are just another way of writing a function, closures can also capture and modify values declared outside of their scope.

Using Closures like Data

Perhaps the most versatile use of closures is to treat them like chunks of data that you can use like any fixed value. That means you can pass a closure as a parameter in a function (or another closure), store closures in data structures like arrays, or assign a closure to a variable.

When you declare a function, you must give that function a unique name such as

```
func addNumbers (x: Int, y: Int) -> Int {
    return x + y
}
```

To call this function, you would use the function name and pass it parameters such as

```
addNumbers(x: 17, y: 9)
```

Likewise, you can assign a closure to a variable name like this:

```
let addNumbers1 = {(x, y) -> Int in return x + y}
let addNumbers2 = {(x: Int, y: Int) in return x + y}
let addNumbers3 = {(x: Int, y: Int) in x + y}
let addNumbers4 = {$0 as Int + $1 as Int}
```

Then you can run this closure by using its name and pass it parameters such as

```
addNumbers1(17, 9)
addNumbers2(17, 9)
addNumbers3(17, 9)
addNumbers4(17, 9)
```

You can pass a closure as data to another closure like this:

```
addNumbers2(17, addNumbers1(17,9))
```

Since the value of addNumbers1(17,9) is 26, the preceding code is equivalent to

```
addNumbers2(17, 26)
```

This calculates the value 43 (17 + 26).

Another interesting use for closures is to store them in data structures. Unlike fixed values, the same closure can represent different values depending on its parameters. Modify the ClosurePlayground as follows and click the Run button:

```
let addNumbers1 = {(x, y) -> Int in return x + y}
let addNumbers2 = {(x: Int, y: Int) in return x + y}
let addNumbers3 = {(x: Int, y: Int) in x + y}
let addNumbers4 = {$0 as Int + $1 as Int}
```

```
let closureArray = [addNumbers1(9,1), addNumbers2(2,3), addNumbers3(7,6),
addNumbers4(10,2)]
print (closureArray.count)
for i in closureArray {
    print(i)
}
```

The first four lines define four different closures that work exactly alike, which is to accept two integers as parameters, add them together, and return the sum. The fifth line creates an array that holds each closure where each closure gets different parameters.

The sixth line prints the total number of items in the closureArray (4), and then the for-in loop prints each item in the closureArray so the output looks like this:

10
5
13
12

Using Trailing Closures

Writing functions as closures has the advantage of simplifying code. When closures consist of single-line calculations, closures can be shorter to write. However, when closures consist of multiple lines, then you can create a trailing closure instead.

A trailing closure is essentially a function that accepts another function as an argument. The simplest closure accepts no arguments and returns no value, which you can define like this:

```
() -> Void
```

To see how to use a simple trailing closure, follow these steps:

1. Choose File ➤ New ➤ Playground and create an iOS Blank playground.

2. Name it **TrailingClosurePlayground**.

3. Type the following:

```swift
func simpleExample(closure: () -> Void) {
    print("1. Wake up")
    closure()
    print("4. Eat breakfast")
}
```

This code defines a trailing closure that performs a single task. Then in between the two print statements, it calls the closure to run.

4. Type the following underneath the simpleExample function:

```swift
simpleExample() {
    print("---2. Go to bathroom")
    print("---3. Brush teeth")
}
```

The preceding code actually calls the function (simpleExample) and also defines the closure's code inside its curly brackets, which define two print statements.

Note   When calling the function, the parameter list (parentheses) can be omitted like this:

```swift
simpleExample {
    print("---2. Go to bathroom")
    print("---3. Brush teeth")
}
```

---

5. Click the Run button. The debug area displays the following:

```
1. Wake up
---2. Go to bathroom
---3. Brush teeth
4. Eat breakfast
```

Notice how the print statements work. The first print statement defined by the simpleExample function prints "1. Wake up". Then it calls the closure.

The closure then prints "---2. Go to the bathroom" and "---3. Brush teeth". Then the second print statement in the simpleExample function prints "4. Eat breakfast".

Passing Parameters to a Trailing Closure

A simple closure that does the same task over and over again isn't as versatile as a closure that can accept data and calculate different values. To define a closure that accepts parameters, you simply need to define the data types for each parameter such as

```
(Int, Int) -> Void
```

The preceding code defines two parameters that must be integer (Int) data types. To see how to pass parameters to a trailing closure, follow these steps:

1. Make sure your TrailingClosurePlayground is loaded into Xcode.

2. Type the following to create a function:

    ```
    func passParameters(closure: (Int, Int) -> Void ) {
        print("First line")
        closure(4, 8)
        print ("Second line")
    }
    ```

    The preceding code defines a parameter list that can accept two integers. In between the two print statements, it calls the closure and passes it two integer values (4, 8).

3. Type the following underneath the passParameters function:

    ```
    passParameters { x, y in
        print ("-- Closure code beginning")
        print ("\(x * y)")
        print ("-- ending")
    }
    ```

The preceding code calls the passParameters function, and then inside the curly brackets, it defines the code for the closure. It creates two arbitrarily named variables (x and y) and prints two lines of text with the sum of x and y in between.

4.   Click the Run button. The debug area displays the following:

```
First line
-- Closure code beginning
32
-- ending
Second line
```

Passing Parameters and Returning a Value from a Trailing Closure

Just as functions can be more versatile when they return a value, so can closures also return values. All you need to do is define the data type to return such as

```
(Int, Int) -> Int
```

The preceding code defines two parameters that must be integer (Int) data types. Then it returns an integer (Int) value. To see how to pass parameters to a trailing closure that returns a value, follow these steps:

1.   Make sure your TrailingClosurePlayground is loaded into Xcode.

2.   Type the following to create a function:

```
func returnValue(closure: (Int, Int) -> Int) {
    print("First line")
    print ("\(closure(5, 2))")
    print ("Second line")
}
```

This code defines a trailing closure that accepts two integers and returns a single integer value. In between its two print statements, it calls the closure, passes it the integers 5 and 2, and then prints that return value.

3. Type the following underneath the returnValue function:

```
returnValue { x, y in
    x + y
}
```

The preceding code calls the returnValue function, and then inside the curly brackets, it defines the code for the closure. It creates two arbitrarily named variables (x and y), adds the two values together, then returns the sum back to the returnValue function.

4. Click the Run button. The debug area displays the following:

```
First line
7
Second line
```

Summary

Closures are nothing more than another way to write a function. Instead of creating a function and then calling that function in a two-step process, you can create and use a closure in one step.

There are different ways to write a closure where each succeeding version gets sparser and more cryptic. Suppose you had a function like this:

```
func multiplyBy2 (x: Int) -> Int {
    return x * 2
}
```

You could rewrite this function as a closure in four different ways:

```
{(x: Int) -> Int in return x * 2}
{x in return x * 2}
{x in x * 2}
{$0 * 2}
```

When passing parameters into a closure, enclose them in parentheses. In case the data type of a closure's parameters might not be clear, explicitly define the data type like this:

```
{(x: Int, y: Int) in return x + y}
{(x: Int, y: Int) in x + y}
{$0 as Int + $1 as Int}
```

Be aware that closures can access and modify variables declared outside of the closure. You can assign closures to a name or simply use closures in place of data. Any place where you can use data, you can use a closure. If you want to pass a function as an argument, you can use a trailing closure.

Just be careful using closures since closures aren't always obvious how they work. Closures offer efficiency in exchange for possible confusion, so use closures sparingly or add comments to explain how a closure works.

CHAPTER 4

Multithreaded Programming Using Grand Central Dispatch

The next time you pay for groceries in a supermarket, look at the lines at the checkout stands. If there's only one open checkout stand, there's likely a long line of customers waiting to pay. That means everyone has to wait their turn before they can leave. However, if there are multiple checkout stands open, more customers can pay at the same time, and the wait time for everyone is much less. That's the basic idea behind multithreaded programming.

In the old days of computers, tasks were fairly simple, so processors were fast enough to handle them one at a time no matter how many there might be. Gradually, as software got more sophisticated and tasks got more complex, processors couldn't handle so many complicated tasks simultaneously. Speeding up the processor by itself could only solve the problem to a limited extent, so processors started offering multiple cores, which were essentially separate processors that could work on different tasks simultaneously.

While multicore processors offered a solution, the bigger problem was none of these multicore processors could work to their full potential unless the software took advantage of these multiple cores. This forced programmers to write code that could run at the same time known as concurrent programming. Writing code was hard enough, and writing additional code to make different parts of a program run at the same time was often confusing and difficult. As a result, most programmers didn't bother, which meant their software wouldn't take full advantage of multicore processors.

To solve the problem of managing code to run in parallel, Apple created a solution called **Grand Central Dispatch** (GCD), which provides support for concurrent code execution on multicore hardware in iOS and macOS. Instead of forcing developers to

63

© Wallace Wang 2023
W. Wang, *Pro iPhone Development with SwiftUI*, https://doi.org/10.1007/978-1-4842-9544-1_4

worry about the details of managing code to run in parallel, known as threads, Grand Central Dispatch lets developers simply identify which chunks of code to run at the same time and Grand Central Dispatch takes care of the actual details to do so.

In the old days, software was mostly self-contained in that it didn't need to rely on anything else. Today, software often depends on external factors that are largely unpredictable such as waiting for a file to load or a network connection to complete. While waiting, the entire program is effectively paused. If this pause is too long, it makes the program look like it's frozen and unresponsive.

That's why you want to use Grand Central Dispatch to allow multiple threads of execution within a program. That way, even if a single thread is stuck waiting for a specific event, the other threads can keep going. By using Grand Central Dispatch, your apps should never feel slow and unresponsive to the user.

Note   Grand Central Dispatch works identically in both iOS and macOS.

Understanding Threads

To fully understand the advantage of Grand Central Dispatch, it's important to see how delays can ruin the responsiveness of an app in the eyes of a user. To do this, we'll see what happens when a process runs for too long, essentially forcing the entire app to wait until the process finishes. During this time, the app appears frozen and unresponsive.

We'll deliberately create an app that will lock up the user interface. To see how to create an app that appears unresponsive, follow these steps:

1. Create a new iOS App project, make sure it uses SwiftUI, and give it a descriptive name (such as ThreadApp).

2. Click the ContentView file in the Navigator pane. The Editor pane displays the contents of the ContentView file.

3. Add three State variables underneath the struct ContentView line like this:

```
@State var message = ""
@State var results = ""
@State var sliderValue = 0.0
```

4. Create a VStack inside the var body: some View and type the
    following to add a Button, TextEditor, Slider, and Text like this:

```
var body: some View {
    VStack {
        Button("Click Me") {

        }
        TextEditor(text: $results)
        Slider(value: $sliderValue)
        Text("Message = \(message)")
    }
}
```

This creates a Button at the top of the screen, a Text Editor in the
middle of the screen, and a Slider at the bottom of the screen.

5. Add the following code above the last curly bracket of the struct
    ContentView:

```
func fetchSomethingFromServer() -> String {
    Thread.sleep(forTimeInterval: 1)
    return "Hi there"
}

func processData(_ data: String) -> String {
    Thread.sleep(forTimeInterval: 2)
    return data.uppercased()
}

func calculateFirstResult(_ data: String) -> String {
    Thread.sleep(forTimeInterval: 3)
    let message = "Number of chars: \(String(data).count)"
    return message
}

func calculateSecondResult(_ data: String) -> String {
    Thread.sleep(forTimeInterval: 4)
    return data.replacingOccurrences(of: "E", with: "e")
}
```

6.   Edit the Button code as follows:

```
Button("Click Me") {
    let startTime = NSDate()
    let fetchedData = fetchSomethingFromServer()
    let processedData = processData(fetchedData)
    let firstResult = calculateFirstResult(processedData)
    let secondResult = calculateSecondResult(processedData)
    let resultsSummary =
    "First: [\(firstResult)]\nSecond: [\(secondResult)]"
    results = resultsSummary
    let endTime = NSDate()
    message = "Completed in \(endTime.timeIntervalSince(startTime
    as Date)) seconds"
}
```

The entire ContentView file should look like this:

```
import SwiftUI

struct ContentView: View {
    @State var message = ""
    @State var results = ""
    @State var sliderValue = 0.0
    var body: some View {
        VStack {
            Button("Click Me") {
                let startTime = NSDate()
                let fetchedData = fetchSomethingFromServer()
                let processedData = processData(fetchedData)
                let firstResult = calculateFirstResult(processed
                Data)
                let secondResult = self.calculateSecondResult
                (processedData)
                let resultsSummary =
                "First: [\(firstResult)]\nSecond:
                [\(secondResult)]"
                results = resultsSummary
```

```swift
                    let endTime = NSDate()
                    message = "Completed in \(endTime.
                    timeIntervalSince(startTime as Date)) seconds"
                }
                TextEditor(text: $results)
                Slider(value: $sliderValue)
                Text("Message = \(message)")
            }
        }
    }

    func fetchSomethingFromServer() -> String {
            Thread.sleep(forTimeInterval: 1)
            return "Hi there"
        }

        func processData(_ data: String) -> String {
            Thread.sleep(forTimeInterval: 2)
            return data.uppercased()
        }

        func calculateFirstResult(_ data: String) -> String {
            Thread.sleep(forTimeInterval: 3)
            let message = "Number of chars: \(String(data).count)"
            return message
        }

        func calculateSecondResult(_ data: String) -> String {
            Thread.sleep(forTimeInterval: 4)
            return data.replacingOccurrences(of: "E", with: "e")
        }

}

struct ContentView_Previews: PreviewProvider {
    static var previews: some View {
        ContentView()

    }
}
```

7. Click the Live icon on the Canvas pane.

8. Drag the slider left and right. Notice that you can easily drag the slider back and forth.

9. Click the Click Me Button at the top of the screen. Notice that the button dims. Try dragging the slider back and forth. Because the app is running a process, the user interface now appears frozen and unresponsive for about ten seconds. After the process completes, it displays the results on the screen as shown in Figure 4-1.

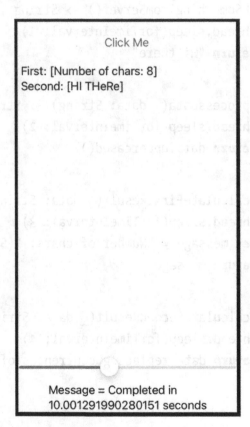

Figure 4-1. *The results after the process runs*

10. Drag the slider left and right. Notice that the slider now easily moves once again.

This example lets you see how a process can freeze an app and make it appear unresponsive even though the app is still running. If you submit an app that freezes its user interface periodically, Apple will reject it from the App Store.

Most modern operating systems (including iOS) support multiple threads of execution. If there's just one processor core, the operating system will switch between all executing threads, much like it switches between all executing processes. If more than one core is available, the threads will be distributed among them.

All threads in a process share the same executable program code and the same global data. Each thread can also have some data that is exclusive to the thread through a special structure called a **mutex** (short for **mutual exclusion**) or a lock. Such a lock ensures that a particular chunk of code can't be run by multiple threads at once, which can keep multiple threads from accessing the same data simultaneously.

When writing code, you need to make sure your code is **thread-safe**. As a general rule, any code that controls the user interface is not thread-safe. Because threads increase the chance of multiple processes interfering with each other, most programmers don't use threads directly. That's why Apple created Grand Central Dispatch (GCD) to help make concurrent programming easier and safer.

Note   To learn more about thread safety, read Apple's documentation:

```
https://developer.apple.com/library/ios/documentation/
Cocoa/Conceptual/Multithreading/ThreadSafetySummary/
ThreadSafetySummary.html
```

Using Grand Central Dispatch

A key concept of GCD is the **queue**. GCD splits tasks into units of work and puts those units into queues for execution. The system manages the queues, executing units of work on multiple threads. We don't need to start or manage the background threads directly, and we are freed from much of the bookkeeping that's usually involved in implementing multithreaded applications.

GCD provides a number of predefined queues, including a queue that's guaranteed to always do its work on the main thread which is perfect for code that manages the user interface. GCD lets you create as many queues as you need. Units of work added to a GCD queue will always be started in the order they were placed in the queue. That said, they may not always finish in the same order, since a GCD queue will automatically distribute its work among multiple threads, if possible.

To use GCD, we first need to create a queue using the DispatchQueue keyword such as

```
let queue1 = DispatchQueue(label: "queue1")
```

Once we've created a queue, we need to define the code to run in that queue. This code runs in a closure and can run synchronously or asynchronously. An asynchronous queue runs whenever the processor has time to complete it. A synchronous queue runs and must complete before any other code can run. In general, asynchronous queues are most useful when you want to run multiple tasks at the same time but the order and time that they complete isn't important.

To make a queue run, we have to define whether it's asynchronous or synchronous and specify the code to run in a closure like this:

```
queue1.sync { () -> Void in
    // Code here
}

Queue2.async { () -> Void in
    // Code here
}
```

To see how asynchronous queues can work, but may complete at different, unpredictable times, follow these steps:

1. Choose File ➤ New ➤ Playground and create a Blank iOS playground. Name this new playground **QueuePlayground**.

2. Edit the playground code so it looks like this:

    ```
    import UIKit

    let queue1 = DispatchQueue(label: "queue1")
    let queue2 = DispatchQueue(label: "queue2")
    let queue3 = DispatchQueue(label: "queue3")
    ```

```
queue1.async { () -> Void in
    print(queue1.label)
}

queue2.async { () -> Void in
    print(queue2.label)
}

queue3.async { () -> Void in
    print(queue3.label)
}

print("Program stopped")
```

This code creates three queues and then runs tasks in each queue that simply prints the name of the queue. Finally, the code ends by printing "Program stopped".

3. Click the Run button. Notice that the debug area displays the output of the code such as

    queue1
    Program stopped
    queue2
    queue3

4. Click the Run button to run the program again. Notice that the output may change such as

    Program stopped
    queue1
    queue3
    queue2

Even though the code is identical, asynchronous queues may complete at different times. Each time you click the Run button, you'll likely see a different result. While you can have multiple tasks running on different asynchronous queues, you cannot predict when any given queue will complete its task.

71

To see how synchronous queues work in the exact same order every time, modify the playground code to change all async calls to sync as follows:

```swift
import UIKit

let queue1 = DispatchQueue(label: "queue1")
let queue2 = DispatchQueue(label: "queue2")
let queue3 = DispatchQueue(label: "queue3")

queue1.sync { () -> Void in
    print(queue1.label)
}

queue2.sync { () -> Void in
    print(queue2.label)
}
queue3.sync { () -> Void in
    print(queue3.label)
}

print("Program stopped")
```

No matter how many times you run this code, the output will always be predictable and in order like this:

queue1
queue2
queue3
Program stopped

The only way you can change the order of the output is to change the position of the queues such as putting queue3 ahead of queue1. Since synchronous queues are little different than not using concurrency at all, asynchronous queues are used most often as long as the order of task completion isn't important.

Now that we know how GCD can run multiple tasks at the same time, we need to use GCD to fix the unresponsive user interface of our ThreadApp. First, we need to identify which code is causing the delay. In our example, it's this code inside the Button:

```swift
let startTime = NSDate()
let fetchedData = fetchSomethingFromServer()
```

```
let processedData = processData(fetchedData)
let firstResult = calculateFirstResult(processedData)
let secondResult = calculateSecondResult(processedData)
let resultsSummary =
"First: [\(firstResult)]\nSecond: [\(secondResult)]"
results = resultsSummary
let endTime = NSDate()
message = "Completed in \(endTime.
timeIntervalSince(startTime as Date)) seconds"
```

Logically, it would seem like we could simply wrap this code inside a closure and run it in a queue. However, look out for this line:

```
results = resultsSummary
```

This line updates the results State variable that appears inside the Text Editor. As a general rule, updating the user interface in a queue is not thread-safe, which means trying to update the user interface in a queue will cause an error. To see what happens when you try to update the user interface within a queue, follow these steps:

1. Make sure the ThreadApp project is loaded in Xcode.

2. Click the ContentView file.

3. Edit the Button code as follows:

```
Button("Click Me") {
    let startTime = NSDate()
    let queue = DispatchQueue.global(qos: .default)
    queue.async {
        let fetchedData = fetchSomethingFromServer()
        let processedData = processData(fetchedData)
        let firstResult = calculateFirstResult
        (processedData)
        let secondResult = calculateSecondResult
        (processedData)
        let resultsSummary =
        "First: [\(firstResult)]\nSecond:
        [\(secondResult)]"
```

```
            results = resultsSummary
            let endTime = NSDate()
            message = "Completed in \(endTime.
            timeIntervalSince(startTime as Date)) seconds"
        }
    }
```

First, we grab a preexisting global queue that's always available, using the DispatchQueue.global() function. That function takes one argument to define a priority. If you specify a different priority in the argument, you will actually get a different global queue, which the system will prioritize differently. For now, we'll stick with the default global queue.

The queue is then passed to the queue.async() function, along with the closure. GCD takes the closure and puts it on the queue, from where it will be scheduled to run on a background thread and executed one step at a time, just as when it was running in the main thread.

Note that we defined a variable called startTime just before the closure is created and then used its value at the end of the closure. The closure can "capture" the value of variables declared ahead of it, allowing access.

The entire ContentView file should look like this:

```
import SwiftUI

struct ContentView: View {
    @State var message = ""
    @State var results = ""
    @State var sliderValue = 0.0
    var body: some View {
        VStack {
            Button("Click Me") {
                let startTime = NSDate()
                let queue = DispatchQueue.global(qos: .default)
                queue.async {
```

```
            let fetchedData = fetchSomethingFromServer()
            let processedData = processData(fetchedData)
            let firstResult = calculateFirstResult
            (processedData)
            let secondResult = calculateSecondResult
            (processedData)
            let resultsSummary =
            "First: [\(firstResult)]\nSecond:
            [\(secondResult)]"
            results = resultsSummary
            let endTime = NSDate()
            message = "Completed in \(endTime.
            timeIntervalSince(startTime as Date)) seconds"
        }
    }
    TextEditor(text: $results)
    Slider(value: $sliderValue)
    Text("Message = \(message)")
  }
}

func fetchSomethingFromServer() -> String {
    Thread.sleep(forTimeInterval: 1)
    return "Hi there"
}

func processData(_ data: String) -> String {
    Thread.sleep(forTimeInterval: 2)
    return data.uppercased()
}

func calculateFirstResult(_ data: String) -> String {
    Thread.sleep(forTimeInterval: 3)
    let message = "Number of chars: \(String(data).count)"
    return message
}
```

```swift
    func calculateSecondResult(_ data: String) -> String {
        Thread.sleep(forTimeInterval: 4)
        return data.replacingOccurrences(of: "E", with: "e")
    }

}

struct ContentView_Previews: PreviewProvider {
    static var previews: some View {
        ContentView()

    }
}
```

4. Click the Live icon on the Canvas pane.

5. Click the Click Me Button at the top of the screen.

6. Drag the slider left and right. Notice that even though the app is processing, the user interface is still responsive. Eventually, the app finishes its processing and displays its results in the text view, but during that entire time, the user could still interact with the interface.

Using Dispatch Groups

In the previous example, we created a background thread and then jumped back to the main thread to update the user interface. While this is acceptable, we can optimize the code a bit further using dispatch groups. Right now, our calculateFirstResult() and calculateSecondResult() methods are called in sequence, yet there's no reason to do this since they're completely independent of each other.

A better solution is to call these two methods in a dispatch group. This lets each function run independent of the other, which can improve performance since the methods are now operating concurrently rather than sequentially. Finally, we can also use dispatch_group_notify() to specify an additional closure that will run only when all the other closures in the group have completed running.

To create a dispatch group, we just need to create a DispatchGroup object like this:

```
let group = DispatchGroup()
```

Then we run each queue inside this dispatch group like this:

```
queue.async(group: group) {
        firstResult = calculateFirstResult(processedData)
}
```

To run a final closure after all other closures have finished, we create a group.notify queue like this:

```
group.notify(queue: queue) {
    let resultsSummary = "First: [\(firstResult!)]\nSecond:
    [\(secondResult!)]"
    let endTime = Date()
    results = resultsSummary
    message = "Completed in \(endTime.timeIntervalSince(startTime))
    seconds"
    }
```

One final difference is that the group.notify and the queue.async queues need to access the firstResult and secondResult variables, so we need to declare them outside of both queues like this:

```
var firstResult: String!
var secondResult: String!
```

To see how to use dispatch groups, follow these steps:

1. Make sure the ThreadApp project is loaded in Xcode.

2. Click the ContentView file in the Navigator pane.

3. Add an HStack right above the Button like this:

```
VStack {
    HStack {
        Button("Click Me") {
```

4. Add a Spacer() after the last curly bracket of the "Click Me" Button.

5. Add a second Button underneath the Spacer() as follows:

```
Button("Dispatch Groups") {
    let startTime = Date()
    let queue = DispatchQueue.global(qos: .default)
    queue.async {
        let fetchedData = self.fetchSomethingFromServer()
        let processedData = self.processData(fetchedData)
        var firstResult: String!
        var secondResult: String!
        let group = DispatchGroup()

        queue.async(group: group) {
            firstResult = self.calculateFirstResult(processedData)
        }
        queue.async(group: group) {
            secondResult = self.calculateSecondResult
            (processedData)
        }

        group.notify(queue: queue) {
            let resultsSummary = "First:
            [\(firstResult!)]\nSecond:
            [\(secondResult!)]"
            let endTime = Date()
            results = resultsSummary
            message = "Completed in \(endTime.
            timeIntervalSince(startTime)) seconds"
        }
    }
}
```

The entire ContentView file should look like this:

```
import SwiftUI

struct ContentView: View {
    @State var message = ""
```

```swift
@State var results = ""
@State var sliderValue = 0.0
var body: some View {
    VStack {
        HStack {
            Button("Click Me") {
                let startTime = NSDate()
                let queue = DispatchQueue.global
                (qos: .default)
                queue.async {
                    let fetchedData =
                    fetchSomethingFromServer()
                    let processedData = processData
                    (fetchedData)
                    let firstResult =
                    calculateFirstResult(processedData)
                    let secondResult = calculateSecondResult
                    (processedData)
                    let resultsSummary =
                    "First: [\(firstResult)]\nSecond:
                    [\(secondResult)]"
                    results = resultsSummary
                    let endTime = NSDate()
                    message = "Completed in \(endTime.
                    timeIntervalSince(startTime as Date))
                    seconds"
                }
            }
            Spacer()
            Button("Dispatch Groups") {
                let startTime = Date()
                let queue = DispatchQueue.global
                (qos: .default)
                queue.async {
                    let fetchedData = self.
                    fetchSomethingFromServer()
```

```swift
                    let processedData = self.
                    processData(fetchedData)
                    var firstResult: String!
                    var secondResult: String!
                    let group = DispatchGroup()

                    queue.async(group: group) {
                        firstResult = self.calculateFirstResult
                        (processedData)
                    }
                    queue.async(group: group) {
                        secondResult = self.calculateSecond
                        Result(processedData)
                    }

                    group.notify(queue: queue) {
                        let resultsSummary = "First:
                        [\(firstResult!)]\nSecond:
                        [\(secondResult!)]"
                        let endTime = Date()
                        results = resultsSummary
                        message = "Completed in \(endTime.
                        timeIntervalSince(startTime)) seconds"
                    }
                }
            }
        }
        TextEditor(text: $results)
        Slider(value: $sliderValue)
        Text("Message = \(message)")
    }
}

func fetchSomethingFromServer() -> String {
    Thread.sleep(forTimeInterval: 1)
    return "Hi there"
}
```

```swift
    func processData(_ data: String) -> String {
        Thread.sleep(forTimeInterval: 2)
        return data.uppercased()
    }

    func calculateFirstResult(_ data: String) -> String {
        Thread.sleep(forTimeInterval: 3)
        let message = "Number of chars: \(String(data).count)"
        return message
    }

    func calculateSecondResult(_ data: String) -> String {
        Thread.sleep(forTimeInterval: 4)
        return data.replacingOccurrences(of: "E", with: "e")
    }
}

struct ContentView_Previews: PreviewProvider {
    static var previews: some View {
        ContentView()

    }
}
```

6. Click the Live icon on the Canvas pane.

7. Click the "Click Me" Button. Notice that when the process completes, the Text view at the bottom of the screen displays a message such as

Completed in 10.00560998916626 seconds

8. Click the second button labeled "Dispatch Group". Notice that when this process completes, the Text view at the bottom of the screen displays a message such as

Completed in 7.014010071754456 seconds

What was once a ten-second operation now takes just seven seconds, thanks to the fact that we're running both of the calculations simultaneously. Obviously, our contrived example gets the maximum effect because these two "calculations" don't actually do anything but cause the thread they're running on to sleep. In a real app, the speedup would depend on what sort of work is being done and what CPU is available.

Summary

Grand Central Dispatch (GCD) is a way to run multiple parts of your code separately. You can do this using threads, but manipulating individual threads can be troublesome and error-prone. Instead of working with threads, you can use GCD instead, which takes care of the details needed to start, run, and stop different threads safely.

As you can see, GCD can help speed up bottlenecks in your code where a single process might take a long time to complete, which can make your app seem to freeze and be unresponsive. By using GCD at points in your app where speed is essential or where your app lags in responses to the user, you can easily provide a better user experience, even in situations where you can't improve the actual performance.

CHAPTER 5

Understanding Concurrency

Most computer programs run instructions sequentially. In many cases, that's fine since computers can process instructions so rapidly that even calculating complex mathematical equations takes so little time that a computer program barely seems to slow down at all.

While the processors in today's iPhone and iPad models rival the processors used in desktop and laptop PCs, there's still a problem running instructions sequentially no matter how fast they can be processed. Suppose a program needs to retrieve data from a server over a network. While waiting for the requested data, a program essentially halts completely because the code waiting for data holds up the entire program. Only until it finishes receiving the data it requested can the program continue executing additional instructions as shown in Figure 5-1.

Figure 5-1. *Sequential processing risks temporarily halting completely to perform time-consuming tasks*

Because time-consuming tasks, such as retrieving data over a network, can temporarily halt a program so it appears to freeze and be unresponsive, a better solution is to run two or more tasks concurrently. That means while the time-consuming task runs, the rest of the program's instructions can run at the same time. That way, the program can always respond to the user no matter how long a particular task may take as shown in Figure 5-2.

© Wallace Wang 2023
W. Wang, *Pro iPhone Development with SwiftUI*, https://doi.org/10.1007/978-1-4842-9544-1_5

Figure 5-2. *Concurrent processing lets two or more tasks run simultaneously*

Concurrency with Async/Await

With synchronous functions, the function must complete before another function can run. With asynchronous functions, the asynchronous function can start running, and then another function can immediately start running before the asynchronous function finishes.

The old way of creating an asynchronous function was to use completion handlers such as

```
func doSomething(completion: (Result<Response, BigError>) -> Void) {
    // Perform task
}
```

To see how to use completion handlers, follow these steps:

1. Create a new iOS Playground file and name it CompletionHandler.

2. Edit the file so that it appears as follows:

```
import UIKit

enum BigError: Error {
    case powerOutage
    case endOfTheWorld
}

enum Response {
    case success
    case failure
}
```

```swift
let startTime = NSDate()

func doSomething(completion: (Result<Response, BigError>)
-> Void) {
    print("Starting task")
    Thread.sleep(forTimeInterval: 2)

    let randomNumber = Int.random(in: 0..<2)

    if randomNumber == 0 {
        completion(.failure(.powerOutage))
        return
    }
    completion(.success(.success))
}

// Calling the function
doSomething { result in
    switch result {
    case .success(let response):
        print("Result = \(response)")
    case .failure(let error):
        print("This is the error = \(error)")
    }
    print("Ending task")
}

let endTime = NSDate()
print("Completed in \(endTime.timeIntervalSince(startTime as
Date)) seconds")
```

3. Move the mouse pointer to the left of the last line and click the
    Run button.

Completion handlers are often called unstructured concurrency because they're hard to read and understand. In particular, look at how the function includes two possible ways to call the completion handler:

```swift
func doSomething(completion: (Result<Response, BigError>) -> Void) {
```

```
    print("Starting task")
    Thread.sleep(forTimeInterval: 2)

    let randomNumber = Int.random(in: 0..<2)

    if randomNumber == 0 {
        completion(.failure(.powerOutage))
        return
    }
    completion(.success(.success))
}
```

If you fail to include all possible ways to exit the function, the function could run endlessly, freezing your program. To make concurrency easier to read and understand, Swift uses the async/await keywords. The async keyword defines a function to run asynchronously. Then to call an asynchronous function, you use the await keyword.

To see how to use async/await, follow these steps:

1. Create a new iOS Playground file and name it AsyncAwait.

2. Edit the file so that it appears as follows:

```
import UIKit

enum BigError: Error {
    case powerOutage
    case endOfTheWorld
}

enum Response {
    case success
    case failure
}

let startTime = NSDate()

func doSomething() async throws -> Response {
    print("Starting task")
    Thread.sleep(forTimeInterval: 2)
```

```
    let randomNumber = Int.random(in: 0..<2)

    if randomNumber == 0 {
        throw BigError.powerOutage
    }
    return Response.success
}

// Calling the function
func callFunction() {
    Task(priority: .low) {
        do {
            let result = try await doSomething()
            print ("Result = \(result)")
        } catch {
            if let whatError = error as? BigError {
                print ("This is the error = \(whatError)")
            } else {
                print ("Unknown error")
            }
        }
    }
    print("Ending task")
}

callFunction()
let endTime = NSDate()
print("Completed in \(endTime.timeIntervalSince(startTime as
Date)) seconds")
```

3. Move the mouse pointer to the left of the last line and click the
   Run button. The result will be similar to the following:

Starting task
Ending task
Completed in 0.010614991188049316 seconds
Result = success

Notice that the doSomething() function prints "Starting task". Then callFunction() prints "Ending task". The last line of the program prints "Completed in 0.010614991188049316 seconds". Finally, the callFunction() task eventually prints "Result = success", which shows that while callFunction() was still running, the rest of the code after callFunction() went ahead and ran (let endTime = NSDate() and print("Completed in 0.010614991188049316 seconds")).

Using Concurrency with User Interfaces

The most visible use of concurrency occurs when interacting with the user interface. Without concurrency, an app might run code that takes a long time, which will temporarily freeze the user interface. Only until a particular task is completed will the app's user interface be responsive again.

Clearly freezing the user interface periodically is unacceptable, which is why we need concurrency to run tasks in the background so the user interface can still remain responsive to the user. To see how an app's user interface can appear frozen and unresponsive without concurrency, follow these steps:

1. Create a new iOS App project and name it ConcurrencyApp.

2. Click ContentView file in the Navigator pane.

3. Add the following State variables underneath the struct ContentView: View line like this:

    ```
    @State var message = ""
    @State var sliderValue = 0.0
    ```

4. Add the following enum underneath the State variables:

    ```
    enum Response {
        case success
    }
    ```

5. Add a VStack underneath the var body: some View line that includes a Button, Spacer(), Slider, and Text view like this:

    ```
    VStack {
        Button("Click Me") {
    ```

```
        }
        Spacer()
        Slider(value: $sliderValue)
        Text("Message = \(message)")
    }
}
```

6. Inside the Button curly brackets, add the following code:

```
let startTime = NSDate()
Thread.sleep(forTimeInterval: 20)
callFunction()
let endTime = NSDate()
message = "Completed in \(endTime.timeIntervalSince(startTime as
Date)) seconds."
```

The most important part of this code is that it halts the program from running for 20 seconds using Thread.sleep(forTimeInterval: 20). This demonstrates the problem of a time-consuming task that will freeze the user interface.

7. Add the following two functions above the last curly bracket in the struct ContentView: View like this:

```
func doSomething() async throws -> Response {
    return Response.success
}

func callFunction() {
    Task(priority: .high) {
        do {
            _ = try await doSomething()
        } catch {
            //
        }
    }
}
```

The callFunction() does nothing more than call the
doSomething() function using the await keyword. Calling a
function with the await keyword only works if that function is
defined with the async keyword as well.

The entire ContentView file should look like this:

```swift
import SwiftUI

struct ContentView: View {
    @State var message = ""
    @State var sliderValue = 0.0
    enum Response {
        case success
    }

    var body: some View {
        VStack {
            Button("Click Me") {
                let startTime = NSDate()
                Thread.sleep(forTimeInterval: 20)
                callFunction()
                let endTime = NSDate()
                message = "Completed in \(endTime.
                timeIntervalSince(startTime as Date)) seconds."
            }
            Spacer()
            Slider(value: $sliderValue)
            Text("Message = \(message)")
        }
    }

    func doSomething() async throws -> Response {
        return Response.success
    }

    func callFunction() {
        Task(priority: .high) {
```

```
        do {
            _ = try await doSomething()
        } catch {
            //
        }
    }
}

struct ContentView_Previews: PreviewProvider {
    static var previews: some View {
        ContentView()
    }
}
```

8. Click the Live icon in the Canvas pane.

9. Click the Click Me Button. Try to drag the Slider left and right.
    Notice that the user interface appears frozen and unresponsive
    until the Thread.sleep(forTimeInterval: 20) ends after 20 seconds.
    After 20 seconds has passed, you'll finally be able to drag the
    Slider back and forth.

The Thread.sleep function mimics a task that takes 20 seconds. During this time
period, the user interface remains frozen. To see how concurrency can avoid this
problem, follow these steps:

1. Create a new iOS App project and name it TryAwaitApp.

2. Click the ContentView file in the Navigator pane.

3. Add the following State variables underneath the struct
    ContentView: View line like this:

```
@State var message = ""
@State var sliderValue = 0.0
@State var taskMessage = ""
```

4. Add the following enum underneath the State variables:

```
enum Response {
    case success
}
```

5. Add a VStack underneath the var body: some View line that
    includes a Button, Spacer(), Slider, and Text view like this:

```
VStack {
    Button("Click Me") {

    }
    Spacer()
    Text("Task message = \(taskMessage)")
    Slider(value: $sliderValue)
    Text("Message = \(message)")
}
```

6. Inside the Button curly brackets, add the following code:

```
let startTime = NSDate()
// Thread.sleep(forTimeInterval: 20)
callFunction()
let endTime = NSDate()
message = "Completed in \(endTime.timeIntervalSince(startTime as
Date)) seconds."
```

This code is largely identical to the previous project with the
exception that it comments out the Thread.sleep function.

7. Add the following two functions above the last curly bracket in the
    struct ContentView: View like this:

```
func doSomething() async throws -> Response {
    try await Task.sleep(nanoseconds: 20_000_000_000)
    taskMessage = "Done now!"
    return Response.success
}
```

```swift
func callFunction() {
    Task(priority: .high) {
        do {
            _ = try await doSomething()
        } catch {
            //
        }
    }
}
```

The doSomething() function uses a Task.sleep function that waits for 20,000,000,000 nanoseconds, which is equal to 20 seconds. After waiting 20 seconds, then it changes the taskMessage variable with the string "Done now!" That means after waiting 20 seconds, the "Done now!" string will appear on the user interface.

Note   To make it easier to read and write large numbers, Swift can optionally use the underscore character to separate three digits of a large number. So 20_000_000_000 is equal to 20,000,000,000.

The entire ContentView file should look like this:

```swift
import SwiftUI

struct ContentView: View {
    @State var message = ""
    @State var sliderValue = 0.0
    @State var taskMessage = ""

    enum Response {
        case success
    }

    var body: some View {
        VStack {
            Button("Click Me") {
                let startTime = NSDate()
```

```
//                  Thread.sleep(forTimeInterval: 20)
                callFunction()
                let endTime = NSDate()
                message = "Completed in \(endTime.
                timeIntervalSince(startTime as Date)) seconds."
            }
            Spacer()
            Text("Task message = \(taskMessage)")
            Slider(value: $sliderValue)
            Text("Message = \(message)")
        }
    }

    func doSomething() async throws -> Response {
        try await Task.sleep(nanoseconds: 20_000_000_000)
        taskMessage = "Done now!"
        return Response.success
    }

    func callFunction() {
        Task(priority: .high) {
            do {
                _ = try await doSomething()
            } catch {
                //
            }
        }
    }

}


struct ContentView_Previews: PreviewProvider {
    static var previews: some View {
        ContentView()
    }
}
```

8. Click the Live icon on the Canvas pane.

9. Click the Click Me Button. Notice the user interface remains responsive while the Text view above the slider remains blank. After 20 seconds has passed, the "Done now!" string appears in this Text view, which shows that the doSomething() function had been running all that time. Because this doSomething() function was running concurrently, the rest of the program could continue running without waiting for the doSomething() function to finish.

Summary

The main idea behind concurrency is that you never want the app to be running code that freezes the user interface and makes it appear unresponsive as if your app had crashed. One way to use concurrency is to rely on completion handlers to run after a function is finished. However, this can be hard to read and understand.

In the latest version of Swift, the new way to define concurrency is to use the async/ await keywords. The await keyword is used to call an asynchronous function that has been defined by the async keyword. Thus, the async/await keywords work together to allow code to run asynchronously, so the user interface is never affected.

CHAPTER 6

Understanding Data Persistence

All but the simplest apps need to store data. The Stocks app lets users track their favorite stocks, so it needs to store the list of stocks to follow that the user chose. Each time the user launches the Stocks app again, it displays the list of stocks the user inputted previously. If the user adds or deletes stocks from this list, the Stocks app needs to store this updated list and retrieve it again the next time the user loads the Stocks app.

Other types of apps may have various settings that allow users to customize an app such as defining its background color or sounds to play when certain events occur such as one sound to represent a text message received and another sound to represent a voicemail someone left you.

Storing and retrieving data when the user starts and stops an app is known as data persistence. Three common ways to store and retrieve data in an iOS app includes

- UserDefaults

- Reading and writing files

- Core Data

Each method offers different advantages and disadvantages, so it depends on what type of data you want to store and its purpose that can define which storage method your app should use.

UserDefaults is generally used to store small amounts of data such as user preferences for a particular app. This method uses a dictionary data structure and saves data in a .plist file, similar to the Info.plist file that every Xcode project includes. It's the simplest method to save common types of data such as strings, numbers, dates, and data structures such as dictionaries or arrays and is best suited for small amounts of data.

97

© Wallace Wang 2023
W. Wang, *Pro iPhone Development with SwiftUI*, https://doi.org/10.1007/978-1-4842-9544-1_6

Reading and writing data to a file can be useful to store longer amounts of data such as several lines of text. However, reading and writing to a file can be slow if you have lots of data, which requires code to search through the entire file to find specific data.

Core Data lets you store different types of data in groups called entities, which are similar to tables or records in a database. If you need to store large amounts of diverse data, use Core Data over the other two options for storing data.

Storing Preferences in UserDefaults

UserDefaults is meant to store small amounts of data such as a number, Boolean value, or a string. This makes UserDefaults best for storing an app's settings such as its default background color. Using UserDefaults involves a two-step process:

- Store data in UserDefaults

- Retrieve data from UserDefaults

To store data using UserDefaults, you need to define a key and the data you want to store in this format where "dataToSave" represents an actual value and "keyString" represents a unique string:

```
UserDefaults.standard.set(dataToSave, forKey: "keyString")
```

The set command saves the key and its associated data. To retrieve previously saved data, you need to know the key value and the type of data stored such as an integer, Boolean, or double data type. Knowing the data type you want to retrieve, you can use one of the following:

- integer(forKey: "keyString") – Returns an integer if the key exists, or 0 if not

- bool(forKey: "keyString") – Returns a Boolean if the key exists, or false if not

- float(forKey: "keyString") – Returns a float value if the key exists, or 0.0 if not

- string(forKey: "keyString") – Returns a string value if the key exists, or nil if not

- double(forKey: "keyString") – Returns a double value if the key exists, or 0.0 if not

- object(forKey: "keyString") – Returns AnyObject? so you'll need to conditionally typecast it to a specific data type, or nil if not

- url(forKey: "keyString") – Returns a URL if the key exists, or nil if not

To see how to save data as UserDefaults, follow these steps:

1. Create a new iOS App project, make sure it uses SwiftUI, and give it a descriptive name such as UserDefaultsApp.

2. Click the ContentView file in the Navigator pane.

3. Add the following three State variables:

```
@State private var myText = ""
@State private var myToggle = true
@State private var mySlider = 0.0
```

4. Add a VStack inside the var body: some View to define a spacing of 25. Make sure the VStack has nothing in it:

```
var body: some View {
    VStack (spacing: 25){

    }
    .padding()

}
```

5. Add a TextField, Toggle, and Slider inside the VStack. These will let the user change them and save their current state as a UserDefault:

```
var body: some View {
    VStack (spacing: 25){
        TextField("Change text here", text: $myText)

        Toggle(isOn: $myToggle, label: {
            Text("Toggle here")
        })
```

```
            Slider(value: $mySlider)
        }
        .padding()

}
```

6. Underneath the Slider, add three Buttons. One Button is to save data, the second Button is to clear or reset the user interface, and the third Button is to retrieve the UserDefaults data:

```
var body: some View {
    VStack (spacing: 25){
        TextField("Change text here", text: $myText)

        Toggle(isOn: $myToggle, label: {
            Text("Toggle here")
        })

        Slider(value: $mySlider)

        Button("Save data") {
            UserDefaults.standard.set(myText, forKey: "Text")
            UserDefaults.standard.set(myToggle, forKey: "Toggle")
            UserDefaults.standard.set(mySlider, forKey: "Slider")
        }

        Button("Clear data") {
            myText = ""
            myToggle = true
            mySlider = 0.0
        }

        Button("Retrieve data") {
            myText = UserDefaults.standard.string
            (forKey: "Text") ?? ""
            myToggle = UserDefaults.standard.bool
            (forKey: "Toggle")
            mySlider = UserDefaults.standard.double
            (forKey: "Slider")
        }
```

```
    }
    .padding()
}
```

Notice that the first Button uses the UserDefaults.standard.
set command to save data. Then the third Button uses the
UserDefaults.standard.string, .bool, or .double command to
retrieve data using the key defined by the first Button.

The entire ContentView file should look like this:

```
import SwiftUI

struct ContentView: View {
    @State private var myText = ""
    @State private var myToggle = true
    @State private var mySlider = 0.0

    var body: some View {
        VStack (spacing: 25) {
            TextField("Change text here", text: $myText)

            Toggle(isOn: $myToggle, label: {
                Text("Toggle here")
            })

            Slider(value: $mySlider)

            Button("Save data") {
                UserDefaults.standard.set(myText, forKey: "Text")
                UserDefaults.standard.set(myToggle, forKey:
                "Toggle")
                UserDefaults.standard.set(mySlider, forKey:
                "Slider")
            }

            Button("Clear data") {
                myText = ""
                myToggle = true
                mySlider = 0.0
            }
```

101

```
            Button("Retrieve data") {
                myText = UserDefaults.standard.string(forKey:
                "Text") ?? ""
                myToggle = UserDefaults.standard.bool(forKey:
                "Toggle")
                mySlider = UserDefaults.standard.double(forKey:
                "Slider")
            }
        }
        .padding()
    }
}

struct ContentView_Previews: PreviewProvider {
    static var previews: some View {
        ContentView()
    }
}
```

7. Click the Live icon in the Canvas pane.

8. Click in the TextField and type some words.

9. Click the Toggle.

10. Drag the Slider to the right.

11. Click the Save data Button to save the current state of the
    TextField, Toggle, and Slider in UserDefaults.

12. Click the Clear data Button to reset the user interface.

13. Click the Retrieve data Button to retrieve the state of the TextField,
    Toggle, and Slider.

Reading and Writing to Files

On ordinary computers like the Macintosh, it's common for a program to read data from a file and write data back to a file. On an iOS device, an iOS app can do that too. Writing data to a file offers another way an app can save data.

Although iOS shields users from the folder hierarchy of the operating system, it still exists. To write a file, we first need to use the FileManager object like this:

```
let fm = FileManager.default
```

Next, we need to define a location for the file, which is the document directory in the home folder:

```
let urls = fm.urls(for: .documentDirectory, in: .userDomainMask)
```

Finally, we need to create a file name (such as "file.txt") to store data like this:

```
let url = urls.last?.appendingPathComponent("file.txt")
```

Once we've stored text in a file, we can retrieve it by using the FileManager again and look for the file in the document directory in the home folder. To see how to write data to a file and then read it back again, follow these steps:

1. Create a new iOS View App and name it ReadWriteApp.

2. Click the ContentView file in the Navigator pane.

3. Add the following two State variables:

    ```
    @State var createText = ""
    @State var displayText = ""
    ```

4. Add a VStack with two TextEditor views, separated by an HStack, inside the var body: some View like this:

    ```
    var body: some View {
        VStack {
            TextEditor(text: $createText)
                .foregroundColor(Color.gray)
                .font(.custom("HelveticaNeue", size: 40))
                .border(Color.red, width: 5)
            HStack {
    ```

```
        } .padding()
        TextEditor(text: $displayText)
            .foregroundColor(Color.purple)
            .font(.custom("Courier", size: 40))
            .border(Color.green, width: 5)

    }
}
```

Both TextEditors have a different foreground color and font to
make the text stand out when displayed. To make it easy to see
where both TextEditors are, we place a border around each of
them with a different color.

5. Inside the HStack, add two Buttons like this:

```
var body: some View {
    VStack {
        TextEditor(text: $createText)
            .foregroundColor(Color.gray)
            .font(.custom("HelveticaNeue", size: 40))
            .border(Color.red, width: 5)
        HStack {
            Button("Write File") {
                let fm = FileManager.default
                let urls = fm.urls(for: .documentDirectory, in:
                .userDomainMask)
                let url = urls.last?.appendingPathComponent
                ("file.txt")
                do {
                    try createText.write(to: url!, atomically:
                    true, encoding: String.Encoding.utf8)
                } catch {
                    print("File writing error")
                }
            }
            Spacer()
            Button("Read File") {
```

```
                let fm = FileManager.default
                let urls = fm.urls(for: .documentDirectory, in:
                .userDomainMask)
                let url = urls.last?.appendingPathComponent
                ("file.txt")
                do {
                    let fileContent = try String(contentsOf: url!,
                    encoding: String.Encoding.utf8)
                    displayText = fileContent
                } catch {
                    print("File reading error")
                }
            }
        } .padding()
        TextEditor(text: $displayText)
            .foregroundColor(Color.purple)
            .font(.custom("Courier", size: 40))
            .border(Color.green, width: 5)
    }
}
```

The entire ContentView file should look like this:

```
import SwiftUI

struct ContentView: View {

    @State var createText = ""
    @State var displayText = ""

    var body: some View {
        VStack {
            TextEditor(text: $createText)
                .foregroundColor(Color.gray)
                .font(.custom("HelveticaNeue", size: 40))
                .border(Color.red, width: 5)
            HStack {
                Button("Write File") {
```

105

```swift
                let fm = FileManager.default
                let urls = fm.urls(for: .documentDirectory,
                in: .userDomainMask)
                let url = urls.last?.appendingPathComponent
                ("file.txt")
                do {
                    try createText.write(to: url!, atomically:
                    true, encoding: String.Encoding.utf8)
                } catch {
                    print("File writing error")
                }
            }
            Spacer()
            Button("Read File") {
                let fm = FileManager.default
                let urls = fm.urls(for: .documentDirectory,
                in: .userDomainMask)
                let url = urls.last?.appendingPathComponent
                ("file.txt")
                do {
                    let fileContent = try String(contentsOf:
                    url!, encoding: String.Encoding.utf8)
                    displayText = fileContent
                } catch {
                    print("File reading error")
                }
            }
        } .padding()
        TextEditor(text: $displayText)
            .foregroundColor(Color.purple)
            .font(.custom("Courier", size: 40))
            .border(Color.green, width: 5)
        }
    }
}
```

```
struct ContentView_Previews: PreviewProvider {
    static var previews: some View {
        ContentView()
    }
}
```

6. Click the Live icon on the Canvas pane.

7. Click in the top TextEditor and type a sentence or two.

8. Click the Write File button. This saves the text in a file.

9. Click the Read File button. Whatever text you saved in the file now appears in the bottom TextEditor.

Using Core Data

If you only need to store small amounts of data, you can store data in UserDefaults. If you need to store large amounts of data that are unstructured, you can store them in a file. However, if you want to store large amounts of structured data, then it's better to use Core Data.

Core Data is a framework to help you manage data in an app. Core Data lets you define the type of data you want to save and the relationships between these different chunks of data. Then Core Data helps you manipulate this data and their relationships without worrying about the actual details of storing and retrieving the data or learning cryptic SQL database commands.

Core Data stores data using entities and attributes. An attribute defines a single chunk of data to store such as a name, address, age, gender, email address, and phone number. An entity represents all of these attributes used to define a single chunk of related data such as a person as shown in Figure 6-1. Think of a Core Data entity like a database record or table and a Core Data attribute like a database field.

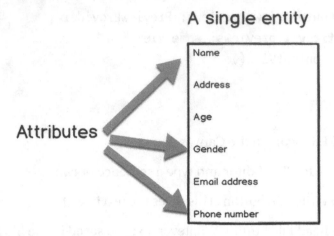

Figure 6-1. *Core Data stores data in attributes, grouped together to represent a single entity*

The basic steps to using Core Data involve

- Creating entities and defining attributes in the Xcode data model editor

- Writing Swift code to manipulate data

There are two ways to add Core Data to a project. First, you can add Core Data after you've created a project. Second, you can include Core Data at the time you create a project. Let's look at both methods to see how they work.

Creating a Data Model File

A data model is a Core Data file that lets you define entities and attributes where an entity represents a single object such as a person and attributes represent details such as a name, phone number, and email address. You can manually add a data model file to any project or let Xcode add a data model file when you create a new project.

To see how to add a Core Data file manually to a project, follow these steps:

1. Choose File ➤ New ➤ Project and create a new iOS App project. Give this project a name such as CoreDataApp. Make sure that the Core Data check box is not selected.

2. Choose File ➤ New ➤ File. A template dialog appears.

3. Click the iOS category.

4. Scroll down and click the Data Model under the Core Data category as shown in Figure 6-2.

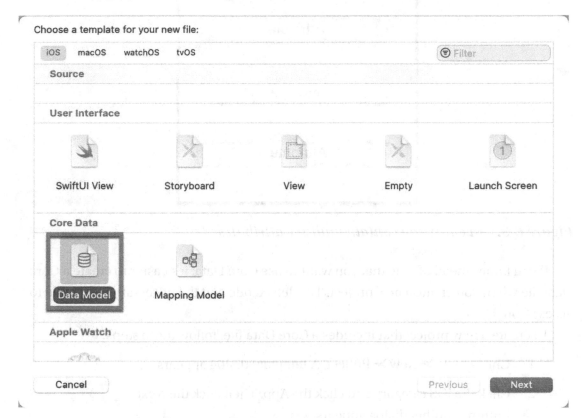

Figure 6-2. *Creating a Core Data data model file*

5. Click the Next button. A dialog appears, letting you choose a name for the Core Data file.

6. Choose a name for your Core Data file, such as DataModel, and click the Create button. Xcode displays your Core Data file in the Navigator pane.

Once you've created a Core Data file, the next step is to define one or more entities. An entity consists of multiple attributes such as holding a name, a price, an age, or a phone number. Think of an entity like a record in a database and attributes like fields as shown in Figure 6-3.

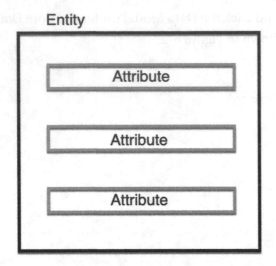

Figure 6-3. *An entity can contain multiple attributes*

If you know ahead of time that you want to use Core Data, it's easier to create a Core Data file when you create a new project. This lets Xcode add the necessary Swift code to access Core Data.

To create a new project that includes a Core Data file, follow these steps:

1.   Choose File ➤ New ➤ Project. A template dialog appears.

2.   Click the iOS category and click the App. Then click the Next button. Another dialog appears.

3.   Click in the Product Name text field and give it a name. (When creating your own projects, choose any name you wish.)

4.   Make sure the Use Core Data check box is selected as shown in Figure 6-4.

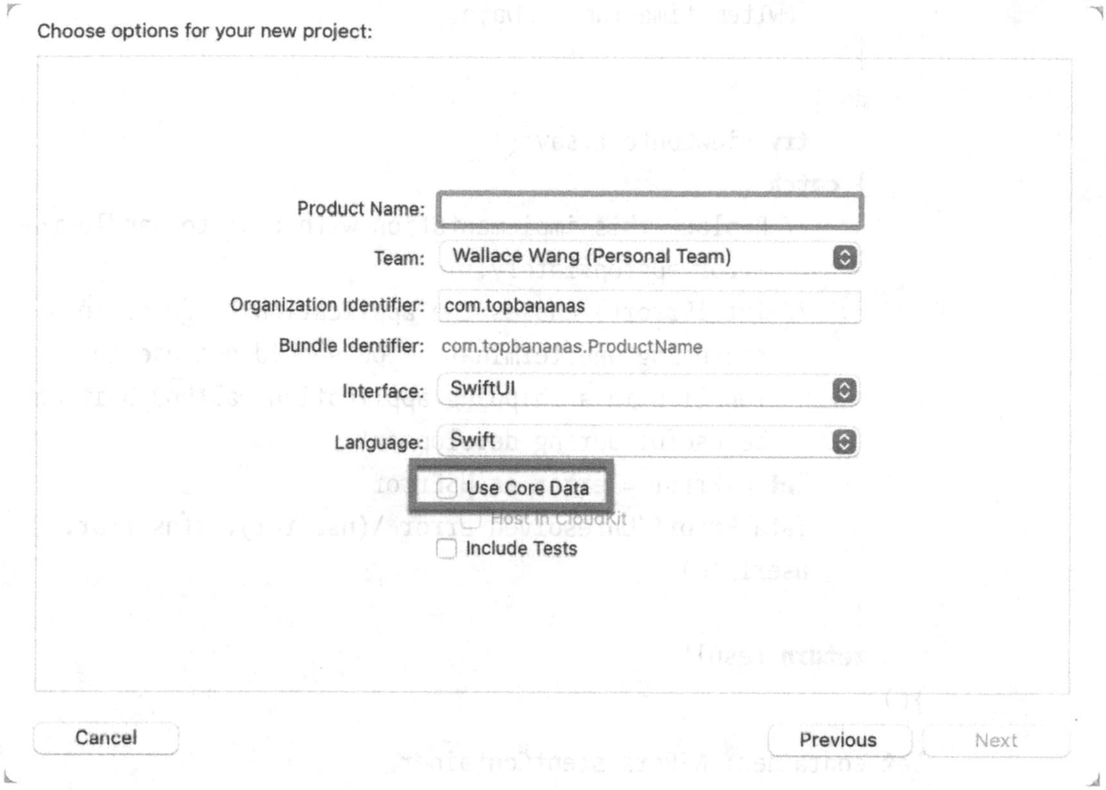

Choose options for your new project:

Product Name:	
Team:	Wallace Wang (Personal Team)
Organization Identifier:	com.topbananas
Bundle Identifier:	com.topbananas.ProductName
Interface:	SwiftUI
Language:	Swift
	☐ Use Core Data
	☐ Host in CloudKit
	☐ Include Tests

Cancel   Previous   Next

Figure 6-4. *Selecting the Use Core Data check box when creating a new project*

5. Click the Next button and then click the Create button.

6. Click the Persistence file in the Navigator pane. When you create a new project using Core Data, Xcode adds the following code in the Persistence file:

```
import CoreData

struct PersistenceController {
    static let shared = PersistenceController()

    static var preview: PersistenceController = {
        let result = PersistenceController(inMemory: true)
        let viewContext = result.container.viewContext
        for _ in 0..<10 {
            let newItem = Item(context: viewContext)
```

```swift
            newItem.timestamp = Date()
        }
        do {
            try viewContext.save()
        } catch {
            // Replace this implementation with code to handle the
            error appropriately.
            // fatalError() causes the application to generate a
            crash log and terminate. You should not use this
            function in a shipping application, although it may
            be useful during development.
            let nsError = error as NSError
            fatalError("Unresolved error \(nsError), \(nsError.
            userInfo)")
        }
        return result
    }()

    let container: NSPersistentContainer

    init(inMemory: Bool = false) {
        container = NSPersistentContainer(name: "DeleteMe")
        if inMemory {
            container.persistentStoreDescriptions.first!.url =
            URL(fileURLWithPath: "/dev/null")
        }
        container.loadPersistentStores(completionHandler: {
        (storeDescription, error) in
            if let error = error as NSError? {
                // Replace this implementation with code to handle
                the error appropriately.
                // fatalError() causes the application to generate
                a crash log and terminate. You should not
                use this function in a shipping application,
                although it may be useful during development.

                /*
```

```
                    Typical reasons for an error here include:
                    * The parent directory does not exist, cannot be
                      created, or disallows writing.
                    * The persistent store is not accessible, due to
                      permissions or data protection when the device
                      is locked.
                    * The device is out of space.
                    * The store could not be migrated to the current
                      model version.
                    Check the error message to determine what the
                    actual problem was.
                    */
                    fatalError("Unresolved error \(error), \(error.
                    userInfo)")
                }
            })
            container.viewContext.automaticallyMergesChanges
            FromParent = true
        }
    }
```

Note   In the preceding code, the line `container = NSPersistentContainer` `(name: "CoreDataApp")` refers to the name of the data model file that defines entities and attributes.

Adding Core Data to an Existing Project

While you can include Core Data when you create a new project, you might prefer to add Core Data to a project later. In this project, we'll design a simple user interface that will consist of two text fields, two buttons, and a label. The two text fields will allow us to input data, the label will display all stored data, and the two buttons will let us add or delete data.

To see how to add Core Data to an existing project, follow these steps:

1. Load the CoreDataApp project created earlier in this chapter. Make sure you have added a data model file to the project by selecting File ➤ New ➤ File ➤ Data Model.

2. Click the Core Data file in the Navigator pane. Xcode displays a data editor as shown in Figure 6-5.

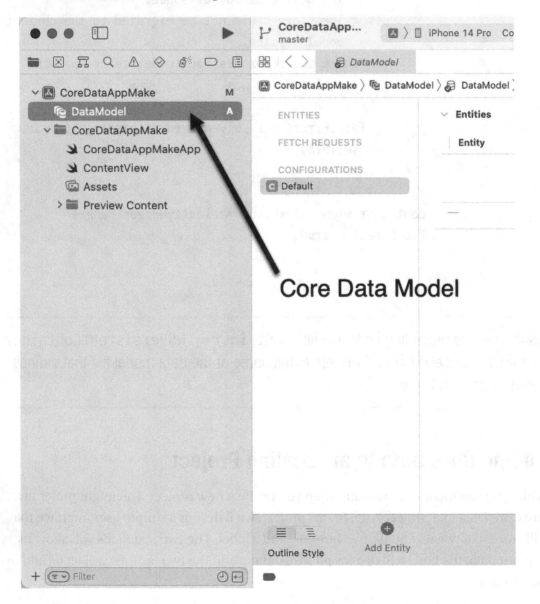

Figure 6-5. *The data editor lets you view and edit entities and attributes*

3. Click the Add Entity icon, or choose Editor ➤ Add Entity. Xcode displays an Entity under the ENTITIES category.

4. Click this Entity to select it and press ENTER to highlight the entire name.

5. Type **Animal** and press ENTER. Entity names must always begin with an uppercase letter such as Item, Person, or Vehicle.

After you've created at least one entity, you'll need to add one or more attributes to hold data. An attribute consists of a descriptive name (typed in lowercase) and the type of data the attribute will hold such as a string, integer, or date.

To define an attribute in an entity, follow these steps:

1. Click the Core Data file in the Navigator pane. Xcode displays the data model editor (see Figure 6-5).

2. Click the entity that you want to modify. Xcode displays an Attributes category as shown in Figure 6-6.

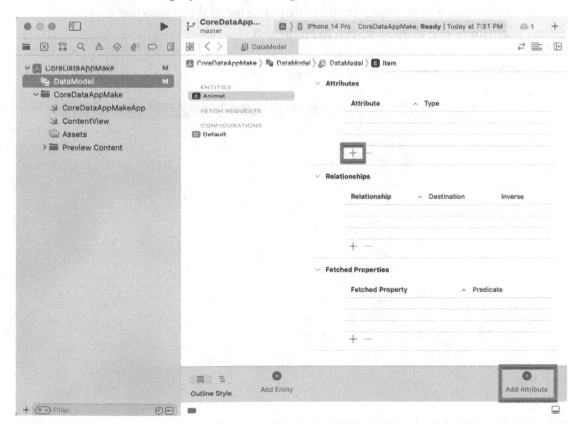

Figure 6-6. *The Add Attributes button appears in two places*

3. Click the Add Attribute button in the bottom of the Xcode window or underneath the Attribute column, or choose Editor ➤ Add Attribute. Xcode displays an attribute and a type as shown in Figure 6-7.

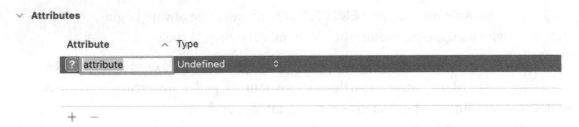

Figure 6-7. *Creating a new attribute*

4. Type **name** and press ENTER. All attribute names must use lowercase letters.

5. Click in the Type popup menu to display a list of data types the attribute can store as shown in Figure 6-8.

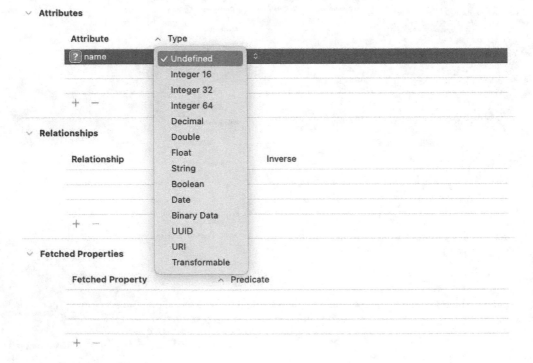

Figure 6-8. *Defining the type of data to store in an attribute*

6. Choose String.

7. Click the Add Attribute button in the bottom of the Xcode window or underneath the Attribute column, or choose Editor ➤ Add Attribute. Xcode displays an attribute and a type (see Figure 6-7).

8. Type **breed** and press ENTER.

9. Click in the Type popup menu and choose String. The two attributes and one entity should look like Figure 6-9.

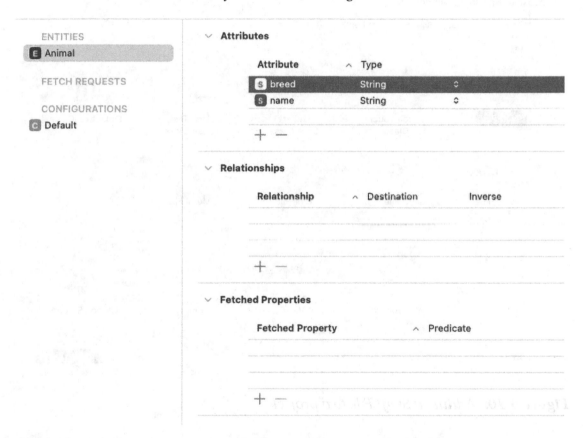

Figure 6-9. *Defining a name and price attribute for an Item entity*

Once you've added a Core Data model to a project and customized this data model to define the entities and attributes of each entity, it's time to add a separate Swift file to add, retrieve, and delete data from Core Data by following these steps:

1. Make sure your Xcode project has a Core Data data model file.

2. Choose File ➤ New ➤ File and choose Swift File as shown in Figure 6-10.

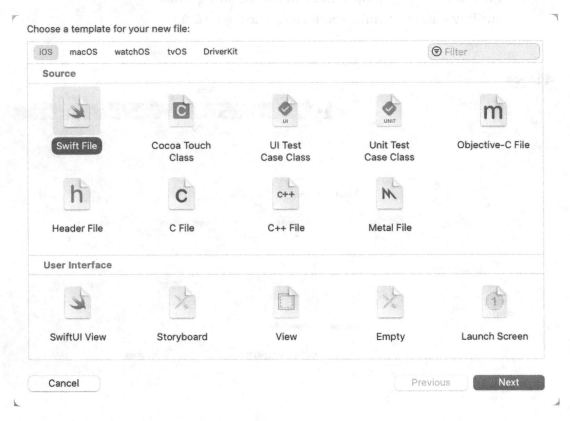

Figure 6-10. *Adding a Swift File to a project*

3. Click Next and give the file a name such as CoreDataManager. Then click Create.

4. Click the Swift file you just created.

5. Add the following underneath the **import** Foundation line:

```
import CoreData
```

6. Create a class called CoreDataManager as follows:

```
class CoreDataManager {
    let persistentContainer: NSPersistentContainer

    init() {
        persistentContainer = NSPersistentContainer(name:
        "DataModel")
        persistentContainer.loadPersistentStores { (description,
        error) in
            if let error = error {
                fatalError("Core Data failed to initialize \
                (error.localizedDescription)")
            }
        }
    }
}
```

This class simply loads the Core Data file. In this case, the Core Data file is named DataModel, so if you gave your Core Data model file a different name, replace "DataModel" with the name of your model file instead.

The preceding code simply loads Core Data, but we still need to write functions to add, delete, and retrieve data from Core Data.

7. Add the following function to save data to the Core Data model:

```
func savePet(name: String, breed: String) {

    let pet = Animal(context: persistentContainer.viewContext)
    pet.name = name
    pet.breed = breed

    do {
        try persistentContainer.viewContext.save()
```

```
        print("Pet saved!")
    } catch {
        print("Failed to save movie \(error)")
    }

}
```

This function accepts a name and a breed (the two attributes defined in the Animal entity of the Core Data model) and tries to save them in the Animal entity.

8. Add the following function to retrieve data:

```
func getAllPets() -> [Animal] {

    let fetchRequest: NSFetchRequest<Animal> = Animal.fetchRequest()
    do {
        return try persistentContainer.viewContext.
        fetch(fetchRequest)
    } catch {
        return []
    }
}
```

This function retrieves all data from the Animal entity defined by the Core Data model file.

9. Add the following function to delete data:

```
func deletePet(animal: Animal) {
    persistentContainer.viewContext.delete(animal)

    do {
        try persistentContainer.viewContext.save()
    } catch {
        persistentContainer.viewContext.rollback()
        print("Failed to save context \(error.
        localizedDescription)")
    }
}
```

This function accepts a single entity and attempts to delete it. The entire CoreDataManager file should look like this:

```swift
import Foundation
import CoreData

class CoreDataManager {
    let persistentContainer: NSPersistentContainer

    init() {
        persistentContainer = NSPersistentContainer(name: "DataModel")
        persistentContainer.loadPersistentStores { (description, error) in
            if let error = error {
                fatalError("Core Data failed to initialize \(error.
                localizedDescription)")
            }
        }
    }

    func deletePet(animal: Animal) {
        persistentContainer.viewContext.delete(animal)

        do {
            try persistentContainer.viewContext.save()
        } catch {
            persistentContainer.viewContext.rollback()
            print("Failed to save context \(error.localizedDescription)")
        }
    }

    func getAllPets() -> [Animal] {

        let fetchRequest: NSFetchRequest<Animal> = Animal.fetchRequest()

        do {
            return try persistentContainer.viewContext.fetch(fetchRequest)
        } catch {
            return []
        }
    }
}
```

```swift
func savePet(name: String, breed: String) {

    let pet = Animal(context: persistentContainer.viewContext)
    pet.name = name
    pet.breed = breed

    do {
        try persistentContainer.viewContext.save()
        print("Pet saved!")
    } catch {
        print("Failed to save movie \(error)")
    }

}
}
```

The final step is to design the user interface that will let users type in two strings (for name and breed), save the data, display the data in a list, and then delete the selected data. To design a user interface, follow these steps:

1. Click the ContentView file in the Navigator pane.

2. Add the following under the struct ContentView: View line:

```swift
let coreDM: CoreDataManager
@State var petName = ""
@State var petBreed = ""
@State var petArray = [Animal]()
```

The first line creates a constant that represents the CoreDataManager file. The first two State variables can hold String values, while the third State variable can hold an array of the Animal entity defined by the Core Data model file.

3. Add the following underneath the var body: some View line:

```swift
VStack {
    TextField("Enter pet name", text: $petName)
    .textFieldStyle(RoundedBorderTextFieldStyle())

    TextField("Enter pet breed", text: $petBreed)
    .textFieldStyle(RoundedBorderTextFieldStyle())
```

```
    Button("Save") {
        coreDM.savePet(name: petName, breed: petBreed)
        displayPets()
        petName = ""
        petBreed = ""
    }
}.padding()
.onAppear(perform: {
    displayPets()
})
```

This creates a vertical stack that displays two TextFields and a Button. When the user taps the Button, it calls the savePet function (stored in the CoreDataManager file) and calls a displayPets() function, which will retrieve the data to display on the user interface.

In addition, the VStack uses the .padding() modifier to space the TextFields and Button apart and also uses .onAppear to display data using the displayPets() function when the user interface appears on the screen.

4. Add the displayPets() function just above the last curly bracket of the var body: some View:

```
func displayPets() {
    petArray = coreDM.getAllPets()
}
```

This function retrieves all data from Core Data and stores it in the petArray variable.

5. Add the following underneath the Button:

```
List {
    ForEach(petArray, id: \.self) { pet in
        VStack {
            Text(pet.name ?? "")
            Text(pet.breed ?? "")
```

```
            }
        }.onDelete(perform: { indexSet in
            indexSet.forEach { index in
                let pet = petArray[index]
                coreDM.deletePet(animal: pet)
                displayPets()
            }
        })
    }

    Spacer()
```

This creates a List that uses a ForEach loop to retrieve each chunk of data from Core Data that gets displayed in a separate VStack. The .onDelete modifier lets users swipe to the left on a chunk of data to display a Delete button. If the user taps this Delete button, the deletePet function gets called to delete the selected data. Then it calls the displayPets() function again. Finally, there's a Spacer at the bottom of the List to push everything up.

6. Edit the struct ContentView_Previews: PreviewProvider code at the bottom of the ContentView file:

```
struct ContentView_Previews: PreviewProvider {
    static var previews: some View {
        ContentView(coreDM: CoreDataManager())
    }
}
```

This gives the preview of the ContentView file access to the CoreDataManager file. The complete ContentView file should look like this:

```
import SwiftUI

struct ContentView: View {

    let coreDM: CoreDataManager
    @State var petName = ""
    @State var petBreed = ""
    @State var petArray = [Animal]()
```

```
var body: some View {
    VStack {
        TextField("Enter pet name", text: $petName)
        .textFieldStyle(RoundedBorderTextFieldStyle())
        TextField("Enter pet breed", text: $petBreed)
        .textFieldStyle(RoundedBorderTextFieldStyle())
        Button("Save") {
            coreDM.savePet(name: petName, breed: petBreed)
            displayPets()
            petName = ""
            petBreed = ""
        }

        List {
            ForEach(petArray, id: \.self) { pet in
                VStack {
                    Text(pet.name ?? "")
                    Text(pet.breed ?? "")
                }
            }.onDelete(perform: { indexSet in
                indexSet.forEach { index in
                    let pet = petArray[index]
                    coreDM.deletePet(animal: pet)
                    displayPets()
                }
            })
        }

        Spacer()
    }.padding()
    .onAppear(perform: {
        displayPets()
    })
}
```

```swift
    func displayPets() {
        petArray = coreDM.getAllPets()
    }

}

struct ContentView_Previews: PreviewProvider {
    static var previews: some View {
        ContentView(coreDM: CoreDataManager())
    }
}
```

The preceding code displays two TextFields and a Button on the screen where users can type a name and a breed type in the two TextFields. Then the user can click the Button to save the data, which appears in a List underneath the Button. Finally, users can swipe left on the displayed data to delete it. To see how this project works, follow these steps:

1. Click the Live icon in the Canvas pane.

2. Click in the top TextField and type a name for a pet such as Fido.

3. Click in the second TextField and type a breed for the pet such as Collie.

4. Click the Save Button. Notice that the data you typed in each TextField now appears underneath the Save Button.

5. Repeat steps 2–4 except type a different name and breed. Make sure you have at least two different chunks of data (name and breed) as shown in Figure 6-11.

Figure 6-11. *Displaying data in a List on the user interface*

6. Swipe left on one chunk of data. A red Delete button appears as shown in Figure 6-12.

Figure 6-12. *Swiping left displays a red Delete button*

7. Click the Delete button. Notice that the selected data now disappears.

8. Repeat steps 6 and 7 on each chunk of data to delete it until all data is gone.

Summary

Storing data and retrieving it again can be important for many apps. For storing simple app settings, store data in UserDefaults that your app can load to retrieve any settings the user chose.

To store longer amounts of data, especially text, save and retrieve data in files. Files can hold multiple lines of text, so they can be handy for large amounts of data.

If you need to store larger amounts of related data, use Core Data to save this information. Whether you store data in UserDefaults, files, or Core Data, you can always retrieve that data again, so an app can display that data automatically without requiring the user to manually load data each time.

CHAPTER 7

Sharing Data Between Structures

When creating a simple iOS app, SwiftUI relies on a single structure to define the user interface. Within this structure, you can define State variables that different user interface items (Sliders, TextFields, Toggles, etc.) can access and modify.

However, more sophisticated apps will likely use multiple structures to define different user interface screens. When you use multiple structures, you need a way to share data between structures, and that requires using more than State variables. In this chapter, you'll learn the different ways to share data between structures whether those structures are in the same file or stored in separate files.

Sharing Data with Bindings

Any structure that creates a user interface can define a State variable. When you declare a State variable, you can give it an initial value and optionally declare it as private. By making a State variable private, you ensure that it can only be modified within the structure. A typical State variable declaration can look like the following:

```
@State private var message = ""
```

For simple apps, you might only need a single structure to define your user interface. However, the more sophisticated your app gets, the more Swift code you'll need to write. Eventually, this can create a cluttered structure that can be hard to read and understand.

The solution is to divide a user interface into multiple structures that you can either store within the same file or in separate files. However, once you separate your user interface into separate structures, those separate structures no longer have access to any State variables declared by the main structure. To get around this problem, we need to use Bindings.

© Wallace Wang 2023
W. Wang, *Pro iPhone Development with SwiftUI*, https://doi.org/10.1007/978-1-4842-9544-1_7

Bindings essentially declare a variable that holds the same data type as a State variable that's defined in a different structure. Now the structure containing the State variable can pass it to a Binding variable defined in the other structure.

To see how to use Bindings, follow these steps:

1. Create an iOS App project and name it BindingApp.

2. Click the ContentView file in the Navigator pane.

3. Modify the struct ContentView: View as follows:

```
struct ContentView: View {
    @State private var message = ""
    var body: some View {
        VStack {
            Text("Hello, \(message)")
            HStack {
                Text("Send a greeting:")
                TextField("Type a message here", text: $message)
            }
        }
    }
}
```

This structure displays a TextField where the user can type a name. Then the TextField stores whatever the user typed into the message State variable, which gets displayed inside the Text view that displays "Hello, " plus whatever the contents of the message State variable might hold.

Although this structure defines a simple user interface, if we keep adding to the user interface, the code inside the ContentView structure will start looking cramped and cluttered. To solve this problem, let's extract the HStack out into a separate structure.

4. Hold down the Command key and click the HStack. A popup menu appears as shown in Figure 7-1.

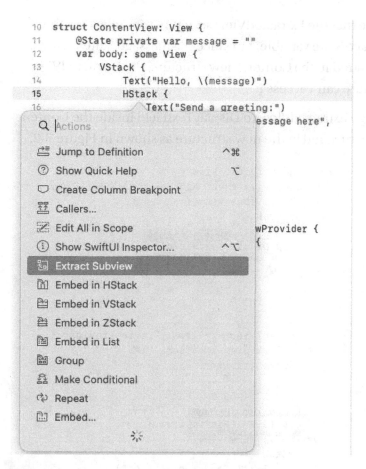

```
10    struct ContentView: View {
11        @State private var message = ""
12        var body: some View {
13            VStack {
14                Text("Hello, \(message)")
15                HStack {
16                    Text("Send a greeting:")
```

Q |Actions

⌷≣ Jump to Definition   ⌃⌘
ⓘ Show Quick Help   ⌥
▽ Create Column Breakpoint
⯭⯭ Callers...
⊠ Edit All in Scope
ⓘ Show SwiftUI Inspector...   ⌃⌥
⯐ Extract Subview
🗔 Embed in HStack
🗔 Embed in VStack
🗔 Embed in ZStack
🗔 Embed in List
🗔 Group
🗅 Make Conditional
↻ Repeat
🗔 Embed...

Figure 7-1. Command-clicking displays a popup menu

5. Choose Extract Subview. Xcode replaces the entire HStack with
    ExtractedView() and displays a new structure at the bottom of the
    ContentView file like this:

```
struct ExtractedView: View {
    var body: some View {
        HStack {
            Text("Send a greeting:")
            TextField("Type a message here", text: $message)
        }
    }
}
```

Notice that the ExtractedView structure tries to access the message State variable, but since the message State variable is declared in the ContentView structure, the ExtractedView structure can't access it.

6. Change ExtractedView to DisplayTextField inside the Content View struct and in the new structure as shown in Figure 7-2.

```
struct ContentView: View {
    @State private var message = ""
    var body: some View {
        VStack {
            Text("Hello, \(message)")
            DisplayTextField()
        }
    }
}


struct ContentView_Previews: PreviewProvider {
    static var previews: some View {
        ContentView()
    }
}

struct DisplayTextField: View {
    var body: some View {
        HStack {
            Text("Send a greeting:")
            TextField("Type a message here",
                text: $message)
        }
    }
}
```

Figure 7-2. *Changing the name of the ExtractedView*

7. Add the following Binding variable inside the DisplayTextField structure and change $message to $newVariable like this:

```
struct DisplayTextField: View {
    @Binding var newVariable: String
    var body: some View {
        HStack {
            Text("Send a greeting:")
```

```
            TextField("Type a message here", text: $newVariable)
        }
    }
}
```

The Binding variable receives the State variable passed to it from the ContentView structure, so we need to modify the DisplayTextField structure call to pass data to the Binding variable.

8. Edit DisplayTextField() inside the ContentView as follows:

```
DisplayTextField(newVariable: $message)
```

This sends the message State variable to the newVariable Binding variable, which is declared inside the DisplayTextField structure. The entire ContentView file should look like this:

```
import SwiftUI

struct ContentView: View {
    @State private var message = ""
    var body: some View {
        VStack {
            Text("Hello, \(message)")
            DisplayTextField(newVariable: $message)
        }
    }
}

struct ContentView_Previews: PreviewProvider {
    static var previews: some View {
        ContentView()
    }
}

struct DisplayTextField: View {
    @Binding var newVariable: String
    var body: some View {
        HStack {
```

```
                     Text("Send a greeting:")
                     TextField("Type a message here", text: $newVariable)
                 }
             }
         }
```

9. Click the Live icon on the canvas pane.

10. Click in the TextField of your user interface and type a name.
    Notice that as you type, the name appears in the Text view
    displaying "Hello, ".

In this example, we created a separate structure stored in the same file
(ContentView). Notice that the State variable defines a variable name and an initial
value. Then the Binding variable gets passed that value. That means the Binding variable
must be defined with the same data type as the State variable.

Binding variables work much like parameters in a function. To pass data from one
structure to another, you must call the structure by name. Then define the Binding
variable (like a parameter name) and pass it a State variable as shown in Figure 7-3.

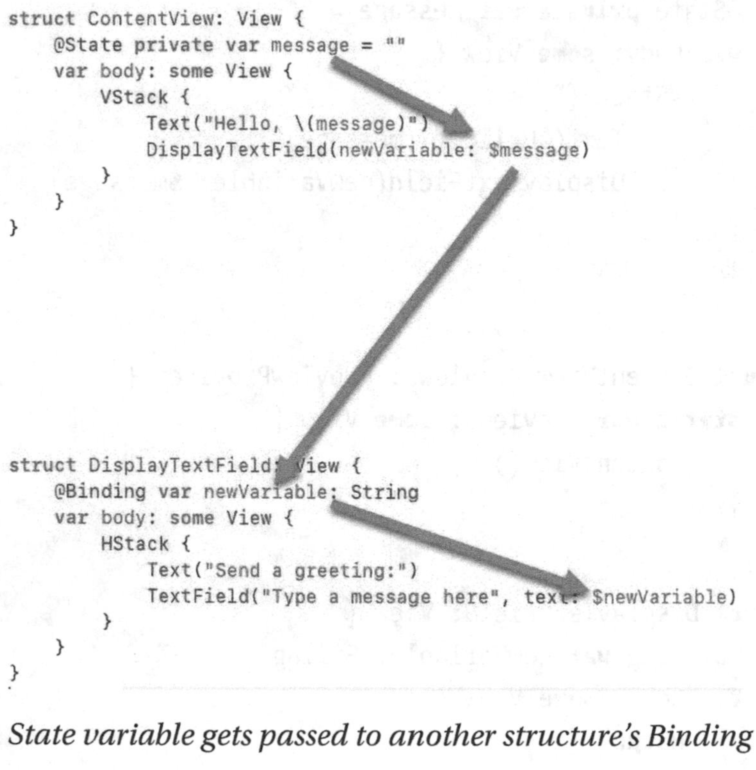

```
struct ContentView: View {
    @State private var message = ""
    var body: some View {
        VStack {
            Text("Hello, \(message)")
            DisplayTextField(newVariable: $message)
        }
    }
}




struct DisplayTextField: View {
    @Binding var newVariable: String
    var body: some View {
        HStack {
            Text("Send a greeting:")
            TextField("Type a message here", text: $newVariable)
        }
    }
}
```

Figure 7-3. *A State variable gets passed to another structure's Binding variable*

Creating separate structures and storing them in the same file can work, but the more structures you create, the more cluttered that single file will get. A better solution is to store a structure in a separate file altogether. To see how to use Binding variables with a structure stored in a separate file, follow these steps:

1. Create an iOS App project and name it BindingFileApp.

2. Choose File ➤ New ➤ File. A template dialog appears as shown in Figure 7-4.

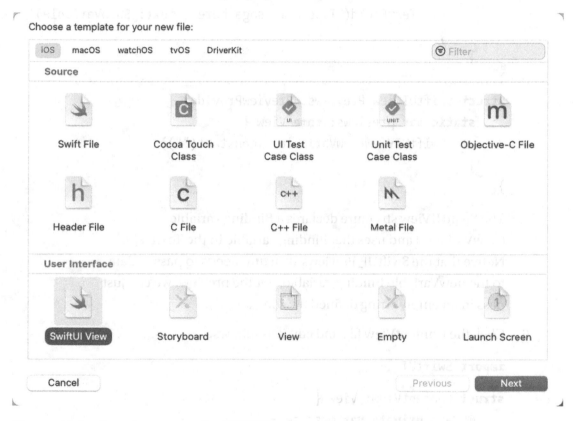

Choose a template for your new file:

iOS   macOS   watchOS   tvOS   DriverKit   Filter

Source

Swift File   Cocoa Touch   UI Test   Unit Test   Objective-C File
              Class   Case Class Case Class

Header File   C File   C++ File   Metal File

User Interface

SwiftUI View   Storyboard   View   Empty   Launch Screen

Cancel   Previous   Next

Figure 7-4. *Creating a new SwiftUI View*

3. Click SwiftUI View and click Next. Another dialog appears.

4. Click Create. Xcode creates a separate file called SwiftUIView (unless you specifically typed in a different name) that appears in the Navigator pane.

5.   Modify the code in the SwiftUIView file as follows:

```swift
import SwiftUI

struct SwiftUIView: View {
    @Binding var newVariable: String
    var body: some View {
        HStack {
            Text("Send a greeting:")
            TextField("Type a message here", text: $newVariable)
        }
    }
}
struct SwiftUIView_Previews: PreviewProvider {
    static var previews: some View {
        SwiftUIView(newVariable: .constant(""))
    }
}
```

The SwiftUIView structure declares a Binding variable
(newVariable) and uses that Binding variable in the TextField.
Notice that the SwiftUI_Previews structure needs to pass in data
to the newVariable Binding variable. For the preview, we can just
pass in an empty string defined by .constant("").

6.   Click the ContentView file and edit it as follows:

```swift
import SwiftUI

struct ContentView: View {
    @State private var message = ""
    var body: some View {
        VStack {
            Text("Hello, \(message)")

            SwiftUIView(newVariable: $message)
        }
    }
}
```

```
struct ContentView_Previews: PreviewProvider {
    static var previews: some View {
        ContentView()
    }
}
```

Notice that the SwiftUIView structure gets passed the message State variable. Inside the SwiftUIView, the newVariable Binding holds the data stored in the message State variable.

7. Click the Live icon in the canvas pane.

8. Click in the TextField and type a name. The Text view displays the name as you type.

As you can see, you can store a structure as either part of the same file or saved in a separate file. Either method works, but if you store structures in separate files, make sure you also pass in data to the Binding variable within the preview structure like this:

```
SwiftUIView(newVariable: .constant(""))
```

Because the Binding variable inside the SwiftUIView structure is a String data type, the preview structure must give it a String value as well such as an empty string.

Sharing Data with StateObject and ObservedObject

State variables are useful for storing individual chunks of data such as integers (Int), decimal numbers (Double or Float), or text (String). Binding variables are useful for modifying State variables from another structure than the structure that defined the State variable.

However, both State and Binding variables can share individual data types. What happens if you want to share an entire object that can consist of multiple properties? Rather than create multiple State/Binding variables, it's far easier to use a StateObject and an ObservedObject instead.

A StateObject is similar to a State variable, and an ObservedObject is similar to a Binding variable. Where a State and a Binding variable can hold a single data type, a StateObject and ObservedObject can hold an entire object where that object can hold multiple properties to store data.

Before you can use a StateObject or ObservedObject, you must create a class with one or more properties. This class must be an ObservableObject like this:

```
class AnimalModel: ObservableObject
```

Within this ObservableObject, you must define one or more variables using the @Published keyword like this:

```
@Published var name: String = ""
```

Then you can create a StateObject and store data in that StateObject's properties like this:

```
@StateObject var cat = AnimalModel()
```

Finally, you can pass the StateObject to another structure that uses an ObservedObject like this:

```
@ObservedObject var creature: AnimalModel
```

To see how to use a StateObject and an ObservedObject, follow these steps:

1. Create an iOS App and name it StateObjectApp.

2. Click the ContentView file in the Navigator pane.

3. Add the following class just below the last curly bracket:

    ```
    class AnimalModel: ObservableObject {
        @Published var name: String = ""
        @Published var breed: String = ""
        @Published var age: Double = 0.0
        @Published var weight: Double = 0.0
    }
    ```

    Notice that each property must include @Published.

4. Modify the struct ContentView: View as follows:

```
struct ContentView: View {

    @StateObject var cat = AnimalModel()

    var body: some View {
        VStack {
            Text("Hello, \(cat.name)")
            Text("Breed: \(cat.breed)")
            Text("Age: \(Int(cat.age))")
            Text("Weight: \(cat.weight)")
            DisplayTextField(creature: cat)
        }
    }
}
```

Notice that this structure creates an AnimalModel object called cat, which is defined as a @StateObject. The DisplayTextField references a separate structure and passes the StateObject of cat into the ObservedObject (creature) stored in the DisplayTextField structure.

5. Add a DisplayTextField structure as follows:

```
struct DisplayTextField: View {

    @ObservedObject var creature: AnimalModel

    var body: some View {
        VStack {
            HStack {
                Text("Name:")
                TextField("Type a name here", text:
                $creature.name)
            }

            HStack {
                Text("Breed:")
                TextField("Type a breed here", text:
                $creature.breed)
            }
```

```
        HStack {
            Text("Age:")
            Slider(value: $creature.age, in: 0...20)
        }

        HStack {
            Text("Weight:")
            Slider(value: $creature.weight, in: 0...200)
        }
    }
}
}
```

Notice that this structure declares an ObservedObject called creature. Now everything inside this DisplayTextField structure can access the AnimalModel properties including name, breed, age, and weight. The entire ContentView file should look like this:

```
import SwiftUI

struct ContentView: View {

    @StateObject var cat = AnimalModel()

    var body: some View {
        VStack {
            Text("Hello, \(cat.name)")
            Text("Breed: \(cat.breed)")
            Text("Age: \(Int(cat.age))")
            Text("Weight: \(cat.weight)")
            DisplayTextField(creature: cat)
        }
    }
}

struct ContentView_Previews: PreviewProvider {
    static var previews: some View {
        ContentView()
    }
}
```

```swift
struct DisplayTextField: View {

    @ObservedObject var creature: AnimalModel

    var body: some View {
        VStack {
            HStack {
                Text("Name:")
                TextField("Type a name here", text:
                $creature.name)
            }

            HStack {
                Text("Breed:")
                TextField("Type a breed here", text:
                $creature.breed)
            }

            HStack {
                Text("Age:")
                Slider(value: $creature.age, in: 0...20)
            }

            HStack {
                Text("Weight:")
                Slider(value: $creature.weight, in: 0...200)
            }
        }
    }
}

class AnimalModel: ObservableObject {
    @Published var name: String = ""
    @Published var breed: String = ""
    @Published var age: Double = 0.0
    @Published var weight: Double = 0.0
}
```

6. Click the Live icon on the Canvas pane.

7. Click in the top TextField and type a name.

8. Click in the second TextField and type a breed.

9. Drag the top Slider to define an age.

10. Drag the bottom Slider to define a weight. All your chosen data
    appears at the top of the user interface as shown in Figure 7-5.

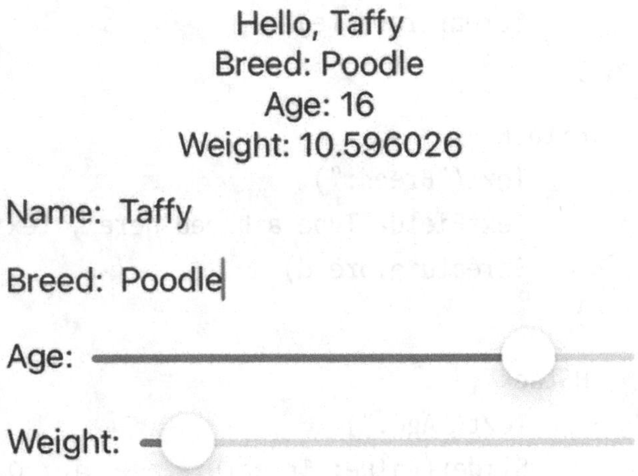

Hello, Taffy
Breed: Poodle
Age: 16
Weight: 10.596026

Name: Taffy

Breed: Poodle

Age:

Weight:

Figure 7-5. *The complete user interface*

Sharing Data with EnvironmentObject

When sharing objects using StateObject and ObservedObject, you must pass a
StateObject to an ObservedObject defined in another structure. For example, suppose
you defined a StateObject in one structure. To share this StateObject with another
structure, you would need to explicitly pass this StateObject to another structure's
ObservedObject as shown in Figure 7-6.

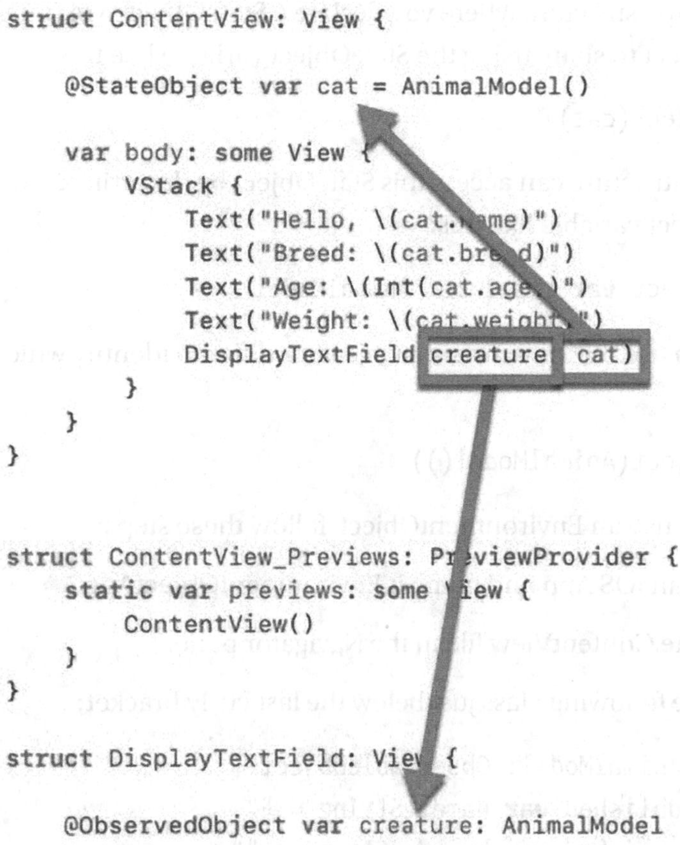

```
struct ContentView: View {

    @StateObject var cat = AnimalModel()

    var body: some View {
        VStack {
            Text("Hello, \(cat.name)")
            Text("Breed: \(cat.breed)")
            Text("Age: \(Int(cat.age))")
            Text("Weight: \(cat.weight)")
            DisplayTextField(creature: cat)
        }
    }
}

struct ContentView_Previews: PreviewProvider {
    static var previews: some View {
        ContentView()
    }
}

struct DisplayTextField: View {

    @ObservedObject var creature: AnimalModel
```

Figure 7-6. *A StateObject must be passed into another structure's ObservedObject*

Any time you want to share an object with another structure, you must pass it to that other structure's ObservedObject. A much simpler method is to use EnvironmentObject instead.

When you use EnvironmentObject, you no longer need to pass a StateObject to each structure. First, you must create a class as an ObservableObject like this:

```
class AnimalModel: ObservableObject
```

Next, you must create an object based on this class using StateObject like this:

```
@StateObject var cat = AnimalModel()
```

Within the same structure where you declare a StateObject, you must also define an .environmentObject to share using the StateObject variable like this:

```
.environmentObject(cat)
```

Finally, each structure can access this StateObject by declaring its own EnvironmentObject variable like this:

```
@EnvironmentObject var creature: AnimalModel
```

You must also use the .environmentObject modifier to identify which class to use such as

```
.environmentObject(AnimalModel())
```

To see how to use an EnvironmentObject, follow these steps:

1.   Create an iOS App and name it EnvironmentObjectApp.

2.   Click the ContentView file in the Navigator pane.

3.   Add the following class just below the last curly bracket:

```
class AnimalModel: ObservableObject {
    @Published var name: String = ""
    @Published var breed: String = ""
    @Published var age: Double = 0.0
    @Published var weight: Double = 0.0
}
```

Notice that each property must include @Published.

4.   Modify the struct ContentView: View as follows:

```
struct ContentView: View {

    @StateObject var cat = AnimalModel()

    var body: some View {
        VStack {
            Text("Hello, \(cat.name)")
            Text("Breed: \(cat.breed)")
            Text("Age: \(Int(cat.age))")
```

```
            Text("Weight: \(cat.weight)")
            DisplayTextField()
        }.environmentObject(cat)
    }
}
```

Notice that this structure creates an AnimalModel object called cat, which is defined as a @StateObject. The DisplayTextField references a separate structure that defines another part of the user interface. Most importantly, notice the .environmentObject(cat) modifier at the end of the VStack. This shares the StateObject with other structures without explicitly requiring you to pass that StateObject to another structure.

5. Modify the struct ContentView_Preview as follows:

```
struct ContentView_Previews: PreviewProvider {
    static var previews: some View {
        ContentView(cat: AnimalModel())
    }
}
```

Notice that the ContentView defines the StateObject (cat) and class (AnimalModel).

6. Add a DisplayTextField structure as follows:

```
struct DisplayTextField: View {

    @EnvironmentObject var creature: AnimalModel

    var body: some View {
        VStack {
            HStack {
                Text("Name:")
                TextField("Type a name here", text:
                $creature.name)
            }
```

```
        HStack {
            Text("Breed:")
            TextField("Type a breed here", text:
            $creature.breed)
        }

        HStack {
            Text("Age:")
            Slider(value: $creature.age, in: 0...20)
        }
        HStack {
            Text("Weight:")
            Slider(value: $creature.weight, in: 0...200)
        }
    }.environmentObject(AnimalModel())
}
}
```

Notice that this structure declares an EnvironmentObject called creature. In addition, the end of the VStack includes the .environ mentObject(AnimalModel()) modifier. Now everything inside this DisplayTextField structure can access the AnimalModel properties including name, breed, age, and weight. The entire ContentView file should look like this:

```
import SwiftUI

struct ContentView: View {

    @StateObject var cat = AnimalModel()

    var body: some View {
        VStack {
            Text("Hello, \(cat.name)")
            Text("Breed: \(cat.breed)")
            Text("Age: \(Int(cat.age))")
            Text("Weight: \(cat.weight)")
            DisplayTextField()
```

```swift
        }.environmentObject(cat)
    }
}

struct ContentView_Previews: PreviewProvider {
    static var previews: some View {
        ContentView(cat: AnimalModel())
    }
}

struct DisplayTextField: View {

    @EnvironmentObject var creature: AnimalModel
    var body: some View {
        VStack {
            HStack {
                Text("Name:")
                TextField("Type a name here", text:
                $creature.name)
            }
            HStack {
                Text("Breed:")
                TextField("Type a breed here", text:
                $creature.breed)
            }
            HStack {
                Text("Age:")
                Slider(value: $creature.age, in: 0...20)
            }
            HStack {
                Text("Weight:")
                Slider(value: $creature.weight, in: 0...200)
            }
        }.environmentObject(AnimalModel())
    }
}
```

```
class AnimalModel: ObservableObject {
    @Published var name: String = ""
    @Published var breed: String = ""
    @Published var age: Double = 0.0
    @Published var weight: Double = 0.0
}
```

7. Click the Live icon on the Canvas pane.

8. Click in the top TextField and type a name.

9. Click in the second TextField and type a breed.

10. Drag the top Slider to define an age.

11. Drag the bottom Slider to define a weight. All your chosen data appears at the top of the user interface (see Figure 7-5).

Summary

Normally, data stays within a structure when you use State variables. To share data between structures, create a State variable in one structure and then use Binding variables in other structures. The State variable typically contains an initial value, while a Binding variable simply defines a variable of the same data type as the State variable.

State and Binding variables can hold individual data types such as integers (Int), decimal numbers (Double or Float), or text (String). If you want to share entire objects that can consist of multiple properties, you need to use StateObject (instead of a State variable) and ObservedObject (instead of a Binding variable). In addition, you need to create a class that's an ObservableObject.

When you use ObservedObjects, you must explicitly pass an object to another structure. To avoid this, you can use EnvironmentObject instead. First, you must create a StateObject within a structure and then use the .environmentObject modifier to share that StateObject.

Within each separate structure, you must declare an EnvironmentObject and also use the .environmentObject modifier to identify the class of the StateObject.

By using State, Binding, StateObject, ObservedObject, and EnvironmentObject, you can easily share data between structures whether those structures are stored in the same file or in a separate file.

CHAPTER 8

Translating with Localization

Most people create apps in their native language, but if you translate your app into other languages, you could sell and distribute your app to other parts of the world. Translating text from one language to another requires an experienced translator, but from a technical point of view, how do you create a single app and let it display different languages?

The hard way is to create separate apps for each language. The easy way is to create a single app and use something called localization. The idea behind localization is that you create your app once, then instead of typing text to appear in the app, you use a special localized string that represents the text to display.

Now you store different text in separate files stored in a localization folder. Depending on the language the user's iOS device uses, your app then yanks out the correct file that matches the user's language. So if you wanted your app to display text in English, Arabic, and Russian, you would create one file containing English words to appear in your app, a second file containing Arabic words that represent equivalent English text, and a third file containing Russian words that represent equivalent text.

If the user switches the settings on their iOS device to display text in Russian, then your app will automatically replace all text with Russian text. If the user switches to Arabic, then your app will automatically replace all text with Arabic text. By creating text in different languages, you can create an app that adapts to different languages.

© Wallace Wang 2023
W. Wang, *Pro iPhone Development with SwiftUI*, https://doi.org/10.1007/978-1-4842-9544-1_8

An app that supports localization will likely need to replace the following to adjust to different languages:

- Text in the user interface such as buttons and labels

- Images

- Text displayed by code

- The name of the app displayed on the home screen

Besides changing text and images that appear on the user interface, localization also needs to adjust the app's user interface as well. For example, buttons that may look perfect when displayed in English may look too small when displaying equivalent text in German or may look too big when displaying equivalent text in Chinese. When designing a user interface, you need to consider the size of displayed text and make sure your user interface adapts to different size text.

Besides the size and text itself, you must also consider how different cultures and regions display dates and numbers. In some areas, people separate decimal numbers with a period such as 3.1415, while in others, people separate decimal numbers with a comma such as 3,1415.

Likewise, some areas display dates with the month first followed by the day and the year like June 4, 2019, while other places display dates differently such as 4 June 2019. So not only must your app display the proper text adjusted on the user interface to appear correctly, but your app must also recognize different number and date formats.

Creating a Localization File

Localization works by creating multiple files to store the text you want to display in other languages. To create localization files, you need to define which languages you want your Xcode project to support. For each language you want your app to support, you'll need to define one localization setting.

For example, if you want your app to support English, Spanish, and French, you'll need to create three separate localization strings for each particular language.

To see how to add localization to a project, follow these steps:

1. Create a new iOS App and give it a name like LocalApp.

2. Click the project name at the top of the Navigator pane as shown in Figure 8-1. Xcode displays information about the project in the middle pane.

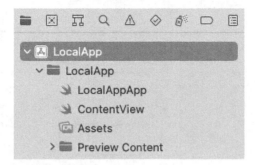

Figure 8-1. *Selecting the project name*

3. Click the project name under the PROJECT heading as shown in Figure 8-2.

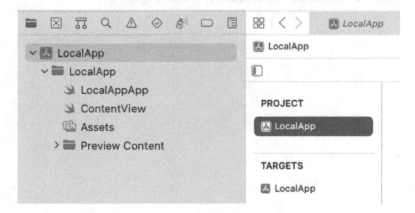

Figure 8-2. *Selecting the project name in the Project pane*

4. Click Info at the top of the middle Xcode pane. Xcode displays an Info pane as shown in Figure 8-3.

Figure 8-3. *The project Info pane*

5. Click the + icon under the Localizations category. A popup menu of different languages appears as shown in Figure 8-4.

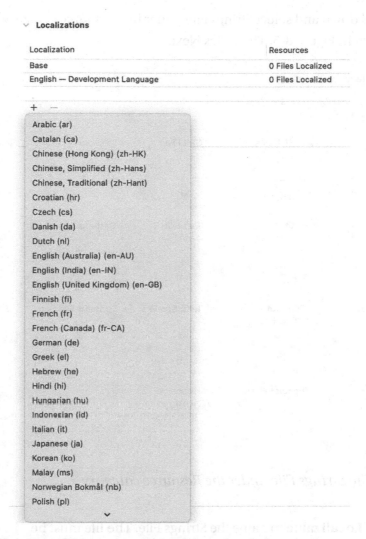

Figure 8-4. *Selecting a language within the project Info pane*

6. Choose a language you want your app to support. For this example, choose French (fr). French appears under English in the Localization column.

7. Repeat steps 5 and 6 except this time choose Spanish (es).

8. Choose File ➤ New ➤ File. A dialog appears.

9. Scroll down and select Strings File under the Resource category as shown in Figure 8-5. Then click Next.

Figure 8-5. *The Strings File under the Resource category*

10. Type **Localizable** to name the Strings File. The file must be named Localizable for Xcode to recognize it as a file that contains translations.

11. Click the Localizable file in the Navigator pane. The contents of the Localizable file appear in the middle Xcode pane.

12. Click the Localize button in the Inspector pane as shown in Figure 8-6. A dialog appears, listing all the different languages you previously defined as shown in Figure 8-7.

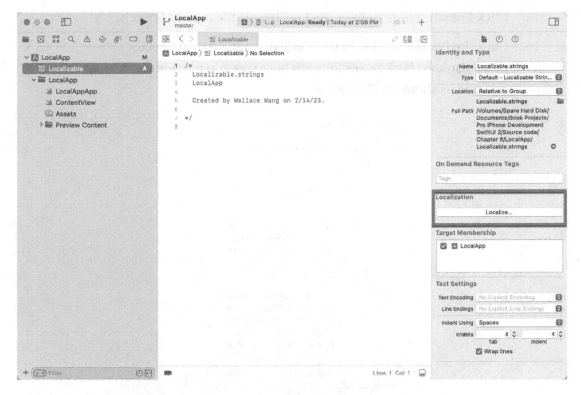

Figure 8-6. *The Localize button appears in the Inspector pane*

Figure 8-7. *The Localize dialog box*

13. Click French. Xcode defines the Localizable file to hold French.

14. Click the Localizable file in the Navigator pane. The Inspector pane displays check boxes for each language you previously selected as shown in Figure 8-8.

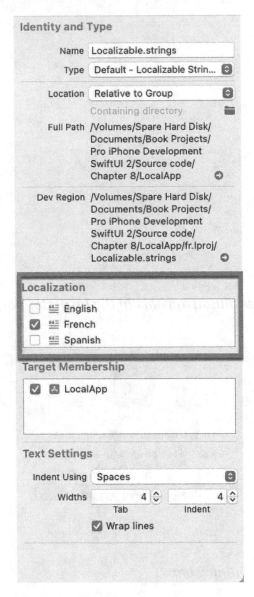

Figure 8-8. *The Inspector pane displaying multiple language check boxes*

15. Select the English, French, and Spanish check boxes. When all check boxes are selected, Xcode creates a Localizable file for French, Spanish, and English as shown in Figure 8-9.

Figure 8-9. *The Navigator pane displays multiple Localizable files*

16. Click the Localizable (English) file and type the following:

```
"greeting-label" = "Hello, world!";
"button labcl" = "Tap me";
```

17. Click the Localizable (Spanish) file and type the following:

```
"greeting-label" = "Hola Mundo";
"button-label" = "Tocame";
```

18. Click the Localizable (French) file and type the following:

```
"greeting-label" = "Bonjour le monde";
"button-label" = "Tape moi";
```

What these localizable files do is define placeholder text with arbitrary names such as "greeting-label" or "button-label". Then depending on which language the app is using, the appropriate translation appears in place of the placeholder text. In this example, we want an app to display text in English, Spanish, and French, so we need to create three separate Localizable files and define translations for each placeholder text.

Defining Multiple Previews

Normally, the Canvas pane displays an app's user interface using the language defined by the current location of your Macintosh. However, you can define multiple previews in the Canvas pane by using the .environment modifier such as

```
.environment(\.locale, .init(identifier: "fr"))
```

In this example, the canvas pane will display French ("fr") by looking for a French Localizable file. You'll need to use a separate .environment modifier for each language you want to display in the canvas pane. In the LocalApp example, we want to use English, French, and Spanish. That means we'll need to define three separate .environment modifiers.

To see how to define multiple language previews in the canvas pane, follow these steps:

1. Make sure the LocalApp project is loaded into Xcode.

2. Click the ContentView file in the Navigator pane.

3. Edit the struct ContentView_Previews structure as follows:

```
struct ContentView_Previews: PreviewProvider {
    static var previews: some View {
        Group {
            ContentView()
                .environment(\.locale, .init(identifier: "en"))
            ContentView()
                .environment(\.locale, .init(identifier: "fr"))
            ContentView()
                .environment(\.locale, .init(identifier: "es"))
        }
    }
}
```

This creates three separate iOS simulated devices in the canvas pane as shown in Figure 8-10.

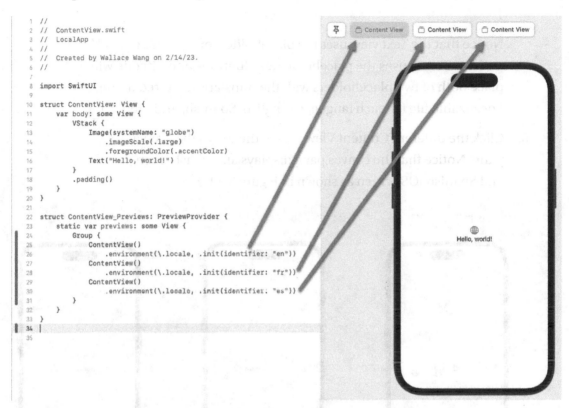

Figure 8-10. *The Canvas pane can display multiple iOS simulated screens in different languages*

4. Edit the struct ContentView structure as follows:

```
struct ContentView: View {

    @State var changeColor = false

    var body: some View {
        VStack {
            Text("greeting-label")
            Button("button-label", action: {
                changeColor.toggle()
            })
```

```
      }.background(changeColor ? Color.red : Color.yellow)
   }
}
```

Notice that the Text view uses the placeholder text "greeting-label" and the Button uses the placeholder text "button-label". Xcode will place both of two placeholders with the translations stored in the Localizable file for each language (English, Spanish, and French).

5. Click the different Content View tabs at the top of the Canvas pane. Notice that the canvas pane displays an English, French, and Spanish iOS screen as shown in Figure 8-11.

Figure 8-11. *Viewing different Canvas panes*

6. Click the Live icon in the Canvas pane for any of the iOS simulated screens and then click the Button to toggle between a red or yellow background in the VStack.

In this simple example, you can see how Xcode lets you create separate translations for different placeholders. By using these placeholders in your user interface, you can let the app replace the placeholder text with the text defined in the appropriate Localizable file.

That's why you need a separate Localizable file for each language, and you need a separate translation for each placeholder text. The more languages you need to support, the more Localizable files you'll need with a separate translation for each placeholder text.

Using a LocalizableStringKey

The Text and Button views let you define placeholder text that will be replaced with different language translations defined in the separate Localizable files. However, if you want to define different language translations for text that appears in something other than a Text or Button view, you need to use something called a LocalizableStringKey.

Normally, when you define a String, you might use code like this:

```
var placeholder = "Type your name here"
```

However, this stores English text in the variable. If you wanted to change this text to French or Spanish, you'd have to rewrite this text in another language such as French or Spanish. Since this isn't practical, SwiftUI lets you declare a String variable or constant as a LocalizedStringKey such as

```
var placeholder: LocalizedStringKey = "placeholder-label"
```

This tells Xcode to replace "placeholder-label" with the appropriate foreign language text defined in the Localizable file. Once you've identified text in your code as LocalizedStringKey, the next step is to edit the Localizable file and define its equivalent word or term in another language.

In the English Localizable file, we can define what text to use in place of "name-label" like this:

```
"placeholder-label" = "Type your name here";
```

In the French Localizable file, we can define what text to use in place of "name-label" like this:

```
"placeholder-label" = "Tapez votre nom ici";
```

161

Now the app will replace "secret-label" with the appropriate text ("Type your name here" or "Tapez votre nom ici") depending on whether the app is displaying English or French. To see how LocalizableStringKey works, follow these steps:

1. Make sure the LocalApp project is loaded into Xcode and that you have created a localization file for French and Spanish (see Figure 8-9).

2. Click the Localizable (English) file so the entire file looks like the following:

```
"greeting-label" = "Hello, world!";
"button-label" = "Tap me";
"placeholder-label" = "Type here";
```

3. Click the Localizable (French) file so the entire file looks like the following:

```
"greeting-label" = "Bonjour le monde";
"button-label" = "Tape moi";
"placeholder-label" = "Écrivez ici";
```

4. Click the Localizable (Spanish) file so the entire file looks like the following:

```
"greeting-label" = "Hola Mundo";
"button-label" = "Tocame";
"placeholder-label" = "Escriba aquí";
```

5. Click the ContentView file and add the following variable:

```
var placeholder: LocalizedStringKey = "placeholder-label"
```

6. Add a TextField underneath the Button as follows:

```
TextField(placeholder, text: $message)
```

The entire ContentView file should look like this:

```swift
import SwiftUI

struct ContentView: View {

    @State var changeColor = false
    @State var message = ""

    var placeholder: LocalizedStringKey = "placeholder-label"

    var body: some View {
        VStack {
            Text("greeting-label")
            Button("button-label", action: {
                changeColor.toggle()
            })
            TextField(placeholder, text: $message)
        }.background(changeColor ? Color.red : Color.yellow)
    }
}

struct ContentView_Previews: PreviewProvider {
    static var previews: some View {
        Group {
            ContentView()
                .environment(\.locale, .init(identifier: "en"))
            ContentView()
                .environment(\.locale, .init(identifier: "fr"))
            ContentView()
                .environment(\.locale, .init(identifier: "es"))
        }
    }
}
```

7. Click each Content View tab at the top of the Canvas pane to see the different translations as shown in Figure 8-12.

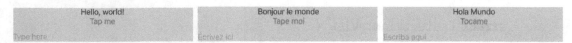

Figure 8-12. *Different languages appear in the Text, Button, and TextField views*

Text and Button views can automatically retrieve translations stored in the Localizable file, but other views, such as the TextField, must declare a LocalizableStringKey variable before they can retrieve translations in the Localizable file.

Using String Interpolation with Localizable Strings

The Localizable file contains a list of placeholder text that will be replaced with actual text in various languages. However, this placeholder text typically represents a fixed string such as

```
"greeting-label" = "Hello, world!";
```

Wherever Xcode finds the string "greeting-label," it will replace that string with the fixed string "Hello, world!" for an English version of the app. However, many times strings combine fixed text with a value inserted inside the string using string interpolation such as

```
Text("You are \(age) years old")
```

If the value of the "age" variable is 26, the preceding Text view would display "You are 26 years old". When you need to use string interpolation within text that may need to appear in different foreign languages, you need to identify where you want to use string interpolation within that text no matter which language may be displayed.

To specify where string interpolation occurs, you need to use a format specifier for that particular data type such as

%@ – For String

%lld – For Int

%lf – For Double

These format specifiers appear in both the placeholder text and the translated text. For example, suppose you wanted to display this text in different languages where "petCount" is an integer:

```
Text("Number of pets = \(petCount)")
```

First, you would need to create placeholder text for the Text view like this:

```
Text("pet-label \(petCount)")
```

Then to define "pet-label" in the Localizable file, you would need to use the format specifier in both the placeholder text to the left of the equal sign and in the actual text on the right of the equal sign like this:

```
"pet-label %lld" = "Number of pets = %lld";
```

Notice that the %lld format specifier appears where string interpolation appears in the string such as at the end. To see how to use string interpolation with localization, follow these steps:

1. Make sure the LocalApp project is loaded into Xcode and that you have created a localization file for French and Spanish (see Figure 8-9).

2. Click the Localizable (English) file so the entire file looks like the following:

   ```
   "greeting-label %@" = "Hello, %@";
   "%lld button-label" = "%lld Tap me";
   "placeholder-label" = "Type here";
   "pi-label %lf" = "Value of pi = %lf";
   ```

3. Click the Localizable (French) file so the entire file looks like the following:

   ```
   "greeting-label %@" = "Bonjour, %@";
   "%lld button-label" = " %lld Tape moi";
   "placeholder-label" = "Écrivez ici";
   "pi-label %lf" = "Valeur de pi = %lf";
   ```

4. Click the Localizable (Spanish) file so the entire file looks like the following:

```
"greeting-label %@" = "Hola, %@";
"%lld button-label" = "%lld Tocame";
"placeholder-label" = "Escriba aquí";
"pi-label %lf" = "Valor de pi = %lf";
```

5. Click the ContentView file and add the following variables and State variables:

```
@State var changeColor = false
@State var name = ""
@State var buttonNumber = 1

var placeholder: LocalizedStringKey = "placeholder-label"
var value = 3.1415
```

6. Modify the var body: some View like this:

```
var body: some View {
    VStack {
        Text("greeting-label \(name)")
        Text("pi-label \(value)")
        Button("\(buttonNumber) button-label", action: {
            changeColor.toggle()
            buttonNumber += 1
        })
        TextField(placeholder, text: $name)
    }.background(changeColor ? Color.red : Color.yellow)
}
```

Notice that the first Text view displays "greeting-label \(name)", so the Localizable file displays the format specifier at the end as "greeting-label %@" and as "Hello, %@". On the other hand, the Button displays "\(buttonNumber) button-label", so the format specifier in the Localizable file must appear in the beginning such as "%lld button-label" and "%lld Tap me".

The entire ContentView file should look like this:

```swift
import SwiftUI

struct ContentView: View {

    @State var changeColor = false
    @State var name = ""
    @State var buttonNumber = 1

    var placeholder: LocalizedStringKey = "placeholder-label"
    var value = 3.1415

    var body: some View {
        VStack {
            Text("greeting-label \(name)")
            Text("pi-label \(value)")
            Button("\(buttonNumber) button-label", action: {
                changeColor.toggle()
                buttonNumber += 1
            })
            TextField(placeholder, text: $name)
        }.background(changeColor ? Color.red : Color.yellow)
    }
}

struct ContentView_Previews: PreviewProvider {
    static var previews: some View {
        Group {
            ContentView()
                .environment(\.locale, .init(identifier: "en"))
            ContentView()
                .environment(\.locale, .init(identifier: "fr"))
            ContentView()
                .environment(\.locale, .init(identifier: "es"))
        }
    }
}
```

7.   Click the Live icon on the Canvas pane.

8.   Click the Content View tabs at the top of the Canvas pane.
     Notice that each Text view displays "Value of pi = 3.1415" in the
     appropriate language.

9.   Click in the TextField and type a name. Notice that the name
     appears in the top Text view.

10. Click the Button. Notice that each time you click the Button, the
     number to the left increments by one.

This project shows how to include string interpolation with text that will be localized
in different languages. By using the right format specifier for String, Int, or Double data
types and placing the format specifier in the front or end of a string, you can make sure
your Localizable file translates text with data displayed by string interpolation.

Formatting Numbers and Dates

Every region tends to display numbers and dates in different ways. To make your app
dates based on the user's language and region, use Apple's DateFormatter. Apple's
various formatters can automatically adjust the appearance of data based on the iOS
device's language and region. Your app just needs to calculate the data to appear on
the user interface. To learn more about the different formatters available, read Apple's
documentation (`https://developer.apple.com/documentation/foundation/`
`formatter`).

The basic steps to using a formatter involve choosing which formatter to use such as

```
let formatter = DateFormatter()
```

Then define one or more settings for how to format the information such as

```
formatter.dateStyle = .full
```

Finally, use the formatter to convert the data such as

```
let myDate = formatter.string(from: Date())
```

To see how to use formatters to display data in different languages and regions, follow these steps:

1. Make sure the LocalApp project is loaded into Xcode with the English, French, and Spanish Localizable files.

2. Click the ContentView file in the Navigator pane.

3. Add the following underneath the existing State variables as follows:

```
let date: Date
let dateFormatter: DateFormatter

init() {
    date = Date()
    dateFormatter = DateFormatter()
    dateFormatter.dateStyle = .long
    dateFormatter.timeStyle = .short
}
```

The available options for dateStyle and timeStyle are .short, .medium, .long, and .full as shown in Table 8-1.

Table 8-1. .dateStyle and .timeStyle options

	.dateStyle	.timeStyle
.full	Sunday, October 24, 2021	1:23:46 PM Pacific Daylight Time
.long	October 24, 2021	1:23:46 PM PDT
.medium	Oct 24, 2021	1:23:46 PM
.short	10/24/21	1:23 PM

4. Add the following Text view underneath the existing TextField:

```
Text(date, formatter: dateFormatter)
```

The entire ContentView file should look like this:

```swift
import SwiftUI

struct ContentView: View {

    @State var changeColor = false
    @State var name = ""
    @State var buttonNumber = 1

    let placeholder: LocalizedStringKey = "placeholder-label"
    let value = 3.1415

    let date: Date
    let dateFormatter: DateFormatter

    init() {
        date = Date()
        dateFormatter = DateFormatter()
        dateFormatter.dateStyle = .long
        dateFormatter.timeStyle = .medium
    }

    var body: some View {
        VStack {
            Text("greeting-label \(name)")
            Text("pi-label \(value)")
            Button("\(buttonNumber) button-label", action: {
                changeColor.toggle()
                    buttonNumber += 1
            })
            TextField(placeholder, text: $name)
            Text(date, formatter: dateFormatter)
        }.background(changeColor ? Color.red : Color.yellow)
    }
}
```

```
struct ContentView_Previews: PreviewProvider {
    static var previews: some View {
        Group {
            ContentView()
                .environment(\.locale, .init(identifier: "en"))
            ContentView()
                .environment(\.locale, .init(identifier: "fr"))
            ContentView()
                .environment(\.locale, .init(identifier: "es"))
        }
    }
}
```

5. Click the Live icon on the Canvas pane. The English, French, and
   Spanish versions of your app appear as shown in Figure 8-13.
   Notice that the English version displays decimal points with a
   period (3.1415), while the French and Spanish versions display
   decimal points with a comma (3,1415).

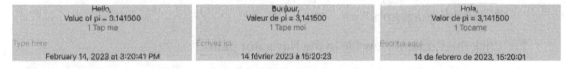

Figure 8-13. *Each region displays numbers, dates, and times differently*

Using Pseudolanguages

When designing apps that will display other languages, keep in mind that translated text
is rarely the same height and length as the text you used to design an app. For example,
text displayed in French might have accent characters above or below certain letters,
increasing the text height. In other cases, text translated into German might appear
longer, while the same text translated into Chinese will appear shorter since each
character in Chinese represents a complete word.

While you could test every possible language to see how it appears within your app's user interface, a much simpler solution is to use pseudolanguage. This lets you see how text will appear in other languages without actually translating text into other languages. The available options for displaying pseudolanguage include

- Double-Length Pseudolanguage – Displays text twice as long

- Right-to-Left Pseudolanguage – Displays text as if starting on the right margin

- Accented Pseudolanguage – Displays text as if it had accent characters above and below text

- Bounded String Pseudolanguage – Wraps text to identify where it may appear truncated

- Right-to-Left Pseudolanguage With Right-to-Left Strings – Simulates right-to-left direction using right-to-left text

To see how to use pseudolanguage to help design your app's user interface, follow these steps:

1. Create a new iOS App SwiftUI project and name it PseudolanguageApp.

2. Click the ContentView file in the Navigator pane.

3. Edit the ContentView file as follows:

```
struct ContentView: View {
    var body: some View {
        VStack {
            Text("Hello, world!")
                .padding()
                .background(Color.yellow)
            Text("This is a lot of text to display in a small
                amount of space to test how well Xcode can truncate
                large amounts of text.")
                .padding()
                .background(Color.mint)
```

```
//                    .lineLimit(2)
        }
    }
}
```

The entire ContentView file should look like this:

```
import SwiftUI

struct ContentView: View {
    var body: some View {
        VStack {
            Text("Hello, world!")
                .padding()
                .background(Color.yellow)
            Text("This is a lot of text to display in a small
            amount of space to test how well Xcode can truncate
            large amounts of text.")
                .padding()
                .background(Color.mint)
//                  .lineLimit(2)
        }
    }
}

struct ContentView_Previews: PreviewProvider {
    static var previews: some View {
        ContentView()
    }
}
```

4. Choose Product ➤ Scheme ➤ Edit Scheme. A dialog appears.

5. Click the Run icon on the left panel and then click the Options tab.

6. Click the App Language list box and choose Double-Length Pseudolanguage as shown in Figure 8-14.

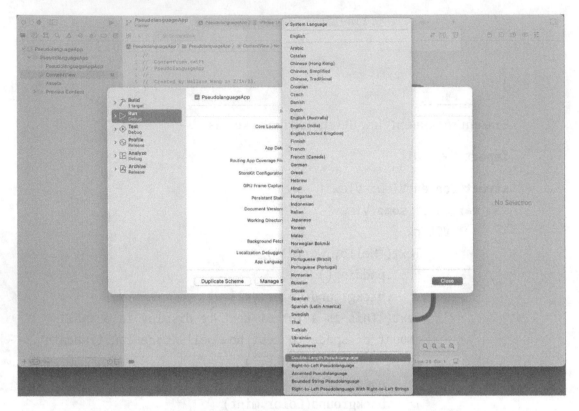

Figure 8-14. *Choosing a pseudolanguage option*

7.   Click the Close button. Xcode displays your app's user interface
      with text twice the length as shown in Figure 8-15.

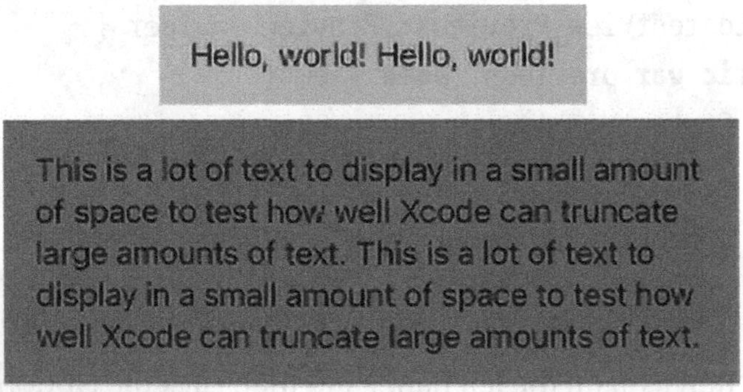

Hello, world! Hello, world!

This is a lot of text to display in a small amount
of space to test how well Xcode can truncate
large amounts of text. This is a lot of text to
display in a small amount of space to test how
well Xcode can truncate large amounts of text.

Figure 8-15. *Displaying text as double-length pseudolanguage*

8. Choose Product ➤ Scheme ➤ Edit Scheme. A dialog appears.

9. Click the Run icon on the left panel and then click the Options tab.

10. Click the App Language list box and choose Right-to-Left Pseudolanguage.

11. Click the Close button and then click the Resume button in the upper-right corner of the canvas pane. Xcode displays your app's user interface with text aligned along the right margin as shown in Figure 8-16.

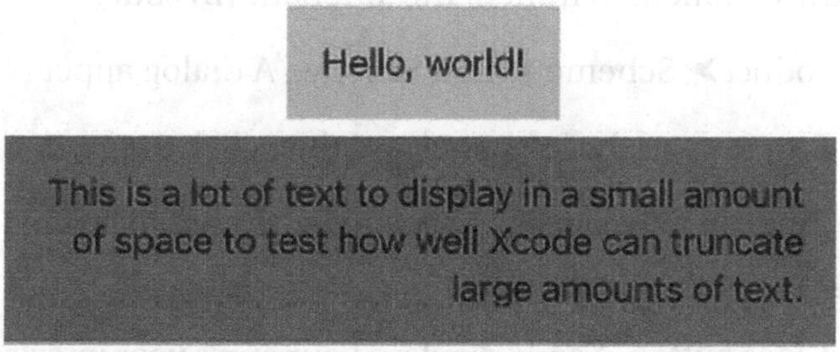

Hello, world!

This is a lot of text to display in a small amount of space to test how well Xcode can truncate large amounts of text.

Figure 8-16. *Displaying text as right-to-left pseudolanguage*

12. Choose Product ➤ Scheme ➤ Edit Scheme. A dialog appears.

13. Click the Run icon on the left panel and then click the Options tab.

14. Click the App Language list box and choose Accented Pseudolanguage.

15. Click the Close button and then click the Resume button in the upper-right corner of the canvas pane. Xcode displays your app's user interface with text displaying accent characters above and below text as shown in Figure 8-17.

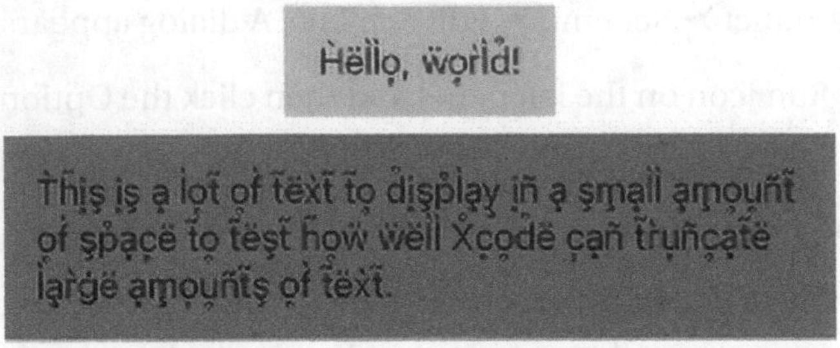

Figure 8-17. *Displaying text as accented pseudolanguage*

16. Remove the comment in front of the .lineLimit(2) code.

17. Choose Product ➤ Scheme ➤ Edit Scheme. A dialog appears.

18. Click the Run icon on the left panel and then click the Options tab.

19. Click the App Language list box and choose Bounded String Pseudolanguage.

20. Click the Close button. Xcode displays your app's user interface. Notice that the square brackets let you see where text begins and ends, but with the .lineLimit(2) modifier, the last square bracket is not visible because text is being cut off as shown in Figure 8-18.

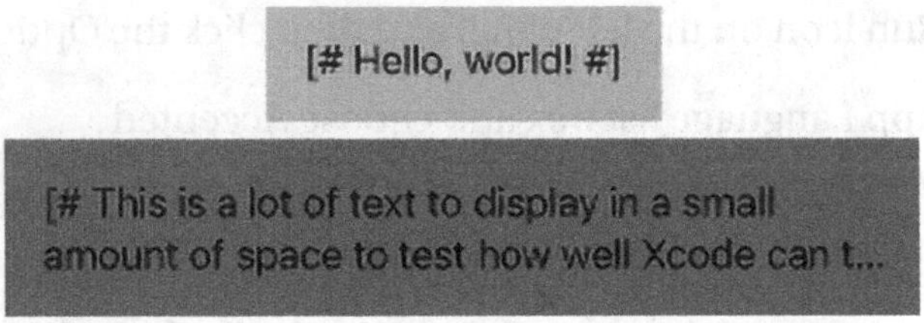

Figure 8-18. *Displaying text as bounded string pseudolanguage*

21. Comment out the .lineLimit(2) line like this:

```
//                    .lineLimit(2)
```

22. Choose Product ➤ Scheme ➤ Edit Scheme. A dialog appears.

23. Click the Run icon on the left panel and then click the Options tab.

24. Click the App Language list box and choose Right-to-Left Pseudolanguage With Right-to-Left Strings Pseudolanguage.

25. Click the Close button. Xcode displays your app's user interface with text reversed and aligned on the right margin as shown in Figure 8-19.

!dlrow ,olleH

tnuoma llams a ni yalpsid ot txet fo tol a si sihT
etacnurt nac edocX llew woh tset ot ecaps fo
.txet fo stnuoma egral

Figure 8-19. *Displaying text as right-to-left pseudolanguage with right-to-left strings*

Pseudolanguage lets you see how your app's user interface adjusts to different types of languages such as those that appear with accent characters and those that appear right to left. By testing how pseudolanguage might affect the appearance of your app, you can make sure that the user interface adapts to all types of languages.

Summary

Creating an app in your native language may be fine, but if you want to reach other markets, you need to translate the text of your app into other languages. By using Xcode's pseudolanguage feature, you can mimic other languages to make sure your user interface adapts to longer or shorter text. You can also display text in other languages to see how specific foreign words and phrases will look on your app's user interface. Don't forget that some languages and regions display data differently such as dates and numbers.

Creating an app can be hard work, so it only makes sense to distribute your app as broadly as possible so it can reach as many people as possible. The more languages your app can support, the bigger your potential market, so always keep foreign markets in mind to increase your app's popularity.

Summary

CHAPTER 9

Displaying Gauges and Progress Views

When a program is busy doing something such as retrieving data or performing a task, it's good practice to let the user know the program is still working. Otherwise, the program may appear frozen as if it crashed or froze. To give visual feedback to the user that a program is busy but likely to finish soon, you can use gauges and progress views.

The main idea behind gauges is to show the user approximately how far along a task might be. This often appears as a horizontal bar that gradually fills up the closer the task gets to completion as shown in Figure 9-1.

Figure 9-1. *Many programs visually display how close a task is to completion*

While a gauge shows approximately how much a task has been completed, a progress view has the option of displaying a horizontal bar or displaying a rotating image to let users know that something is happening but there's no definite idea when that task will finish. Progress views simply give visual feedback that the program hasn't crashed but is still working as shown in Figure 9-2.

Figure 9-2. *A spinning progress view shows activity without identifying when that activity will finish*

© Wallace Wang 2023
W. Wang, *Pro iPhone Development with SwiftUI*, https://doi.org/10.1007/978-1-4842-9544-1_9

Creating a Gauge

A Gauge visually represents a numeric value. By default, this numeric value ranges between zero and one, but you can define any range of values you want. The most basic Gauge requires a value like this, which creates a simple horizontal Gauge as shown in Figure 9-3:

```
Gauge(value: aNumericValue) {

}
```

Figure 9-3. *A basic appearance of a Gauge*

Inside the curly brackets of a Gauge is where you can display descriptive text or an image to help users better understand the purpose of the Gauge and what it's measuring as shown in Figure 9-4.

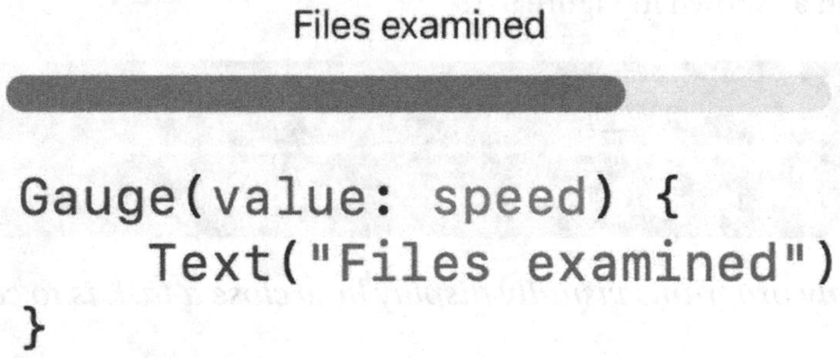

Files examined

```
Gauge(value: speed) {
    Text("Files examined")
}
```

Figure 9-4. *Adding descriptive text to a Gauge*

Instead of a Text view, you can also use an Image or Label view such as

```
Gauge(value: speed) {
    Text("Text view")
}

Gauge(value: speed) {
    Image(systemName: "hare")
}
```

```
Gauge(value: speed) {
    Label {
        Text("Text view")
    } icon: {
        Image(systemName: "tortoise")
    }
}
```

Although a Gauge represents a value of zero to one, you can define your own minimum and maximum values by defining a range like this:

```
Gauge(value: speed, in: 25...100) {
    Text("Text view")
}
```

To make the current value of the Gauge appear underneath the Gauge, you can define the currentValueLabel like this:

```
Gauge(value: speed, in: -25...100) {
    Text("Descriptive text")
} currentValueLabel: {
    Text("\(speed)")
}
```

The preceding code defines the Gauge's range from –25 to 100, displays "Descriptive text" above the Gauge, and displays the current value of the Gauge underneath as shown in Figure 9-5.

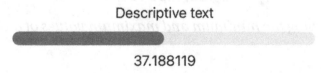

Descriptive text

37.188119

Figure 9-5. *Displaying descriptive text on top and its current numeric value underneath a Gauge*

To make it clear what the minimum and maximum values of a Gauge represent, you can use the minimumValueLabel and maximumValueLabel properties to define these values at the left and right ends of the Gauge like this:

```
Gauge(value: speed, in: minimumValue...maximumValue) {
    Text("Descriptive text")
} currentValueLabel: {
    Text("\(speed)")
} minimumValueLabel: {
    Text("\(Int(minimumValue))")
} maximumValueLabel: {
    Text("\(Int(maximumValue))")
}
```

The preceding code assumes the minimumValue and maximumValue variables have been defined such as

```
@State var minimumValue = 0.0
 @State var maximumValue = 100.0
```

Since the Gauge represents a decimal number, the Text views defined under both the minimumValueLabel and maximumValueLabel properties convert these values to integers that appear on the far left and right of the Gauge as shown in Figure 9-6.

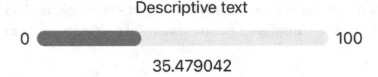

Figure 9-6. *Displaying the minimum and maximum values of a Gauge at the far ends*

By default, a Gauge displays a fill color using blue. To customize this color, you can use the .tint modifier like this:

```
Gauge(value: speed, in: minimumValue...maximumValue) {
    Text("Descriptive text")
}.tint(.green)
```

When you add descriptive text and the currentValueLabel property, the descriptive text and current value appear centered above and below the Gauge (see Figure 9-6). If you want to push this descriptive text and current value to the far left, you can modify the Gauge using the .gaugeStyle modifier like this:

```
.gaugeStyle(.accessoryLinearCapacity)
```

This pushes the descriptive text and current value to the left as shown in Figure 9-7.

Figure 9-7. *Changing the location of descriptive text and current values of a Gauge*

To see how to use a Gauge, follow these steps:

1. Create a new iOS App and give it a name like GaugeApp.

2. Click the ContentView file.

3. Add the following State variables:

```
@State var speed = 50.0
@State var minimumValue = 0.0
@State var maximumValue = 100.0
```

4. Modify the VStack to add spacing and delete anything inside like this:

```
VStack (spacing: 50) {

}
.padding()
```

5. Add a Gauge and a Slider view inside the VStack like this:

```
VStack (spacing: 50) {

    Gauge(value: speed, in: minimumValue...maximumValue) {
        Text("Current speed")
    } currentValueLabel: {
        Text("\(speed)")
```

```
            } minimumValueLabel: {
                Text("\(Int(minimumValue))")
            } maximumValueLabel: {
                Text("\(Int(maximumValue))")
            }.tint(.green)
            .gaugeStyle(.accessoryLinearCapacity)

            Slider(value: $speed, in: minimumValue...maximumValue)
        }
        .padding()
```

The entire ContentView file should look like this:

```
import SwiftUI

struct ContentView: View {

    @State var speed = 50.0
    @State var minimumValue = 0.0
    @State var maximumValue = 100.0

    var body: some View {
        VStack (spacing: 50) {

            Gauge(value: speed, in: minimumValue...maximumValue) {
                Text("Current speed")
            } currentValueLabel: {
                Text("\(speed)")
            } minimumValueLabel: {
                Text("\(Int(minimumValue))")
            } maximumValueLabel: {
                Text("\(Int(maximumValue))")
            }.tint(.green)
            .gaugeStyle(.accessoryLinearCapacity)

            Slider(value: $speed, in: minimumValue...maximumValue)
        }
        .padding()
    }
}
```

```
struct ContentView_Previews: PreviewProvider {
    static var previews: some View {
        ContentView()
    }
}
```

6. Click the Live icon on the Canvas pane.

7. Drag the Slider left and right to change the value of the Gauge.
    Notice how the currentValueLabel property displays the Gauge's
    current value underneath.

Creating a Circular Gauge

A Gauge normally appears as a horizontal line, but you can also create a circular Gauge.
Two circular style Gauges are shown in Figure 9-8:

- .accessoryCircular

- .accessoryCircularCapacity

.accessoryCircular   .accessoryCircularCapacity

Figure 9-8. *The two types of circular Gauges*

To define a circular Gauge, you must create a Gauge view and then
add the .gaugeStyle modifier that specifies either .accessoryCircular or
.accessoryCircularCapacity. Notice how the descriptive text appears in both
circular Gauges.

With .accessoryCircular, the text appears at the bottom and keeps the Gauge from
completing forming a closed circle.

With .accessoryCircularCapacity, the text appears inside the circular Gauge, which
allows the Gauge to form a complete circle.

To see how to create a circular Gauge, follow these steps:

1. Create a new iOS App and give it a name like CircularGaugeApp.

2. Click the ContentView file.

3. Add the following State variables:

```
@State var speed = 50.0
@State var minimumValue = 0.0
@State var maximumValue = 100.0
```

4. Modify the VStack to add a Gauge and Slider like this:

```
VStack {
    Gauge(value: speed, in: minimumValue...maximumValue) {
        Text("RPMs")
    } currentValueLabel: {
        Text("\(speed)")
    } minimumValueLabel: {
        Text("\(Int(minimumValue))")
    } maximumValueLabel: {
        Text("\(Int(maximumValue))")
    }.tint(.purple)
    .gaugeStyle(.accessoryCircular)

    Slider(value: $speed, in: minimumValue...maximumValue)
}
.padding()
```

The entire ContentView file should look like this:

```
import SwiftUI

struct ContentView: View {

    @State var speed = 50.0
    @State var minimumValue = 0.0
    @State var maximumValue = 100.0

    var body: some View {
        VStack {
```

```
Gauge(value: speed, in: minimumValue...maximumValue) {
    Text("RPMs")
} currentValueLabel: {
    Text("\(speed)")
} minimumValueLabel: {
    Text("\(Int(minimumValue))")
} maximumValueLabel: {
    Text("\(Int(maximumValue))")
}.tint(.purple)
.gaugeStyle(.accessoryCircular)

Slider(value: $speed, in: minimumValue...maximumValue)
}
    .padding()
    }
}

struct ContentView_Previews: PreviewProvider {
    static var previews: some View {
        ContentView()
    }
}
```

5. Click the Live icon on the Canvas pane.

6. Drag the Slider left and right to see how the circular Gauge works
   as shown in Figure 9-9.

Figure 9-9. *The appearance of a circular Gauge*

7. Edit the .gaugeStyle modifier as follows:

    `.gaugeStyle(.accessoryCircularCapacity)`

8. Click the Live icon on the Canvas pane.

9. Drag the Slider left and right. Notice that the circular Gauge looks different as shown in Figure 9-10.

Figure 9-10. *The different appearance of the circular Gauge*

Use a Progress View

The simplest Progress view displays a spinning animation (see Figure 9-2) just by specifying a Progress view like this:

`ProgressView()`

Besides displaying a spinning animation, the Progress view can also display text underneath as shown in Figure 9-11.

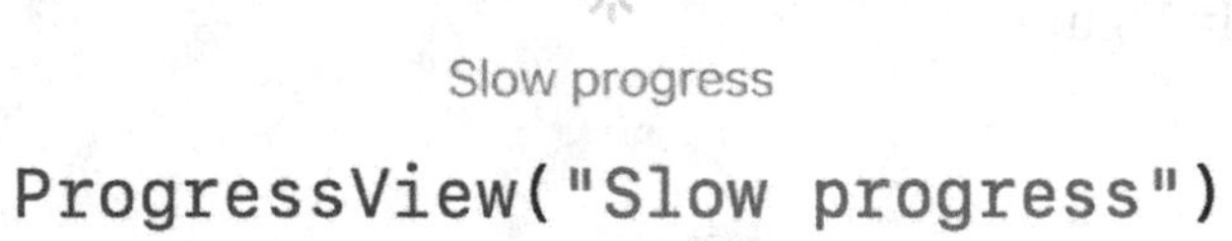

Slow progress

`ProgressView("Slow progress")`

Figure 9-11. *A Progress view can display text*

If you specify a value and a total, the Progress view can look like a Gauge as a horizontal line that gradually fills up. The value parameter defines the current value that the Progress view represents, and the total parameter defines the value representing 100% completion such as

`ProgressView("Slow progress", value: 50, total: 100)`

To see how to use a Progress view, follow these steps:

1. Create a new iOS App and give it a name like ProgressViewApp.

2. Click the ContentView file.

3. Add the following State variables:

    ```
    @State var sliderValue = 0.0
    ```

4. Modify the VStack as follows:

    ```
    VStack (spacing: 75) {
        ProgressView()

        ProgressView("Text added")

        ProgressView("Horizontal Progress view", value: sliderValue,
        total: 100)

        Slider(value: $sliderValue, in: 0...100)
    }
    .padding()
    ```

    The entire ContentView file should look like this:

    ```
    import SwiftUI

    struct ContentView: View {
        @State var sliderValue = 0.0

        var body: some View {
            VStack (spacing: 75) {
                ProgressView()

                ProgressView("Text added")

                ProgressView("Horizontal Progress view", value:
                sliderValue, total: 100)
    ```

```
                Slider(value: $sliderValue, in: 0...100)
            }
            .padding()
        }
    }

    struct ContentView_Previews: PreviewProvider {
        static var previews: some View {
            ContentView()
        }
    }
```

5. Click the Live icon on the Canvas pane. Notice that the top
    Progress view displays a spinning animation, while the second
    Progress view displays a spinning animation with "Text added"
    appearing underneath. When a Progress view represents a value,
    it appears as a horizontal line.

Summary

When an app needs to perform a lengthy task, it can appear frozen or unresponsive.
That's why apps use visual clues like Gauges and Progress views to show that the app is
still working and even how close it might be to completion.

Gauges can appear as a horizontal line or as a circular image. To customize
the appearance of a Gauge, you can change the .tint color, .gaugeStyle, and
minimumValueLabel/maximumValueLabel.

Progress views can appear as spinning animation by themselves or with explanatory
text underneath. If a Progress view represents a numeric value, then it appears as a
horizontal line much like a linear Gauge.

Both Gauges and Progress views are ways to give feedback to the user so they know
that the app is continuing to work and is getting closer to completion.

CHAPTER 10

Adding Search to an App

If you open the Contacts app on an iPhone, you'll see a list of people whose names and contact information you've saved. When you want to find a particular person, you could scroll through your list or jump to a specific area alphabetically. However, it's much faster to just search for that data by typing text into a search bar as shown in Figure 10-1.

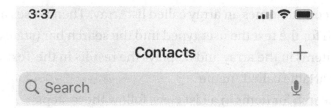

Figure 10-1. *The search bar appears in the Contacts app on an iPhone*

Swift now lets you create your own search bar to search through data stored in a list. Essentially, all you need to do is store data in a List view and then add a .searchable modifier to that List. That will allow users to search for specific data stored in that List view.

Adding a Search Bar to a List View

SwiftUI can add a search bar to the top of any List. To create a search bar, you just need to create a NavigationView and then modify this NavigationStack using the .searchable modifier like this:

```
NavigationStack{

}.searchable(text: $stateVariable)
```

© Wallace Wang 2023
W. Wang, *Pro iPhone Development with SwiftUI*, https://doi.org/10.1007/978-1-4842-9544-1_10

You'll also need to declare a State variable to use within the .searchable modifier like this:

```
@State var stateVariable = ""
```

Whatever you type inside the search bar will get stored in the State variable. Then you'll need to filter out the List to match whatever the user typed using code like this:

```
.searchable(text: $stateVariable) {
    ForEach(listArray.filter {$0.hasPrefix(stateVariable)},
    id: \.self) { name in
  Text(name)
}
```

The preceding code assumes an array called listArray. Then it uses a ForEach loop with .filter to search for the text the user typed into the search bar (stateVariable). This filters out the items in the array and displays the results in the Text view using an arbitrarily named variable called "name".

To see how to search for items in a List view, follow these steps:

1. Create a new iOS App project and name it SearchApp.

2. Click the ContentView file in the Navigator pane.

3. Add the following State variable and array under struct ContentView: View like this:

```
@State var searchText = ""
let petArray = ["Cat", "Dog", "Fish", "Donkey", "Canary",
"Camel", "Frog"]
```

This code creates a State variable to work with the search bar. In addition, it creates an array of strings. Notice that each string begins with a capital letter. That's because the search bar always capitalizes the first letter of any text typed in.

4. Create a separate structure to display a List view:

```
struct PetListView: View {
    let animals: [String]
    var body: some View {
```

```
        List(animals, id: \.self) { x in
            Text(x)
        }
    }
}
```

5. Add the following underneath var body: some View like this:

```
NavigationStack{
    PetListView(animals: petArray)
      }.searchable(text: $searchText) {
    ForEach(petArray.filter {$0.hasPrefix(searchText)},
    id: \.self) { name in
        Text(name)
    }
}
```

This creates a NavigationStack that displays the List defined by the PetListView structure. The .searchable modifier uses the searchText State variable to hold any text typed into the search bar. When the user types text into the search bar, the .searchable modifier runs a ForEach loop to constantly filter out items in the List that do not match the text typed in the search bar (the searchText State variable).

The entire ContentView file should look like this:

```
import SwiftUI

struct ContentView: View {
    @State var searchText = ""
    let petArray = ["Cat", "Dog", "Fish", "Donkey", "Canary",
    "Camel", "Frog"]

    var body: some View {
        NavigationStack{
            PetListView(animals: petArray)
        }.searchable(text: $searchText) {
```

```
            ForEach(petArray.filter {$0.hasPrefix(searchText)},
            id: \.self) { name in
                Text(name)
            }
        }
    }
}

struct PetListView: View {
    let animals: [String]
    var body: some View {
        List(animals, id: \.self) { x in
            Text(x)
        }
    }
}

struct ContentView_Previews: PreviewProvider {
    static var previews: some View {
        ContentView()
    }
}
```

6. Click the Live icon on the Canvas pane. The canvas pane displays
    the List view containing all the strings defined in the petArray
    variable.

7. Click in the search bar and type C. Notice that the List view
    now filters out only those items that contain "C" as shown in
    Figure 10-2.

| 🔍 d | ✖ | Cancel |

Cat

Canary

Camel

Figure 10-2. *Filtering out items in the List view through the search bar*

8. Continue typing Can. The List view will display the only text that matches "Can" which is Canary.

Changing the Placeholder Text in the Search Bar

By default, the search bar always displays "Search" as placeholder text whenever the search bar is visible and the user has not typed any text in it (see Figure 10-1). While displaying "Search" makes the purpose of the search bar clear, you may want to customize this placeholder text with your own text.

To define placeholder text in the search bar, just add text after the prompt: parameter in the .searchable modifier like this:

```
.searchable(text: $searchText, prompt: "Look for a pet")
```

Any text that appears after the prompt parameter appears as placeholder text in the search bar as shown in Figure 10-3.

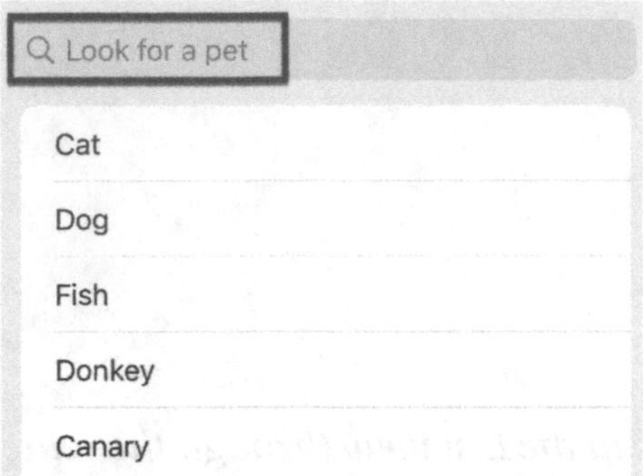

```
NavigationStack{
    PetListView(animals: petArray)
}.searchable(text: $searchText, prompt: "Look for a pet") {
    ForEach(petArray.filter {$0.hasPrefix(searchText)}, id: \.self) { name in
        Text(name)
    }
}
```

Figure 10-3. Defining placeholder text in the search bar

To see how to change this placeholder text in the search bar, follow these steps:

1. Make sure the SearchApp project is loaded into Xcode.

2. Click the ContentView file in the Navigator pane.

3. Modify the .searchable modifier code like this:

    ```
    .searchable(text: $searchText, prompt: "Look for a pet")
    ```

4. Click the Live icon in the Canvas pane. Notice that the placeholder text now displays the text you defined after the prompt parameter in the .searchable modifier (see Figure 10-3).

Adding Suggestions to the Search Bar

Oftentimes, a search bar in an app displays a list of suggestions that might be frequently or recently searched for text. If you want to add suggestions underneath the search bar, you need to add one or more Text views that display the suggested text, followed by the .searchComplete modifier like this:

```
Text("Croaking").searchCompletion("Frog")
```

The .searchCompletion modifier contains text that will appear in the search bar if the user selects the suggested text (displayed by the Text view). In the preceding example, "Croaking" will appear underneath the search bar, and if the user clicks "Croaking," then the .searchCompletion modifier will display "Frog" in the search bar.

To see how to add suggestions to a search bar, follow these steps:

1. Create a new iOS App project and name it SearchSuggestionsApp.

2. Click the ContentView file in the Navigator pane.

3. Add the following State variable and array under struct ContentView: View like this:

```
@State var searchText = ""
let petArray = ["Cat", "Dog", "Fish", "Donkey", "Canary",
"Camel", "Frog"]
```

This code creates a State variable to work with the search bar. In addition, it creates an array of strings. Notice that each string begins with a capital letter. That's because the search bar always capitalizes the first letter of any text typed in.

4. Create a separate structure to display a List view:

```
struct PetListView: View {
    let animals: [String]
    var body: some View {
        List(animals, id: \.self) { x in
            Text(x)
        }
    }
}
```

5. Add the following underneath var body: some View like this:

```
NavigationStack{
    PetListView(animals: petArray)
}
```

6. Add the .searchable modifier to the NavigationStack like this:

```
.searchable(text: $searchText, prompt: "Look for a pet") {
    Text("Singing").searchCompletion("Canary")
    Text("Croaking").searchCompletion("Frog")
    Text("Grumpy").searchCompletion("Cat")
    Divider()
    ForEach(petArray.filter {$0.hasPrefix(searchText)},
    id: \.self) { name in
        Text(name)
    }
}
```

The entire ContentView file should look like this:

```
import SwiftUI

struct ContentView: View {
    @State var searchText = ""
    let petArray = ["Cat", "Dog", "Fish", "Donkey", "Canary",
    "Camel", "Frog"]

    var body: some View {
        NavigationStack{
            PetListView(animals: petArray)
        }.searchable(text: $searchText, prompt: "Look for
        a pet") {
            Text("Singing").searchCompletion("Canary")
            Text("Croaking").searchCompletion("Frog")
            Text("Grumpy").searchCompletion("Cat")
            Divider()
            ForEach(petArray.filter {$0.hasPrefix(searchText)},
            id: \.self) { name in
                Text(name)
            }
        }
    }
}
```

```
struct PetListView: View {
    let animals: [String]
    var body: some View {
        List(animals, id: \.self) { x in
            Text(x)
        }
    }
}

struct ContentView_Previews: PreviewProvider {
    static var previews: some View {
        ContentView()
    }
}
```

Notice the Divider() that appears right above the ForEach loop. This Divider() view simply adds a horizontal line separating the suggestions from the actual items displayed in the List view.

7.   Click the Live icon in the Canvas pane.

8.   Click in the search bar. Notice that the search bar now displays suggestions in a different color as shown in Figure 10-4.

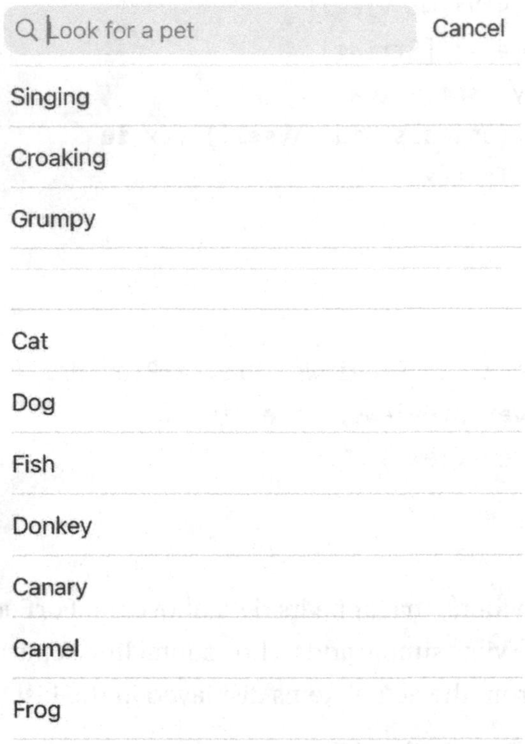

| Q Look for a pet | Cancel |

Singing

Croaking

Grumpy

Cat

Dog

Fish

Donkey

Canary

Camel

Frog

Figure 10-4. *Displaying suggestions underneath the search bar*

9. Click one of the suggestions under the search bar. Notice that when you select a suggestion, it automatically displays the text defined by that Text view's .searchCompletion modifier.

Summary

A search bar can make it easy to find items in a List view, especially if there are multiple items that may not be visible in the screen. Creating a list of suggestions can be helpful to simplify searching. Text views combined with the .searchComplete modifier can create these suggestions. By using variables in these Text views instead of strings, you could make this list of suggestions dynamic so they constantly adapt to the user's behavior. Search bars can make finding items in a List view fast and easy, so consider using them whenever you can.

CHAPTER 11

Detecting Motion and Orientation

Mobile computer devices like the iPhone and iPad essentially put a PC in your pocket, letting you use a computer wherever you happen to be. However, unlike a desktop or even a laptop PC, mobile computers can track movement and orientation. This can come in handy for tracking the user's arm movements in a game or helping you measure angles.

To track motion and orientation, every iOS device comes with a built-in accelerometer that can detect movement. In addition to the accelerometer, the iOS devices also include a gyroscope to detect positions of the iOS device. By adding motion and orientation detection, you can create apps that respond to physical gestures as well as touch gestures.

Understanding Core Motion

To detect movement beyond simple shakes, Apple provides a software framework called Core Motion. Core Motion lets an app access the following types of motion data:

- Acceleration in three dimensions

- Rotation around the x, y, and z axes

- Magnetometer data that measures the device's orientation relative to the Earth's magnetic field

- Device motion data such as its orientation relative to gravity

© Wallace Wang 2023
W. Wang, *Pro iPhone Development with SwiftUI*, https://doi.org/10.1007/978-1-4842-9544-1_11

Note   To test motion and orientation, you need a real iOS device connected to your Macintosh through a USB cable. The Simulator and Canvas pane cannot detect changes in physical movements and different orientations.

To use Core Motion in an app, you need to import the CoreMotion framework and then create a CMMotionManager object like this:

```
import CoreMotion

let motionManager = CMMotionManager()
```

Finally, you need to check for data updates on a special queue called OperationQueue. Without this OperationQueue, motion-detecting data could arrive faster than the app could process it, making the app feel frozen or unresponsive. You can define this OperationQueue() as a constant like this:

```
let queue = OperationQueue()
```

Detecting Acceleration

The accelerometer can measure both acceleration and gravity in three dimensions. The accelerometer can determine not only how an iOS device is being held but also whether it's lying face down or face up on a flat surface such as a table. Accelerometers measure g-forces (**g** for gravity), so a value of 1.0 returned by the accelerometer means that 1 g is sensed in a particular direction, as in these examples:

- If the device is being held perfectly upright, in portrait orientation, it will detect and report about 1 g of force exerted on its y axis.

- If the device is being held at an angle, that 1 g of force will be distributed along different axes depending on how it is being held. When held at a 45-degree angle, the 1 g of force will be split roughly equally between two of the axes.

Sudden movement can be detected by looking for accelerometer values considerably larger than 1 g. In normal usage, the accelerometer does not detect significantly more than 1 g on any axis. If you shake, drop, or throw your device, the accelerometer will detect a greater amount of force on one or more axes as shown in Figure 11-1.

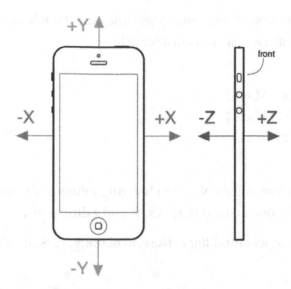

Figure 11-1. *The iPhone accelerometer's axes in three dimensions. The front view of an iPhone on the left shows the x and y axes. The side view on the right shows the z axis*

To see how to use the accelerometer, follow these steps:

1. Create a new iOS App project and name it AccelerateApp.

2. Click the ContentView file in the Navigator pane.

3. Add the following underneath the import SwiftUI line to import the CoreMotion library like this:

   ```
   import CoreMotion
   ```

4. Underneath the struct ContentView: View line, add the following State variables and constants:

   ```
   let motionManager = CMMotionManager()
   let queue = OperationQueue()

   @State private var x: Double = 0.0
   @State private var y: Double = 0.0
   @State private var z: Double = 0.0
   ```

5. Underneath the var body: some View line, add the following
    VStack with three Text views inside:

```
VStack{
    Text("x: \(x)")
    Text("y: \(y)")
    Text("z: \(z)")
}
```

These Text views will display the changing values as the user
moves the iPhone in the different x, y, and z directions.

6. Add the .onAppear modifier at the end of the VStack like this:

```
.onAppear {
    motionManager.startAccelerometerUpdates(to: queue) { (data:
    CMAccelerometerData?, error: Error?) in
        guard let data = data else {
            print("Error: \(error!)")
            return
        }
        let trackMotion: CMAcceleration = data.acceleration
        motionManager.accelerometerUpdateInterval = 2.5
        DispatchQueue.main.async {
            x = trackMotion.x
            y = trackMotion.y
            z = trackMotion.z
        }
    }
}
```

The .startAccelerometerUpdates checks to make sure it can access
the accelerometer. If so, then it retrieves data and stores it in a
trackMotion constant. The DispatchQueue.main.async changes
the State variables defined earlier. Since these State variables
affect the user interface, it must run within the main thread
(DispatchQueue.main.async).

To prevent the x, y, and z values from changing too rapidly, the accelerometerUpdateInterval is set to 2.5 seconds, but you can define any value you wish.

The entire ContentView file should look like this:

```
import SwiftUI
import CoreMotion

struct ContentView: View {
    let motionManager = CMMotionManager()
    let queue = OperationQueue()

    @State private var x: Double = 0.0
    @State private var y: Double = 0.0
    @State private var z: Double = 0.0

    var body: some View {
        VStack{
            Text("x: \(x)")
            Text("y: \(y)")
            Text("z: \(z)")
        }
        .onAppear {
            motionManager.startAccelerometerUpdates(to: queue) {
            (data: CMAccelerometerData?, error: Error?) in
                guard let data = data else {
                    print("Error: \(error!)")
                    return
                }
                let trackMotion: CMAcceleration = data.
                acceleration
                motionManager.accelerometerUpdateInterval = 2.5
                DispatchQueue.main.async {
                    x = trackMotion.x
                    y = trackMotion.y
                    z = trackMotion.z
                }
```

```
            }
        }
    }
}

struct ContentView_Previews: PreviewProvider {
    static var previews: some View {
        ContentView()
    }
}
```

7. Connect an iPhone (or iPad) to your Macintosh through a USB cable and unlock the iPhone (or iPad).

8. Choose Product ➤ Destination and then select the iOS device connected to your Macintosh under the iOS Device category as shown in Figure 11-2. You can also click the current target displayed at the top of the Xcode window to display a menu where you can also select an iOS device under the iOS Device category as shown in Figure 11-3.

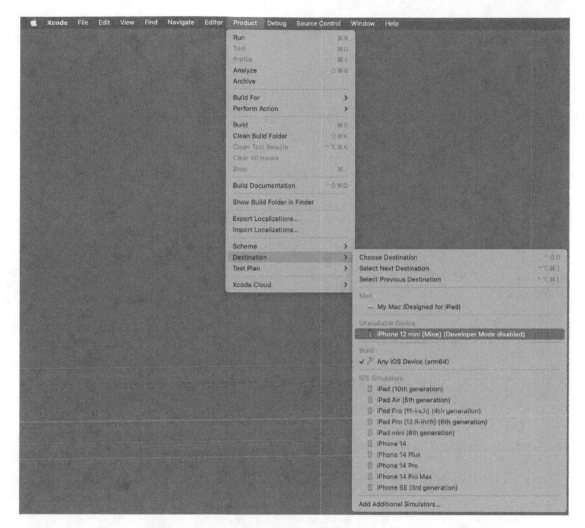

Figure 11-2. *Choosing an actual iOS device through the Product menu*

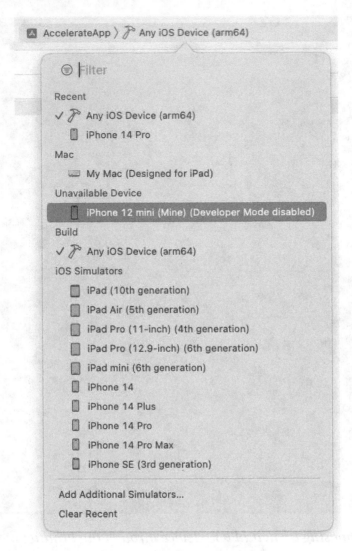

Figure 11-3. *Choosing an actual iOS device through a popup menu*

9. On your iOS device, choose Settings ➤ Privacy & Security. Scroll down to Developer Mode under the SECURITY category as shown in Figure 11-4.

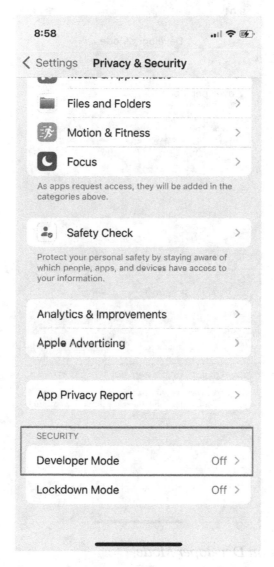

Figure 11-4. *The Developer Mode setting on an iOS device*

10. Tap Developer Mode. A Developer Mode screen appears as shown in Figure 11-5.

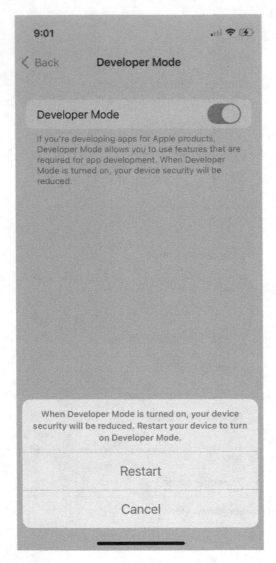

Figure 11-5. *Turning on Developer Mode*

11. Tap the Developer Mode toggle. An action sheet appears at the bottom of the screen, asking you to select Restart or Cancel.

12. Tap Restart. Your iOS device will shut off and turn on again.

13. Make sure your iOS device is connected to Xcode (see Figure 11-3) and connected to your Macintosh through a USB cable.

14. Click the Run icon or choose Product ➤ Run.

15. Lay your iOS device flat on a table. The z value should be near 1 or –1.

16. Hold the iPhone in portrait mode. The y value should be 1 or –1.

17. Hold the iPhone in landscape mode. The x value should be 1 or –1.

18. Click the Stop button in Xcode (or choose Product ➤ Stop) to stop running the app.

Detecting Rotation with the Gyroscope

A gyroscope measures orientation and rotation around the x, y, and z axes. Rotation around the x axis occurs when the iOS device tumbles backward or forward around its horizontal center. Rotation around the y axis occurs when the iOS device twists around its vertical center. Rotation around the z axis occurs when the iOS device rotates clockwise or counter-clockwise as if pierced by a line through its front and back as shown in Figure 11-6.

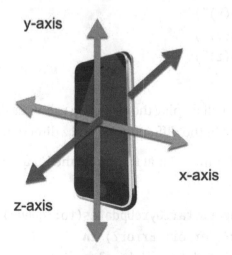

Figure 11-6. *Rotation around the x, y, and z axes*

To see how to use the gyroscope to detect and measure rotation, follow these steps:

1. Create a new iOS App project and name it GyroApp.

2. Click the ContentView file in the Navigator pane.

3. Add the following underneath the import SwiftUI line to import the CoreMotion library like this:

```
import CoreMotion
```

4. Underneath the struct ContentView: View line, add the following State variables and constants:

```
let motionManager = CMMotionManager()
let queue = OperationQueue()

@State private var x: Double = 0.0
@State private var y: Double = 0.0
@State private var z: Double = 0.0
```

5. Underneath the var body: some View line, add the following VStack with three Text views inside:

```
VStack{
    Text("x: \(x)")
    Text("y: \(y)")
    Text("z: \(z)")
}
```

These Text views will display the changing values as the user moves the iPhone in the different x, y, and z directions.

6. Add the .onAppear modifier at the end of the VStack like this:

```
.onAppear {
    motionManager.startGyroUpdates(to: queue) { (data:
    CMGyroData?, error: Error?) in
        guard let data = data else {
            print("Error: \(error!)")
            return
        }
```

```swift
        let trackMotion: CMRotationRate = data.rotationRate
        motionManager.gyroUpdateInterval = 2.5
        DispatchQueue.main.async {
            x = trackMotion.x
            y = trackMotion.y
            z = trackMotion.z
        }
    }
}
```

The .startGyroUpdates checks to make sure it can access
the gyroscope. If so, then it retrieves data and stores it in a
trackMotion constant. The DispatchQueue.main.async changes
the State variables defined earlier. Since these State variables
affect the user interface, it must run within the main thread
(DispatchQueue.main.async).

To prevent the x, y, and z values from changing too rapidly, the
gyroUpdateInterval is set to 2.5 seconds, but you can define any
value you wish.

The entire ContentView file should look like this:

```swift
import SwiftUI
import CoreMotion

struct ContentView: View {
    let motionManager = CMMotionManager()
    let queue = OperationQueue()

    @State private var x: Double = 0.0
    @State private var y: Double = 0.0
    @State private var z: Double = 0.0

    var body: some View {
        VStack{
            Text("x: \(x)")
            Text("y: \(y)")
            Text("z: \(z)")
```

```swift
                }
                .onAppear {
                    motionManager.startGyroUpdates(to: queue) { (data:
                    CMGyroData?, error: Error?) in
                        guard let data = data else {
                            print("Error: \(error!)")
                            return
                        }
                        let trackMotion: CMRotationRate = data.
                        rotationRate
                        motionManager.gyroUpdateInterval = 2.5
                        DispatchQueue.main.async {
                            x = trackMotion.x
                            y = trackMotion.y
                            z = trackMotion.z
                        }
                    }
                }
            }
        }

struct ContentView_Previews: PreviewProvider {
    static var previews: some View {
        ContentView()
    }
}
```

7. Connect an iPhone to your Macintosh through a USB cable and unlock your iPhone.

8. Choose Product ➤ Destination and then select the iOS device connected to your Macintosh under the iOS Device category (see Figure 11-2). You can also click the current target displayed at the top of the Xcode window to display a menu where you can also select an iOS device under the iOS Device category (see Figure 11-3).

9. Rapidly dip your iOS device forward and backward across its horizontal center (x axis). Notice that the x value displayed on the screen changes drastically away from 0 such as reaching a value of –8 or 10.

10. Twist your iOS device around its vertical center (y axis). Notice that the y value displayed on the screen changes drastically away from 0 such as reaching a value of 7 or –6.

11. Rotate your iOS device clockwise and counter-clockwise around its z axis that pierces the front and back of the device. Notice that the z value displayed on the screen changes drastically away from 0 such as reaching a value of –6 or 5.

12. Click the Stop button in Xcode (or choose Product ➤ Stop) to stop running the app.

Detecting Magnetic Fields

A magnetometer measures the Earth's magnetic field relative to the iOS device that contains the magnetometer. The values returned measure the Earth's magnetic field in microteslas where the x value measures horizontal displacement to the nearest magnetic field, the y value measures the vertical displacement, and the z value measures the altitude above/below the Earth's magnetic field.

To see how to get data from the magnetometer, follow these steps:

1. Create a new iOS App project and name it MagnetApp.

2. Click the ContentView file in the Navigator pane.

3. Add the following underneath the import SwiftUI line to import the CoreMotion library like this:

    ```
    import CoreMotion
    ```

4. Underneath the struct ContentView: View line, add the following
    State variables and constants:

```
let motionManager = CMMotionManager()
let queue = OperationQueue()

@State private var x: Double = 0.0
@State private var y: Double = 0.0
@State private var z: Double = 0.0
```

5. Underneath the var body: some View line, add the following
    VStack with three Text views inside:

```
VStack{
    Text("x: \(x)")
    Text("y: \(y)")
    Text("z: \(z)")
}
```

These Text views will display the changing values as the user
moves the iPhone in the different x, y, and z directions.

6. Add the .onAppear modifier at the end of the VStack like this:

```
.onAppear {
    motionManager.startMagnetometerUpdates(to: queue) { (data:
    CMMagnetometerData?, error: Error?) in
        guard let data = data else {
            print("Error: \(error!)")
            return
        }
        let trackMotion: CMMagneticField = data.magneticField
        motionManager.magnetometerUpdateInterval = 2.5
        DispatchQueue.main.async {
            x = trackMotion.x
            y = trackMotion.y
            z = trackMotion.z
        }
    }
}
```

The .startMagnetometerUpdates checks to make sure it can access the magnetometer. If so, then it retrieves data and stores it in a trackMotion constant. The DispatchQueue.main.async changes the State variables defined earlier. Since these State variables affect the user interface, it must run within the main thread (DispatchQueue.main.async).

The entire ContentView file should look like this:

```swift
import SwiftUI
import CoreMotion

struct ContentView: View {
    let motionManager = CMMotionManager()
    let queue = OperationQueue()

    @State private var x: Double = 0.0
    @State private var y: Double = 0.0
    @State private var z: Double = 0.0

    var body: some View {
        VStack{
            Text("x: \(x)")
            Text("y: \(y)")
            Text("z: \(z)")
        }
        .onAppear {
            motionManager.startMagnetometerUpdates(to: queue) {
            (data: CMMagnetometerData?, error: Error?) in
                guard let data = data else {
                    print("Error: \(error!)")
                    return
                }
                let trackMotion: CMMagneticField = data.
                magneticField
                motionManager.magnetometerUpdateInterval = 2.5
                DispatchQueue.main.async {
                    x = trackMotion.x
```

```
                    y = trackMotion.y
                    z = trackMotion.z
                }
            }
        }
    }
}

struct ContentView_Previews: PreviewProvider {
    static var previews: some View {
        ContentView()
    }
}
```

7. Connect an iPhone to your Macintosh through a USB cable and unlock your iPhone.

8. Choose Product ➤ Destination and then select the iOS device connected to your Macintosh under the iOS Device category (see Figure 11-2). You can also click the current target displayed at the top of the Xcode window to display a menu where you can also select an iOS device under the iOS Device category (see Figure 11-3).

9. Move your iPhone around to see how the different values change.

10. Click the Stop button in Xcode (or choose Product ➤ Stop) to stop running the app.

Detecting Device Motion Data

Detecting device motion data lets you retrieve roll, pitch, and yaw data. Roll measures the rotation around the vertical axis, pitch measures the rotation around the horizontal axis, and yaw measures the rotation around an axis that pierces through the front and back of an iOS device as shown in Figure 11-7.

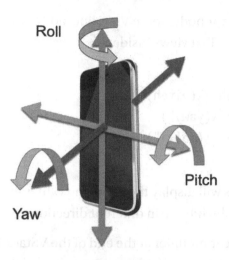

Figure 11-7. *Identifying roll, pitch, and yaw on an iOS device*

To see how to detect roll, pitch, and yaw, follow these steps:

1. Create a new iOS App project and name it DeviceMotionApp.

2. Click the ContentView file in the Navigator pane.

3. Add the following underneath the import SwiftUI line to import the CoreMotion library like this:

   import CoreMotion

4. Underneath the struct ContentView: View line, add the following State variables and constants:

   let motionManager = CMMotionManager()
   let queue = OperationQueue()

   @State **private var** pitch: Double = 0.0
   @State **private var** yaw: Double = 0.0
   @State **private var** roll: Double = 0.0

5. Underneath the var body: some View line, add the following
    VStack with three Text views inside:

```
VStack{
    Text("Pitch: \(pitch)")
    Text("Yaw: \(yaw)")
    Text("Roll: \(roll)")
}
```

These Text views will display the changing values as the user
rotates and tilts the iPhone in different directions.

6. Add the .onAppear modifier at the end of the VStack like this:

```
.onAppear {
    motionManager.startDeviceMotionUpdates(to: queue) { (data:
    CMDeviceMotion?, error: Error?) in
        guard let data = data else {
            print("Error: \(error!)")
            return
        }
        let trackMotion: CMAttitude = data.attitude
        motionManager.deviceMotionUpdateInterval = 2.5
        DispatchQueue.main.async {
            pitch = trackMotion.pitch
            yaw = trackMotion.yaw
            roll = trackMotion.roll
        }
    }
}
```

The .startDeviceMotionUpdates checks to make sure it can access
the accelerometer. If so, then it retrieves data and stores it in a
trackMotion constant. The DispatchQueue.main.async changes
the State variables defined earlier. Since these State variables
affect the user interface, it must run within the main thread
(DispatchQueue.main.async).

To prevent the x, y, and z values from changing too rapidly, the deviceMotionUpdateInterval is set to 2.5 seconds, but you can define any value you wish.

The entire ContentView file should look like this:

```
import SwiftUI
import CoreMotion

struct ContentView: View {
    let motionManager = CMMotionManager()
    let queue = OperationQueue()

    @State private var pitch: Double = 0.0
    @State private var yaw: Double = 0.0
    @State private var roll: Double = 0.0

    var body: some View {
        VStack{
            Text("Pitch: \(pitch)")
            Text("Yaw: \(yaw)")
            Text("Roll: \(roll)")
        }
        .onAppear {
            motionManager.startDeviceMotionUpdates(to: queue)
            { (data: CMDeviceMotion?, error: Error?) in
                guard let data = data else {
                    print("Error: \(error!)")
                    return
                }
                let trackMotion: CMAttitude = data.attitude
                motionManager.deviceMotionUpdateInterval = 2.5
                DispatchQueue.main.async {
                    pitch = trackMotion.pitch
                    yaw = trackMotion.yaw
                    roll = trackMotion.roll
                }
            }
```

```
                  }
             }
        }

        struct ContentView_Previews: PreviewProvider {
            static var previews: some View {
                ContentView()
            }
        }
```

7. Connect an iPhone to your Macintosh through a USB cable and unlock your iPhone.

8. Choose Product ➤ Destination and then select the iOS device connected to your Macintosh under the iOS Device category as shown in Figure 11-2. You can also click the current target displayed at the top of the Xcode window to display a menu where you can also select an iOS device under the iOS Device category as shown in Figure 11-3.

9. Twist your iOS device around its vertical axis. The Roll value should deviate from 0 such as –2 or 3.

10. Flip the front of your iOS device back and forward. The Pitch value should deviate from 0 such as 1 or –2.

11. Rotate your iOS device on the flat surface clockwise and counter-clockwise. The Yaw value should deviate from 0 such as –2 to 1.

12. Click the Stop button in Xcode (or choose Product ➤ Stop) to stop running the app.

Summary

Every iOS device comes with built-in sensors to measure movement. To detect movements of an iOS device, you need to use the CoreMotion framework.

Some of the different types of motion data an app can detect include acceleration, rotation, and even nearby magnetic fields. Detecting the movement of an iOS device lets an app respond appropriately, giving movement another way to control an app.

CHAPTER 12

Using Location and Maps

One of the most useful features of mobile computers like smartphones and tablets is the ability to identify their location in the real world. Just this feature alone has made possible ride-sharing services that allow devices to track the position of both cars and waiting passengers in real time.

Tracking the location of an iOS device involves Global Positioning System (GPS), cell ID location, and WiFi positioning service (WPS). By using three different services, Apple's Core Location framework can pinpoint the location of an iOS device with varying degrees of accuracy.

Fortunately, Core Location hides the details of using these various technologies. Instead, Core Location lets you simply specify the degree of accuracy you wish, such as finding the location of an iOS device within 10 or 200 meters while also detecting any changes in the location of an iOS device. By tracking locations within a specified degree of accuracy and the distance an iOS device must travel before detecting movement, Core Location makes it easy for any app to identify the location of any iOS device.

Note The more accurate and more often you need to track the movement of an iOS device's location, the more battery power the app will require, so you need to trade off between greater accuracy and constant updates against longer battery life.

Using MapKit

The first step to defining a location is to import the MapKit framework into an app like this:

```
import MapKit
```

© Wallace Wang 2023
W. Wang, *Pro iPhone Development with SwiftUI*, https://doi.org/10.1007/978-1-4842-9544-1_12

MapKit will allow us to display a map on the screen. To display a particular location, we need to access the location manager with any arbitrary name such as locationManager like this:

```
let locationManager = CLLocationManager()
```

To display a map on the user interface, we can just use the following code that displays a map using specific latitude and longitude coordinates:

```
Map(coordinateRegion: $region)
```

This region must be an MKCoordinateRegion that defines the latitude, longitude, and a desired zoom level defined by MKCoordinateSpan like this:

```
@State private var region: MKCoordinateRegion =
MKCoordinateRegion(center: CLLocationCoordinate2D(latitude: 48.856613,
longitude: 2.352222), span: MKCoordinateSpan(latitudeDelta: 0.05,
longitudeDelta: 0.05))
```

Note   Visit www.latlong.net to type in a specific address or location and retrieve the latitude and longitude coordinates.

Defining Accuracy

When using Core Location, you need to define the amount of accuracy you want. Remember, the greater the accuracy, the more power the iOS device will require, so it's best to choose the level of accuracy your app absolutely needs. If you just need to identify the user's geographical location such as a city, then you don't need specific accuracy. However, if your app needs to know the iOS device's precise location to locate the user such as for a ride-sharing service that needs to know where to pick up a passenger, then you'll need greater precision.

You can define a specific level of accuracy in meters such as 150 meters. However, Core Location provides several constants you can use that define varying degrees of accuracy:

- kCLLocationAccuracyBestForNavigation – The highest possible accuracy used for navigation apps

- kCLLocationAccuracyBest – The best accuracy available

- kCLLocationAccuracyNearestTenMeters – Accurate to within ten meters

- kCLLocationAccuracyHundredMeters – Accurate to within one hundred meters

- kCLLocationAccuracyKilometer – Accurate to the nearest kilometer

- kCLLocationAccuracyThreeKilometers – Accurate to the nearest three kilometers

- kCLLocationAccuracyReduced – Uses the best accuracy possible when the app is not authorized to access full accuracy location data

To define accuracy, you need to set the desiredAccuracy property to a value or to one of the preceding constants like this:

```
locationManager.desiredAccuracy = kCLLocationAccuracyNearestTenMeters
```

Defining a Distance Filter

In addition to defining the accuracy you want, you can also define a distance filter that specifies how far the iOS device needs to move to detect movement. The default value is stored in a constant called kCLDistanceFilterNone, which tells an app to be notified of all movement.

However, if you define a specific value in meters, you can modify this distance filter such as only detecting movement when an iOS device travels 100 meters such as

```
locationManager.distanceFilter = 100
```

Requesting a Location

Core Location gives you two ways to request the location of an iOS device. The first method requests the location once. This can be useful for apps that don't need constant updating to track movement. To request a location once, use the requestLocation method like this:

```
locationManager.requestLocation()
```

Because the requestLocation method only checks for a location once, it requires far less power than the second method, which requests locations continuously. To track locations continuously, you need to use the startUpdatingLocation and stopUpdatingLocation methods like this:

```
locationManager.startUpdatingLocation()
locationManager.stopUpdatingLocation()
```

Core Location also offers two Boolean values you can modify as follows:

- pausesLocationUpdatesAutomatically – Allows an app to temporarily pause updating a location

- allowsBackgroundLocationUpdates – Defines whether an app can continue receiving location updates even when the app is suspended

Retrieving Location Data

When Core Location retrieves the location of an iOS device, it provides several different types of values:

- coordinate.latitude and coordinate.longitude – Returns the latitude and longitude of a location

- horizontalAccuracy – Returns a distance of how accurate Core Location believes the defined location might be, measured in meters

- altitude – Returns the distance above or below sea level, measured in meters

- verticalAccuracy – Returns a distance of how accurate Core Location believes the altitude might be, measured in meters

- floor – Returns the floor of a building where the iOS device is located

- timestamp – Returns the time the location was retrieved

Requesting Authorization

Apps often need to request permission to access many hardware features of an iOS device. By forcing an app to request permission, Apple wants to make sure users authorize an app's access to features such as the camera, the microphone, and the device's location. Requesting authorization provides privacy for users and allows them to know exactly when an app might need to request access to specific hardware features.

Any app that uses Core Location must request authorization to track an iOS device's location. Core Location provides two ways to request authorization:

- requestWhenInUseAuthorization() – Uses location services only when your app is running

- requestAlwaysAuthorization() – Uses location services all the time

In most cases, you'll only want to use location services while your app is running. Besides using one of the preceding methods, an app also needs to modify its Info.plist file and add the Privacy – Location Always and When In Use Usage Description key as shown in Figure 12-1. In addition, you'll need to add descriptive text explaining why your app needs to access location services.

Key		Type	Value	
Application supports indirect input events	◇	Boolean	YES	◇
Bundle identifier	◇	String	$(PRODUCT_BUNDLE_IDENTIFIER)	
Bundle name	◇	String	$(PRODUCT_NAME)	
InfoDictionary version	◇	String	6.0	
Bundle version	◇	String	$(CURRENT_PROJECT_VERSION)	
> Supported interface orientations (iPhone)	◇	Array	(3 items)	
> Application Scene Manifest	◇	Dictionary	(2 items)	
Application requires iPhone environment	◇	Boolean	YES	◇
Executable file	◇	String	$(EXECUTABLE_NAME)	
Privacy - Location Always and When In Use Usage... ◇ ⊕ ⊖		String ◇	Need to use location data	
Privacy - Health Share Usage Description		String	$(PRODUCT_BUNDLE_PACKAGE_TYPE)	
Privacy - Health Update Usage Description				
Privacy - HomeKit Usage Description	◇	Dictionary	(1 item)	
Privacy - Identity Usage Description		String	$(DEVELOPMENT_LANGUAGE)	
Privacy - Local Network Usage Description	◇	Array	(4 items)	
Privacy - Location Always and When In Use Usage De...	◇	String	$(MARKETING_VERSION)	
Privacy - Location Always Usage Description				
Privacy - Location Default Accuracy Reduced				
Privacy - Location Temporary Usage Description Dicti...				
Privacy - Location Usage Description				
Privacy - Location When In Use Usage Description				

Figure 12-1. *Requesting to use location services in the Info.plist file*

To see how to display a specific location on a map, follow these steps:

1. Create a new iOS App project and name it MapApp.

2. Click the ContentView file in the Navigator pane.

3. Add the following underneath the import SwiftUI line:

```
import MapKit
```

4. Add the following constant and State variables underneath the struct ContentView: View line:

```
let locationManager = CLLocationManager()

@State var message = "Map of Paris"
@State private var region: MKCoordinateRegion =
MKCoordinateRegion(center: CLLocationCoordinate2D
(latitude: 48.856613, longitude: 2.352222), span:
MKCoordinateSpan(latitudeDelta: 0.05, longitudeDelta: 0.05))
```

The preceding latitude and longitude will display Paris, but you can enter any latitude and longitude coordinates you wish.

5. Inside var body: some View, add a VStack, a Map, and a TextEditor like this:

```
VStack{
    Map(coordinateRegion: $region)
    TextEditor(text: $message)
        .frame(width: .infinity, height: 100)
}
```

This displays the map at the top of the screen and a TextEditor underneath.

6. Add the .onAppear modifier to the VStack like this:

```
.onAppear {
    locationManager.desiredAccuracy = kCLLocationAccuracyBest
    locationManager.distanceFilter = kCLDistanceFilterNone
```

```
    locationManager.requestWhenInUseAuthorization()
    locationManager.startUpdatingLocation()
}
```

The entire ContentView file should look like this:

```swift
import SwiftUI
import MapKit

struct ContentView: View {
    let locationManager = CLLocationManager()

    @State var message = "Map of Paris"
    @State private var region: MKCoordinateRegion =
    MKCoordinateRegion(center: CLLocationCoordinate2D
    (latitude: 48.856613, longitude: 2.352222), span:
    MKCoordinateSpan(latitudeDelta: 0.05, longitudeDelta: 0.05))

    var body: some View {
        VStack{
            Map(coordinateRegion: $region)
            TextEditor(text: $message)
                .frame(width: .infinity, height: 100)
        }
        .onAppear {
            locationManager.desiredAccuracy =
            kCLLocationAccuracyBest
            locationManager.distanceFilter = kCLDistanceFilterNone
            locationManager.requestWhenInUseAuthorization()
            locationManager.startUpdatingLocation()
        }
    }
}

struct ContentView_Previews: PreviewProvider {
    static var previews: some View {
        ContentView()
    }
}
```

7. Click the Live icon in the Canvas pane. The map of Paris (or whatever latitude and longitude coordinates you entered) now appears on the screen as shown in Figure 12-2.

Map of Paris

Figure 12-2. *Displaying a location on a map*

The preceding steps display a map in the canvas pane. However, if you want to run this project in the Simulator or on an actual iOS device, we must go through the additional step of changing a privacy setting in the Info file. To do this, follow these steps:

1. Make sure the MapApp project is loaded in Xcode.

2. Click the project name at the top of the Navigator pane. Then click the Info tab to display a list of properties as shown in Figure 12-3.

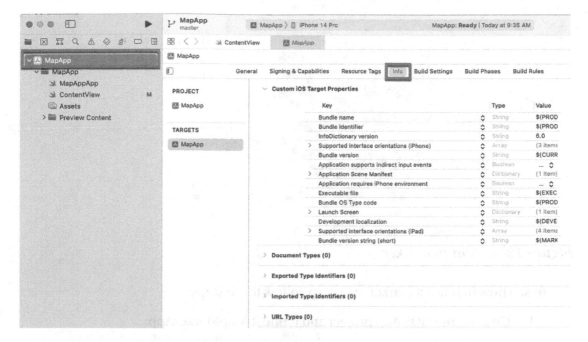

Figure 12-3. *A project's list of properties*

3. Move the mouse over the up/down arrow in any line in the Key column. The + and – icons appear.

4. Click the + icon to insert a new property into the property list.

5. Click "Privacy – Location Always and When in Use Usage Description".

6. Type "Need to use location data" in the Value column.

7. Click the Run button or choose Product ➤ Run.

8. Choose Simulator ➤ Quit Simulator.

Adding a Map Marker

When a map appears on the screen, it displays a large area that the user can scroll through. To identify certain locations, you may want to add a map marker, which appears as a balloon-shaped image that can highlight a specific area on the map in different colors as shown in Figure 12-4.

Figure 12-4. *A map marker*

To see how to place a marker on a map, follow these steps:

1. Create a new iOS App project and name it MapMarkerApp.

2. Click the ContentView file in the Navigator pane.

3. Add import MapKit underneath import SwiftUI like this:

```
import MapKit
```

4. Add the following State variables and constant:

```
let locationManager = CLLocationManager()

@State var message = "Map of Paris"
@State private var region: MKCoordinateRegion =
MKCoordinateRegion(center: CLLocationCoordinate2D
(latitude: 48.856613, longitude: 2.352222), span:
MKCoordinateSpan(latitudeDelta: 0.05, longitudeDelta: 0.05))
```

5. Add the following structure underneath the State variables:

```
struct IdentifiablePlace: Identifiable {
    let id: UUID
    let location: CLLocationCoordinate2D
    init(id: UUID = UUID(), lat: Double, long: Double) {
        self.id = id
```

```
    self.location = CLLocationCoordinate2D(
        latitude: lat,
        longitude: long)
    }
}
```

This structure holds a location defined as a latitude and longitude.

6. Underneath this structure, declare a variable to represent this structure like this:

```
let place = IdentifiablePlace(lat: 48.856613, long: 2.352222)
```

Add the latitude and longitude for a specific location within the map.

7. In the VStack, define the Map view with both a coordinateRegion parameter and an annotationItems parameter like this:

```
Map(coordinateRegion: $region,
    annotationItems: [place])
{ place in
    MapMarker(coordinate: place.location,
            tint: Color.purple)
}
```

The annotationItems parameter accepts an array of IdentifiablePlaces that have different latitudes and longitudes. In the preceding example, we're just using a single item. After the annotationItems parameter, the MapMarker uses the place constant's latitude and longitude to define where to place the marker along with a color to use (Color.purple).

8. Add a TextEditor like this:

```
TextEditor(text: $message)
    .frame(width: .infinity, height: 100)
```

9.   Add the following to the VStack:

```
.onAppear {
    locationManager.desiredAccuracy = kCLLocationAccuracyBest
    locationManager.distanceFilter = kCLDistanceFilterNone
    locationManager.requestWhenInUseAuthorization()
    locationManager.startUpdatingLocation()
}
```

The entire ContentView file should look like this:

```
import SwiftUI
import MapKit

struct ContentView: View {
    let locationManager = CLLocationManager()

    @State var message = "Map of Paris"
    @State private var region: MKCoordinateRegion =
    MKCoordinateRegion(center: CLLocationCoordinate2D
    (latitude: 48.856613, longitude: 2.352222), span:
    MKCoordinateSpan(latitudeDelta: 0.05, longitudeDelta: 0.05))

    struct IdentifiablePlace: Identifiable {
        let id: UUID
        let location: CLLocationCoordinate2D
        init(id: UUID = UUID(), lat: Double, long: Double) {
            self.id = id
            self.location = CLLocationCoordinate2D(
                latitude: lat,
                longitude: long)
        }
    }

    let place = IdentifiablePlace(lat: 48.856613, long: 2.352222)

    var body: some View {
        VStack{
            Map(coordinateRegion: $region,
                annotationItems: [place])
```

```
            { place in
                MapMarker(coordinate: place.location,
                        tint: Color.purple)
            }
            TextEditor(text: $message)
                .frame(width: .infinity, height: 100)
        }
        .onAppear {
            locationManager.desiredAccuracy =
            kCLLocationAccuracyBest
            locationManager.distanceFilter = kCLDistanceFilterNone
            locationManager.requestWhenInUseAuthorization()
            locationManager.startUpdatingLocation()
        }
    }
}

struct ContentView_Previews: PreviewProvider {
    static var previews: some View {
        ContentView()
    }
}
```

Try experimenting with different latitudes and longitudes for both the map and the map marker.

10. Click the Live icon in the Canvas pane to see the map marker placed on the map (see Figure 12-4).

Adding a Map Annotation

Another way to identify specific locations on a map is to use a map annotation, which lets you define a shape, color, and line thickness to highlight certain areas on the map as shown in Figure 12-5.

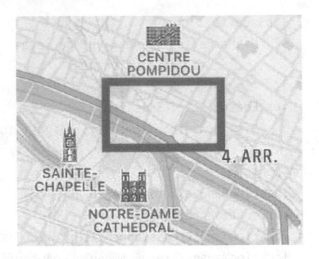

Figure 12-5. A map annotation

To see how to place an annotation on a map, follow these steps:

1. Create a new iOS App project and name it MapAnnotationApp.

2. Click the ContentView file in the Navigator pane.

3. Add import MapKit underneath import SwiftUI like this:

    ```
    import MapKit
    ```

4. Add the following State variables and constant:

    ```
    let locationManager = CLLocationManager()

    @State var message = "Map of Paris"
    @State private var region: MKCoordinateRegion =
    MKCoordinateRegion(center: CLLocationCoordinate2D
    (latitude: 48.856613, longitude: 2.352222), span:
    MKCoordinateSpan(latitudeDelta: 0.05, longitudeDelta: 0.05))
    ```

5. Add the following structure underneath the State variables:

    ```
    struct IdentifiablePlace: Identifiable {
        let id: UUID
        let location: CLLocationCoordinate2D
        init(id: UUID = UUID(), lat: Double, long: Double) {
    ```

```
        self.id = id
        self.location = CLLocationCoordinate2D(
            latitude: lat,
            longitude: long)
    }
}
```

This structure holds a location defined as a latitude and longitude.

6. Underneath this structure, declare a variable to represent this
    structure like this:

```
let place = IdentifiablePlace(lat: 48.856613, long: 2.352222)
```

Add the latitude and longitude for a specific location within
the map.

7. In the VStack, define the Map view with both a coordinateRegion
    parameter and an annotationItems parameter like this:

```
Map(coordinateRegion: $region,
    annotationItems: [place])
{ place in
    MapAnnotation(coordinate: place.location) {
        Rectangle().stroke(Color.purple, lineWidth: 5)
            .frame(width: 70, height: 40)
    }
}
```

The annotationItems parameter accepts an array of
IdentifiablePlaces that have different latitudes and longitudes. In
the preceding example, we're just using a single item. After the
annotationItems parameter, the MapAnnotation uses the place
constant's latitude and longitude to define where to place a shape
(rectangle) including its color (Color.purple), line width, width,
and height.

The entire ContentView file should look like this:

```swift
import SwiftUI
import MapKit

struct ContentView: View {
    let locationManager = CLLocationManager()

    @State var message = "Map of Paris"
    @State private var region: MKCoordinateRegion =
    MKCoordinateRegion(center: CLLocationCoordinate2D
    (latitude: 48.856613, longitude: 2.352222), span:
    MKCoordinateSpan(latitudeDelta: 0.05, longitudeDelta: 0.05))

    struct IdentifiablePlace: Identifiable {
        let id: UUID
        let location: CLLocationCoordinate2D
        init(id: UUID = UUID(), lat: Double, long: Double) {
            self.id = id
            self.location = CLLocationCoordinate2D(
                latitude: lat,
                longitude: long)
        }
    }

    let place = IdentifiablePlace(lat: 48.856613, long: 2.352222)

    var body: some View {
        VStack{
            Map(coordinateRegion: $region,
                annotationItems: [place])
            { place in
                MapAnnotation(coordinate: place.location) {
                    Rectangle().stroke(Color.purple, lineWidth: 5)
                        .frame(width: 70, height: 40)
                }
            }
            TextEditor(text: $message)
```

```
                .frame(width: .infinity, height: 100)
        }
        .onAppear {
            locationManager.desiredAccuracy =
            kCLLocationAccuracyBest
            locationManager.distanceFilter = kCLDistanceFilterNone
            locationManager.requestWhenInUseAuthorization()
            locationManager.startUpdatingLocation()
        }
    }
}

struct ContentView_Previews: PreviewProvider {
    static var previews: some View {
        ContentView()
    }
}
```

Try experimenting with different latitudes and longitudes for both the map and the map marker.

8. Click the Live icon in the Canvas pane to see the map annotation placed on the map (see Figure 12-5).

Summary

Mobile devices such as the iPhone and iPad can be especially useful when tracking the user's current location. When combined with a map display, an app can show the location of the user and the locations of other places or people as well.

When identifying a user's location, you can define the accuracy you want and whether to use markers, pins, or annotations to identify and highlight certain areas on the map.

Remember that the greater the accuracy you need, the more power the app will require, which can drain the iOS device's battery, so only use greater accuracy when you need it. Also, make sure that any app that uses location services requests permission to do so as well.

CHAPTER 13

Playing Audio and Video

Not every app needs audio and video, but playing audio and video within an app can create an interesting way to deliver information to the user. For example, an app might want to play music or different sounds to alert the user or play a video to demonstrate steps for the user to follow. With both audio and video, an app can provide a more dynamic user experience.

When working with audio and video files, it's important to identify the file format. Some popular audio formats supported by iOS include

- .mp3 – Popular format that compresses audio files

- .aac – Advanced Audio Coding format that improves upon the mp3 format

- .aif – Audio Interchange File Format

- .wav – Waveform Audio file mostly found on Windows PCs

- .mp4 – MPEG-4 audio file

Some popular video formats supported by iOS include

- .mov – QuickTime media format

- .mp4 – MPEG-4 video file

- .m4v – An MPEG-4 video file, often called an iTunes video file because this is the format of videos downloaded from the iTunes Store

---

Note   If you have an audio or video file stored in a different format, you'll need to convert it to a format that iOS can recognize.

© Wallace Wang 2023
W. Wang, *Pro iPhone Development with SwiftUI*, https://doi.org/10.1007/978-1-4842-9544-1_13

Playing an Audio File

To play audio, you need to import AVFoundation into your project like this:

```
import AVFoundation
```

After you've imported AVFoundation into your project, you can create a variable to represent the AVAudioPlayer such as

```
var audioPlayer: AVAudioPlayer?
```

To play an audio file, you need to drag and drop an audio file into the Navigator pane. Then you need to write code that loads the audio file into the AVAudioPlayer variable. Finally, you can use the play(), pause(), and stop() methods to control the playing of the audio file.

To complete this example, you'll need an audio file stored in a supported file format such as .mp3 or .mov. If you don't have any audio files stored on your Macintosh, you can download free audio files from the following sites:

- soundbible.com

- archive.org

- freesound.org

- gamesounds.xyz

You can also record audio files on a Macintosh by loading the QuickTime Player program and choosing File ➤ New Audio Recording. Once you have an audio file, either one you downloaded or created through QuickTime Player program, you can test how to play an audio file in an iOS app.

When working with files of any type, you need to specify the file name and the file path. The file name is the complete name of the file and its file extension such as HappyBirthday.mp3 or JingleBells.mov. The file path defines the location of the file within your app.

To retrieve the file path, you need to identify the file name and type you want to find such as

```
let audioFilePath = Bundle.main.path(forResource: "Streetlife",
ofType: "mp3")
```

Once you know the path of the file you want to play, then you can load that file and path into the AVAudioPlayer to play it.

To see how to play an audio file, follow these steps:

1. Create a new iOS App project and name this new project AudioApp.

2. Choose File ➤ New ➤ File, select Swift File as shown in Figure 13-1, and then click Next. A dialog appears.

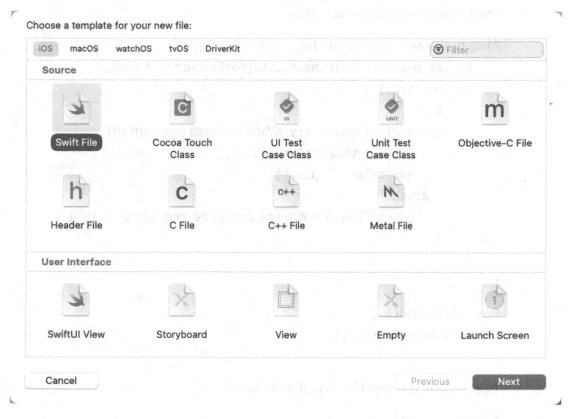

Figure 13-1. *Creating a Swift File*

3. Give your Swift File a descriptive name such as PlaySound and then click Create.

4. Inside this newly created Swift file, add the following line underneath import Foundation:

```
import AVFoundation
```

5. Underneath the import AVFoundation line, declare an AVAudioPlayer variable like this:

```
var audioPlayer: AVAudioPlayer?
```

6. Create the following two functions:

```
func playSound(sound: String, type: String) {
    if let path = Bundle.main.path(forResource: sound,
    ofType: type) {
        do {
            audioPlayer = try AVAudioPlayer(contentsOf:
            URL(fileURLWithPath: path))
            audioPlayer?.play()
        } catch {
            print("Could not find and play the sound file")
        }
    }
}

func stopSound() {
    audioPlayer?.stop()
}
```

The entire PlaySound file should look like this:

```
import Foundation
import AVFoundation

var audioPlayer: AVAudioPlayer?

func playSound(sound: String, type: String) {
    if let path = Bundle.main.path(forResource: sound,
    ofType: type) {
        do {
```

```
            audioPlayer = try AVAudioPlayer(contentsOf:
            URL(fileURLWithPath: path))
            audioPlayer?.play()
        } catch {
            print("Could not find and play the sound file")
        }
    }
}

func stopSound() {
    audioPlayer?.stop()
}
```

7. Drag and drop an audio file into the Navigator pane as shown in Figure 13-2. A dialog appears.

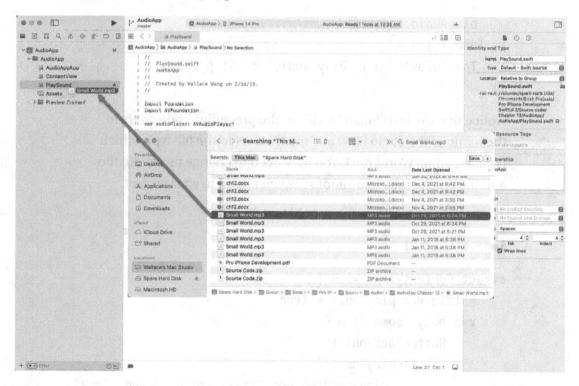

Figure 13-2. *Adding an audio file to the Navigator pane*

8. Click Finish. Your audio file now appears in the Navigator pane.

9. Click the ContentView file in the Navigator pane and add the
    following State variable underneath the struct ContentView:
    View line:

```
@State var playAudio = true
```

10. Add the following Button inside the var body: some View line
    like this:

```
Button(action: {
    if playAudio {
        playSound(sound: "Small World", type: "mp3")
    } else {
        stopSound()
    }
    playAudio.toggle()
}, label: {
    Text(playAudio ? "Play audio" : "Stop audio")
})
```

Notice that the text "Small World" in the preceding code refers to
the name of the audio file, and "mp3" refers to the file type, which
is called Small World.mp3. You may need to change this audio file
and file type to match the audio file you added to your project.

The entire ContentView file should look like this:

```
import SwiftUI

struct ContentView: View {
    @State var playAudio = true
    var body: some View {
        Button(action: {
            if playAudio {
                playSound(sound: "Small World", type: "mp3")
            } else {
                stopSound()
            }
```

```
              playAudio.toggle()
         }, label: {
              Text(playAudio ? "Play audio" : "Stop audio")
         })
    }
}

struct ContentView_Previews: PreviewProvider {
    static var previews: some View {
         ContentView()
    }
}
```

11.   Click the Live icon in the Canvas pane.

12.   Click the Play audio button. Notice that the audio file starts
      playing, and the Button changes from "Play audio" to "Stop audio".

13.   Click the Stop audio button. Notice that the audio stops playing,
      and the Button changes from "Stop audio" to "Play audio".

Experiment with different audio files and file formats such as a .wav or .mov audio
file. Remember to modify your code to use the exact name and file format of each new
audio file you test in this project.

Playing Video

Videos can display tutorials or tips for how to use an app. Just keep in mind that video
files tend to be much larger than audio files, so you'll generally want to use short videos
to avoid taking up too much space.

To play video, your app needs to import the AVKit framework like this:

import AVKit

Then you need to create a State variable that represents an AVPlayer like this:

@State **var** player: AVPlayer?

This player is an optional variable because we have no guarantee that it will be able to load a video file or not.

To actually display video in an app, we just need the VideoPlayer view that displays the AVPlayer like this:

```
VideoPlayer(player: player)
```

At this point, we still need to load a video file into the player (AVPlayer). To do that, we can use an .onAppear modifier to load the video file as soon as the VideoPlayer appears. The first step is to use a guard statement to make sure we can load a specific video file stored in the Xcode project like this:

```
guard let videoURL = Bundle.main.url(forResource: "SaturnV",
withExtension: "mov") else {
    print ("Video file not found")
    return
}
```

This guard statement looks for a video file named SaturnV.mov. If this file exists, then it loads that video file into the videoURL constant. Otherwise, the guard statement exits out to prevent the player (AVPlayer) from trying to run a nonexistent video file.

After the guard statement confirms that the video file exists, we can safely load it into the player like this:

```
player = AVPlayer(url: videoURL as URL)
```

To complete the following exercise, you'll need a video file. You can record your own videos using the QuickTime Player on a Macintosh or record a video on an iOS device such as an iPhone or iPad. You can also find free video files at the following sites:

- nasa.gov

- publicdomainfiles.com

- archive.org

To see how to play a video, follow these steps:

1. Create a new iOS App project and name it VideoApp.

2. Click the ContentView file in the Navigator pane.

3. Drag and drop a video file into the Navigator pane (see Figure 13-2).

4. Add the import AVKit line underneath the import SwiftUI line like this:

```
import AVKit
```

5. Add the following State variable underneath the struct ContentView: View line like this:

```
@State var player: AVPlayer?
```

6. Add a VideoPlayer view underneath the var body: some View line like this:

```
VideoPlayer(player: player)
```

7. Add an .onAppear modifier to the VideoPlayer view:

```
VideoPlayer(player: player)
    .onAppear {

    }
```

8. Inside the .onAppear curly brackets, add the following guard statement to check if a specific video file exists. You will need to modify the file name and file type to match the video file you added to your project in step #3:

```
VideoPlayer(player: player)
    .onAppear {
        guard let videoURL = Bundle.main.url(forResource:
        "SaturnV", withExtension: "mov") else {
            print ("Video file not found")
            return
        }
    }
```

9. Add the following code at the end of the .onAppear block to finally
    load the video file into the AVPlayer:

```
VideoPlayer(player: player)
    .onAppear {
        guard let videoURL = Bundle.main.url(forResource:
        "SaturnV", withExtension: "mov") else {
            print ("Video file not found")
                return
        }
        player = AVPlayer(url: videoURL as URL)
}
```

The complete ContentView file should look like this:

```
import SwiftUI
import AVKit

struct ContentView: View {

    @State var player: AVPlayer?

    var body: some View {
        VideoPlayer(player: player)
            .onAppear {
                guard let videoURL = Bundle.main.url(forResource:
                "SaturnV", withExtension: "mov") else {
                    print ("Video file not found")
                    return
                }
                player = AVPlayer(url: videoURL as URL)
            }
    }
}
struct ContentView_Previews: PreviewProvider {
    static var previews: some View {
        ContentView()
    }
}
```

Note   The preceding code tries to load a video file named SaturnV.mov, so make sure you modify the file name and file extension in your code to match the video file you added to your project.

10.   Click the Live icon in the Canvas pane. Your video file appears.

11.   Click the Play button to play the video file. Notice that you can pause the video or drag the slider to view a different part of the video at any time as shown in Figure 13-3.

Figure 13-3. *Playing a video on an iOS device*

Overlaying Text on Video

When playing video, you can overlay text that can appear on top of the video. This text can act like a watermark that people will see as the video plays. To create this overlay text, you need to use the overlay parameter in the VideoPlayer like this:

```
VideoPlayer(player: player, videoOverlay: {

        })
```

Within the videoOverlay's curly brackets, you can define a Text view to display text such as

```
VideoPlayer(player: player, videoOverlay: {
        Text("Overlay text to appear")
    })
```

By default, the videoOverlay places the Text view in the center of the video and displays text in black. To change the color of the text, just modify the Text view with the .foregroundColor modifier like this:

```
VideoPlayer(player: player, videoOverlay: {
        Text("Overlay text to appear")
            .foregroundColor(.white)
})
```

To adjust the position of the Text view over the video, move the Text view using a Spacer(), which means we'll need to enclose the entire Text view inside a VStack like this:

```
VideoPlayer(player: player, videoOverlay: {
    VStack {
        Spacer()
        Text("Overlay text to appear")
            .foregroundColor(.white)
    }
})
```

To further adjust the placement of the Text view, we can use a .padding() and .frame modifier as well like this:

```
VideoPlayer(player: player, videoOverlay: {
    VStack {
        Spacer()
        Text("Overlay text to appear")
            .foregroundColor(.white)
    }.padding()
}).frame(height: 320)
```

You can vary the exact frame height based on what you think looks best. Rather than or in addition to using the Spacer(), you could also use the .offset modifier or any other technique to adjust the spacing and position of the Text view.

To see how to overlay text on a video, follow these steps:

1. Create a new iOS App project and name it VideoOverlayApp.

2. Click the ContentView file in the Navigator pane.

3. Drag and drop a video file into the Navigator pane (see Figure 13-2).

4. Add the import AVKit line underneath the import SwiftUI line like this:

   import AVKit

5. Add the following State variable underneath the struct ContentView: View line like this:

   @State **var** player: AVPlayer?

6. Add a VideoPlayer view underneath the var body: some View line like this:

   ```
   VideoPlayer(player: player, videoOverlay: {
   }).frame(height: 320)
   ```

7. Add a VStack inside the videoOverlay curly brackets and place a Text view inside like this:

```
VideoPlayer(player: player, videoOverlay: {
    VStack {
        Spacer()
        Text("Overlay text to appear")
            .foregroundColor(.white)
    }.padding()
}).frame(height: 320)
```

8. Add an .onAppear modifier to the VideoPlayer view:

```
VideoPlayer(player: player)
    .onAppear {

    }
```

9. Inside the .onAppear curly brackets, add the following guard statement to check if a specific video file exists. You will need to modify the file name and file type to match the video file you added to your project in step #3:

```
VideoPlayer(player: player)
    .onAppear {
        guard let videoURL = Bundle.main.url(forResource:
        "SaturnV", withExtension: "mov") else {
            print ("Video file not found")
            return
        }
    }
```

10. Add the following code at the end of the .onAppear block to finally load the video file into the AVPlayer:

```
VideoPlayer(player: player)
    .onAppear {
        guard let videoURL = Bundle.main.url(forResource:
        "SaturnV", withExtension: "mov") else {
```

```
            print ("Video file not found")
            return
        }
        player = AVPlayer(url: videoURL as URL)
    }
```

The complete ContentView file should look like this:

```
import SwiftUI
import AVKit

struct ContentView: View {

    @State var player: AVPlayer?

    var body: some View {
        VideoPlayer(player: player, videoOverlay: {
            VStack {
                Spacer()
                Text("Overlay text to appear")
                    .foregroundColor(.white)
            }.padding()
        }).frame(height: 320)
            .onAppear {
                guard let videoURL = Bundle.main.url(forResource:
                "SaturnV", withExtension: "mov") else {
                    print ("Video file not found")
                    return
                }
                player = AVPlayer(url: videoURL as URL)
            }
    }
}

struct ContentView_Previews: PreviewProvider {
    static var previews: some View {
        ContentView()
    }
}
```

Note   The preceding code tries to load a video file named SaturnV.mov, so make sure you modify the file name and file extension in your code to match the video file you added to your project.

11.   Click the Live icon in the Canvas pane. Your video file appears.

12.   Click the Play button to play the video file. Notice that the text appears underneath the video as shown in Figure 13-4.

Figure 13-4.   *Displaying overlay text on a video*

Summary

Any app can enhance the user's experience by playing audio or video. Audio lets your app play music, sound effects, or spoken speech. Video files let you display movies that users can watch. Since video files can take up large amounts of space, use video files sparingly, or else the size of your app can dramatically increase each time you add another video file to your app.

By overlaying text on a video, you can provide additional information about that video. When defining overlay text, simply use standard SwiftUI views such as Text, Spacer(), and modifiers to position the overlay text where you want it to appear over the video.

CHAPTER 14

Using Speech

The Speech framework lets apps recognize audio commands as a supplement to taps and gestures. In addition, the Speech framework can also transcribe speech into text. By adding speech recognition features, your app can offer more ways for the user to interact in a natural manner that's easy for everyone to do.

Before an app can use speech recognition, the user must give permission for the app to access the microphone and use speech recognition. You may also want to make your users aware that speech recognition may send audio data to Apple's servers over the Internet to improve accuracy. That's why it's important to get the user's permission to use the microphone and use speech recognition due to privacy concerns.

By adding speech recognition to your app, your user interface is no longer limited to the touch screen. Speech recognition may never replace the touch screen, but it can give users another way to interact with your app by just speaking to it out loud.

Note   You can only test speech recognition on an actual iOS device. You cannot test speech recognition with the canvas pane or the Simulator program.

Converting Speech to Text

The Speech framework that Apple provides can convert spoken words into printed text, even in different languages based on your current location. To do this, we need to import the Speech framework, use the AVAudioEngine, and then define the location and language such as English spoken in the United States or Spanish spoken in Spain since the same languages are spoken slightly differently around the world.

257

© Wallace Wang 2023
W. Wang, *Pro iPhone Development with SwiftUI*, https://doi.org/10.1007/978-1-4842-9544-1_14

To see how this speech to text recognition feature works, follow these steps:

1. Create a new iOS App project and name it Speech2TextApp.

2. Click the project name at the top of the Navigator pane and then click the Info tab to display the properties.

3. Move the mouse pointer over any row in the Key column until the + and – icons appear.

4. Click the + icon so a popup menu appears and choose Privacy – Microphone Usage Description as shown in Figure 14-1.

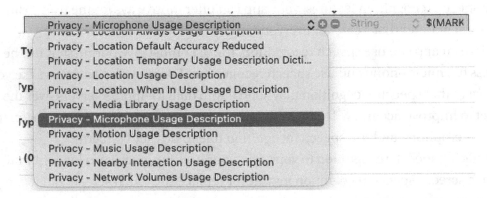

Figure 14-1. *Adding the microphone usage setting*

5. Click the ContentView file in the Navigator pane.

6. Add the following underneath the import SwiftUI line:

```
import Speech
```

7. Under the struct ContentView: View line, add the following to create an instance of the AVAudioEngine class:

```
let audioEngine = AVAudioEngine()
```

8. Add a speech recognizer and define a location to detect a specific type of language like this:

```
let speechRecognizer = SFSpeechRecognizer(locale:
Locale(identifier: "en-US"))
```

9. Add a request to detect spoken audio:

```
@State var request = SFSpeechAudioBufferRecognitionRequest()
```

10. Add an optional variable to store the recognition task. Since the
    task may or may not succeed, it needs to be an optional variable:

```
@State var recognitionTask : SFSpeechRecognitionTask?
```

11. Add a String State variable to display the transcribed text:

```
@State var message = ""
```

At this point, we need to write two functions: recognizeSpeech()
and stopSpeech().

12. Add the stopSpeech() function as follows:

```
func stopSpeech() {
    audioEngine.stop()
    request.endAudio()
    recognitionTask?.cancel()
    audioEngine.inputNode.removeTap(onBus: 0)
}
```

13. Add a recognizeSpeech() function as follows:

```
func recognizeSpeech() {
    let node = audioEngine.inputNode

    request = SFSpeechAudioBufferRecognitionRequest()
    request.shouldReportPartialResults = true

    let recordingFormat = node.outputFormat(forBus: 0)
    node.installTap(onBus: 0, bufferSize: 1024, format:
    recordingFormat) { (buffer, _) in
        self.request.append(buffer)
    }

    audioEngine.prepare()
    do {
```

```
        try audioEngine.start()
    } catch {
        return print (error)
    }

    guard let recognizeMe = SFSpeechRecognizer() else {
        return
    }

    if !recognizeMe.isAvailable {
        return
    }
    recognitionTask = speechRecognizer?.recognitionTask(with:
    request, resultHandler: {result, error in
        if let result = result {
            let transcribedString = result.bestTranscription.
            formattedString
            self.textLabel.text = transcribedString
        } else if let error = error {
            print(error)
        }
    })

}
```

The first few lines of the recognizeSpeech() function require an audio engine to process data in nodes, so we need to get that data and create a request to recognize speech. The first few lines of code in the recognizeSpeech function do this:

```
let node = audioEngine.inputNode

request = SFSpeechAudioBufferRecognitionRequest()
request.shouldReportPartialResults = true

let recordingFormat = node.outputFormat(forBus: 0)
node.installTap(onBus: 0, bufferSize: 1024, format:
recordingFormat) { (buffer, _) in
```

```
    self.request.append(buffer)
}
```

Next, we need to catch potential errors in case the audio engine can't start or if the speech recognizer cannot be accessed:

```
audioEngine.prepare()
do {
    try audioEngine.start()
} catch {
    return print (error)
}
guard let recognizeMe = SFSpeechRecognizer() else {
    return
}

if !recognizeMe.isAvailable {
    return
}
```

Finally, we need to recognize the spoken speech and transcribe it to text, which will appear in the textLabel:

```
recognitionTask = speechRecognizer?.recognitionTask(with: request,
resultHandler: {result, error in
    if let result = result {
        let transcribedString = result.bestTranscription.
        formattedString
        self.textLabel.text = transcribedString
    } else if let error = error {
        print(error)
    }
})
```

14. Define the user interface underneath the var body: some View line
     as follows:

```
VStack (spacing: 25) {
    Button {
        recognizeSpeech()
    } label: {
        Text("Start recording")
    }

    TextField("Spoken text appears here", text: $message)

    Button {
        message = ""
        stopSpeech()
    } label: {
        Text("Stop recording")
    }
}
```

The entire ContentView file should look like this:

```
import SwiftUI
import Speech

struct ContentView: View {

    let audioEngine = AVAudioEngine()
    let speechRecognizer = SFSpeechRecognizer(locale:
    Locale(identifier: "en-US"))
    @State var request = SFSpeechAudioBufferRecognitionRequest()
    @State var recognitionTask : SFSpeechRecognitionTask?
    @State var message = ""

    var body: some View {
        VStack (spacing: 25) {
            Button {
                recognizeSpeech()
            } label: {
```

```
            Text("Start recording")
        }

        TextField("Spoken text appears here", text: $message)

        Button {
            message = ""
            stopSpeech()
        } label: {
            Text("Stop recording")
        }
    }
}

func stopSpeech() {
    audioEngine.stop()
    request.endAudio()
    recognitionTask?.cancel()
    audioEngine.inputNode.removeTap(onBus: 0)
}

func recognizeSpeech() {
    let node = audioEngine.inputNode

    request = SFSpeechAudioBufferRecognitionRequest()
    request.shouldReportPartialResults = true

    let recordingFormat = node.outputFormat(forBus: 0)
    node.installTap(onBus: 0, bufferSize: 1024, format:
    recordingFormat) { (buffer, _) in
        self.request.append(buffer)
    }
    audioEngine.prepare()
    do {
        try audioEngine.start()
    } catch {
        return print (error)
    }
```

```
    guard let recognizeMe = SFSpeechRecognizer() else {
        return
    }

    if !recognizeMe.isAvailable {
        return
    }

    recognitionTask = speechRecognizer?.recognitionTask(with:
    request, resultHandler: {result, error in
        if let result = result {
            let transcribedString = result.bestTranscription.
            formattedString
            message = transcribedString
        } else if let error = error {
            print(error)
        }
    })

}


}

struct ContentView_Previews: PreviewProvider {
    static var previews: some View {
        ContentView()
    }
}
```

15. Connect an iOS device to your Macintosh through its USB cable.

16. Choose Product ➤ Destination and then select the iOS device connected to your Macintosh under the iOS Device category. You can also click the current target displayed at the top of the Xcode window to display a menu where you can also select an iOS device under the iOS Device category.

17. Click the Run button or choose Product ➤ Run. The first time you run the app, it will ask permission to access the microphone.

18.   Tap the Start recording Button.

19.   Speak a sentence and the transcribed text should appear in the TextField. Then tap the Stop recording Button when you're done. The transcribed text may make mistakes, but in general, you'll find it's fairly accurate in transcribing common words into text as shown in Figure 14-2.

5:38   ..ll 🛜 ▣

Start recording

Cats are the best animals in the world

Stop recording

Figure 14-2. *Running the Speech2TextApp project on an iPhone*

20.   Click the Stop button in Xcode, or choose Product ➤ Stop.

Recognizing Spoken Commands

Besides transcribing spoken speech into text, the Speech framework can also recognize specific spoken words that you must define ahead of time. This gives your app the ability to respond to spoken commands as a way to interact with the user.

Just be aware that in most languages, words may sound alike but be spelled differently. For example, in English, "red" and "read" sound the same, and "too," "to," and "two" also sound alike. When identifying spoken commands, be aware of words that sound alike but may have completely different meanings.

To recognize spoken commands, we simply need to use a switch statement to detect a specific word or phrase. To see how to recognize spoken commands, follow these steps:

1. Make sure the Speech2TextApp project is loaded into Xcode.

2. Click the ContentView file in the Navigator pane.

3. Add the following State variable:

    ```
    @State var newColor: Color = .white
    ```

4. Add the following function to define specific words to recognize as spoken commands:

    ```
    func checkSpokenCommand (commandString: String) {
        switch commandString {
        case "Purple":
            newColor = .purple
        case "Green":
            newColor = .green
        case "Yellow":
            newColor = .yellow
        default:
            newColor = .white
        }
    }
    ```

If the user says "purple," "green," or "yellow," the app will change the UILabel background to a different color. If the user says anything else, the UILabel background will turn to white. Now we need to call this checkSpokenCommand function inside the recognizeSpeech function like this:

```
checkSpokenCommand(commandString: transcribedString)
```

5. Modify the recognizeSpeech() function as follows:

```swift
func recognizeSpeech() {
    let node = audioEngine.inputNode

    request = SFSpeechAudioBufferRecognitionRequest()
    request.shouldReportPartialResults = true

    let recordingFormat = node.outputFormat(forBus: 0)
    node.installTap(onBus: 0, bufferSize: 1024, format:
    recordingFormat) { (buffer, _) in
        self.request.append(buffer)
    }

    audioEngine.prepare()
    do {
        try audioEngine.start()
    } catch {
        return print (error)
    }

    guard let recognizeMe = SFSpeechRecognizer() else {
        return
    }

    if !recognizeMe.isAvailable {
        return
    }

    recognitionTask = speechRecognizer?.recognitionTask(with:
    request, resultHandler: {result, error in
        if let result = result {
```

```
            let transcribedString = result.bestTranscription.
            formattedString
            message = transcribedString
            checkSpokenCommand(commandString: transcribedString)
        } else if let error = error {
            print(error)
        }
    })

}
```

6. Add the following inside the Stop recording Button code:

```
Button {
    message = ""
    newColor = .white
    stopSpeech()
} label: {
    Text("Stop recording")
}
```

7. Add a .background(newColor) modifier to the VStack:

```
.background(newColor)
```

The entire ContentView file should look like this:

```
import SwiftUI
import Speech

struct ContentView: View {

    let audioEngine = AVAudioEngine()
    let speechRecognizer = SFSpeechRecognizer(locale:
    Locale(identifier: "en-US"))
    @State var request = SFSpeechAudioBufferRecognitionRequest()
    @State var recognitionTask : SFSpeechRecognitionTask?
    @State var message = ""
    @State var newColor: Color = .white
```

```
var body: some View {
    VStack (spacing: 25) {
        Button {
            recognizeSpeech()
        } label: {
            Text("Start recording")
        }

        TextField("Spoken text appears here", text: $message)

        Button {
            message = ""
            newColor = .white
            stopSpeech()
        } label: {
            Text("Stop recording")
        }
    }.background(newColor)
}

func checkSpokenCommand (commandString: String) {
    switch commandString {
    case "Purple":
        newColor = .purple
    case "Green":
        newColor = .green
    case "Yellow":
        newColor = .yellow
    default:
        newColor = .white
    }
}

func stopSpeech() {
    audioEngine.stop()
    request.endAudio()
    recognitionTask?.cancel()
```

```
            audioEngine.inputNode.removeTap(onBus: 0)
    }

    func recognizeSpeech() {
        let node = audioEngine.inputNode

        request = SFSpeechAudioBufferRecognitionRequest()
        request.shouldReportPartialResults = true

        let recordingFormat = node.outputFormat(forBus: 0)
        node.installTap(onBus: 0, bufferSize: 1024, format:
        recordingFormat) { (buffer, _) in
            self.request.append(buffer)
        }

        audioEngine.prepare()
        do {
            try audioEngine.start()
        } catch {
            return print (error)
        }
        guard let recognizeMe = SFSpeechRecognizer() else {
            return
        }

        if !recognizeMe.isAvailable {
            return
        }

        recognitionTask = speechRecognizer?.recognitionTask(with:
        request, resultHandler: {result, error in
            if let result = result {
                let transcribedString = result.bestTranscription.
                formattedString
                message = transcribedString
                checkSpokenCommand(commandString:
                transcribedString)
            } else if let error = error {
```

```
            print(error)
        }
    })

}

}

struct ContentView_Previews: PreviewProvider {
    static var previews: some View {
        ContentView()
    }
}
```

8. Connect an iOS device to your Macintosh through its USB cable.

9. Choose Product ➤ Destination and then select the iOS device connected to your Macintosh under the iOS Device category. You can also click the current target displayed at the top of the Xcode window to display a menu where you can also select an iOS device under the iOS Device category.

10. Click the Run button or choose Product ➤ Run.

11. Tap the Start recording Button.

12. Say one of the three words ("purple," "green," or "yellow") that will change the background color of the VStack. When the app recognizes one of these three command words, it changes the VStack background color as shown in Figure 14-3.

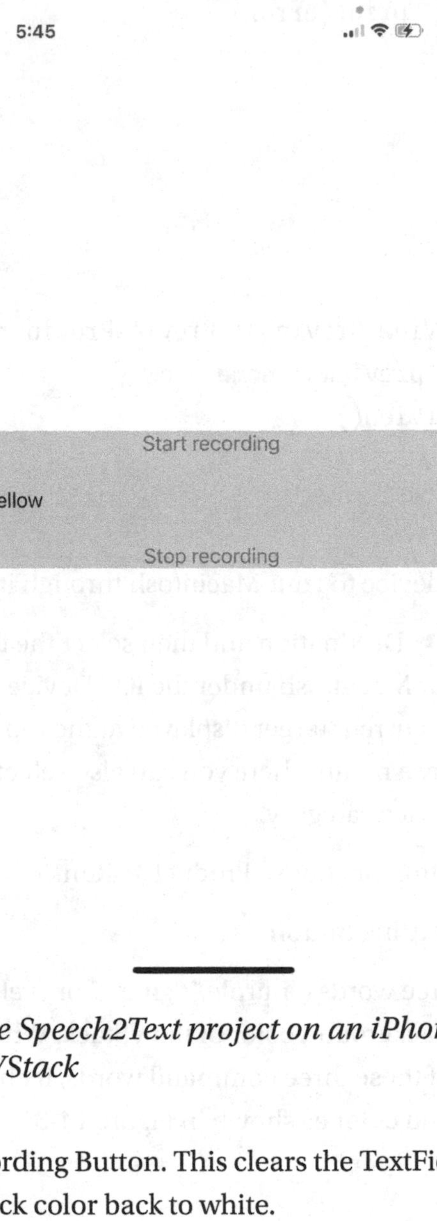

5:45   .ıl 🗢 🔋

Start recording

Yellow

Stop recording

Figure 14-3. *Running the Speech2Text project on an iPhone to change the background color of the VStack*

13. Tap the Stop recording Button. This clears the TextField and changes the VStack color back to white.

14. Click the Stop button in Xcode, or choose Product ➤ Stop.

Turning Text to Speech

Just as Swift can recognize spoken commands and convert spoken words into text, so can Swift do it the other way around by reading text out loud. To read text out loud, you need to use the AVFoundation framework, which gives your app access to a speech synthesizer.

This speech synthesizer is based on your current location and default language such as American English, Australian English, or United Kingdom English. Then the speech synthesizer can read text stored in a string that can be read at a fast or slow rate.

To see how to use the speech synthesizer, follow these steps:

1. Create a new iOS App project and name it Text2SpeechApp.

2. Click the ContentView file in the Navigator pane.

3. Add the following underneath the import SwiftUI line:

   ```
   import AVFoundation
   ```

4. Add the following constants and State variables underneath the struct ContentView: View line:

   ```
   let audio = AVSpeechSynthesizer()
   @State var convertText = AVSpeechUtterance(string: "")
   @State var textToRead = "This is a test of the emergency
   broadcast system"
   @State var sliderValue: Float = 0.5
   ```

5. Add a VStack with a spacing of 25 under the var body: some View line:

   ```
   var body: some View {
       VStack (spacing: 25) {

       }
   }
   ```

6. Add a TextEditor inside the VStack:

   ```
   VStack (spacing: 25) {
   ```

273

```
    TextEditor(text: $textToRead)
        .frame(width: 250, height: 200)
}
```

7. Add a Slider underneath the TextEditor in the VStack:

```
VStack (spacing: 25) {
    TextEditor(text: $textToRead)
        .frame(width: 250, height: 200)
    Slider(value: $sliderValue, in: 0...1)
}
```

8. Add a Button underneath the Slider in the VStack:

```
VStack (spacing: 25) {
    TextEditor(text: $textToRead)
        .frame(width: 250, height: 200)
    Slider(value: $sliderValue, in: 0...1)
    Button {
        convertText = AVSpeechUtterance(string: textToRead)
        convertText.rate = sliderValue
        audio.speak(convertText)
    } label: {
        Text("Read Text Out Loud")
    }
}
```

The entire ContentView file should look like this:

```
import SwiftUI
import AVFoundation

struct ContentView: View {

    let audio = AVSpeechSynthesizer()
    @State var convertText = AVSpeechUtterance(string: "")
    @State var textToRead = "This is a test of the emergency
    broadcast system"
```

```
    @State var sliderValue: Float = 0.5

    var body: some View {
        VStack (spacing: 25) {
            TextEditor(text: $textToRead)
                .frame(width: 250, height: 200)
            Slider(value: $sliderValue, in: 0...1)
            Button {
                convertText = AVSpeechUtterance(string:
                textToRead)
                convertText.rate = sliderValue
                audio.speak(convertText)
            } label: {
                Text("Read Text Out Loud")
            }
        }
    }
}

struct ContentView_Previews: PreviewProvider {
    static var previews: some View {
        ContentView()
    }
}
```

9. Click the Live icon in the Canvas pane.

10. Click the Read Text Out Loud Button. The app reads the text in
    the TextEditor, which is "This is a test of the emergency broadcast
    system."

11. Edit the text in the TextEditor and click the Read Text Out
    Loud Button again. Notice that this time the app reads the text
    you typed.

12. Drag the Slider left or right. Then click the Read Text Out Loud
    Button again. Notice that this time the app reads the text faster
    or slower.

Summary

Adding speech recognition requires the Speech framework, while adding a speech synthesizer to read text out loud requires the AVFoundation framework. Speech recognition gives users another way to interact with your app, while the speech synthesizer lets your app read short strings or even long amounts of text out loud. This can be handy for people with visibility problems or to provide information to users if they can't look at the iPhone screen, such as when they're driving.

By adding speech recognition and speech synthesizer, your app can use audio as another part of its user interface to allow users to give and receive data from your app.

CHAPTER 15

Integrating SwiftUI with UIKit

The previous way to create user interfaces was to rely on storyboards and the UIKit framework. While storyboards and UIKit have been around for years, Apple is encouraging developers to migrate to SwiftUI. Not only is SwiftUI adaptable to different screen sizes without requiring a lot of work, but SwiftUI can create user interfaces with far less code than storyboards or UIKit.

Although SwiftUI is clearly the future for developing apps in all of Apple's operating systems, there's still a problem. SwiftUI isn't as mature as UIKit, which means many features are still not available in SwiftUI that you can find in UIKit.

There are two solutions. One is to wait until Apple adds more features to SwiftUI. However, if you need certain features now, the second solution is to combine SwiftUI with UIKit. Not only does this give you the best of both worlds, but it also allows you to add SwiftUI to existing apps created with UIKit.

The first step is to import UIKit in any SwiftUI project like this:

```
import UIKit
```

Next, you need to create a structure that encloses the UIKit view you want to use using the UIViewRepresentable protocol like this:

```
struct Wrapper: UIViewRepresentable {

}
```

© Wallace Wang 2023
W. Wang, *Pro iPhone Development with SwiftUI*, https://doi.org/10.1007/978-1-4842-9544-1_15

The name of the structure can be any descriptive name you want, so feel free to replace "Wrapper" with a name of your own choosing. Inside this structure, we need two functions called makeUIView and updateUIView like this:

```
struct Wrapper: UIViewRepresentable {
    func makeUIView(context: Context) -> some UIView {

    }

    func updateUIView(_ uiView: UIViewType, context: Context) {

    }
}
```

The makeUIView function runs once to create the specific UIView, so you must replace UIView with the specific UIKit view you want to integrate into SwiftUI. The updateUIView function runs to keep updating the UIView within the SwiftUI project. Whatever UIView you defined in the makeUIView function is the same UIView you need to use to replace "UIViewType" in the updateUIView function.

Finally, to display the UIKit view in a SwiftUI project, just reference the structure name. In the preceding example, the structure has an arbitrary name of "Wrapper," so to make it appear in SwiftUI, just use its name like this:

```
var body: some View {
    Wrapper()
}
```

Displaying a PDF File

Apple provides numerous frameworks that provide code you can use in your own projects. By relying on Apple's numerous frameworks, you can write apps that do a lot while writing as little Swift code as possible. One of Apple's frameworks is called PDFKit, which allows you to view a PDF file.

Although SwiftUI does not support PDFKit yet, we can still use PDFKit by wrapping it inside a UIViewRepresentable structure. To see how to display a PDF file using PDFKit, follow these steps:

1. Create a new iOS App project and name it PDFApp.

2. Drag and drop a PDF file in the Navigator pane. You may also want to rename the PDF file to something simple and easy to type for your convenience.

3. Click the ContentView file in the Navigator pane.

4. Underneath the import SwiftUI line, add the following:

    import PDFKit

5. Create a structure and give it any name you wish:

    struct ViewMe: UIViewRepresentable {

    }

6. Inside the structure, add the following constant:

    let url: URL

    To open a PDF file, we'll need to pass in the file name and location, which is a URL data type. The preceding "url" constant will let us call the structure (called ViewMe) by sending it a url that specifies the PDF file name and location.

7. Add the following makeUIView function inside the structure:

    ```
    func makeUIView(context: UIViewRepresentableContext<ViewMe>) ->
    PDFView {
        let pdfView = PDFView()
        pdfView.document = PDFDocument(url: url)
        return pdfView
    }
    ```

PDFView is a class defined in the PDFKit framework (`https://developer.apple.com/documentation/pdfkit`). So this function needs to return a PDFView. More importantly, the .document property needs the "url" constant to load the actual PDF file name. Finally, notice that this function uses the structure name (ViewMe) to define the UIViewRepresentableContext like this:

```
UIViewRepresentableContext<ViewMe>)
```

8. Add the following updateUIView function inside the structure:

```
func updateUIView(_ uiView: PDFView, context: UIViewRepresentable
Context<ViewMe>) {

}
```

Notice that this function specifies the object that the makeUIView function returns:

```
_ uiView: PDFView
```

In addition, this updateUIView function also uses the structure name (ViewMe) to define the UIViewRepresentableContext like this:

```
UIViewRepresentableContext<ViewMe>
```

9. Under the struct ContentView: View line, add the following constant that loads the PDF file added to the Navigator pane. You'll need to modify the file name text to match the name of the PDF file stored in the Navigator pane:

```
let fileURL = Bundle.main.url(forResource: "ds11",
withExtension: "pdf")
```

10. Under the var body: some View line, add the following:

```
ViewMe(url: fileURL!)
```

Notice that this is the name of the UIViewRepresentable structure and that it passes in the fileURL constant to the structure's url property. Because the file name may not exist, fileURL is optional that must be unwrapped using the exclamation mark.

The entire Content View file should look like this:

```swift
import SwiftUI
import PDFKit

struct ViewMe: UIViewRepresentable {
    let url: URL

    func makeUIView(context: UIViewRepresentableContext<ViewMe>)
    -> PDFView {
        let pdfView = PDFView()
        pdfView.document = PDFDocument(url: url)
        return pdfView
    }

    func updateUIView(_ uiView: PDFView, context:
    UIViewRepresentableContext<ViewMe>) {

    }
}

struct ContentView: View {

    let fileURL = Bundle.main.url(forResource: "ds11",
    withExtension: "pdf")
    var body: some View {
        ViewMe(url: fileURL!)
    }
}

struct ContentView_Previews: PreviewProvider {
    static var previews: some View {
        ContentView()
    }
}
```

11. Click the Live icon in the Canvas pane. The canvas pane displays the PDF file you added to the Navigator pane as shown in Figure 15-1. The page may appear cut off, so you may need to scroll side to side to view the entire width of each PDF page. If the PDF file contains multiple pages, you can view all the pages by scrolling up or down.

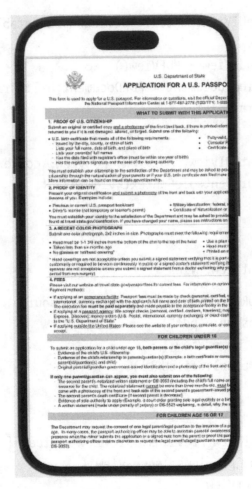

Figure 15-1. *Displaying a PDF file within an app*

Displaying a Website

Another Apple framework that isn't available to SwiftUI is WebKit, which can load a website within an app. To use WebKit, just wrap it inside a UIViewRepresentable structure. To see how to display a website using WebKit, follow these steps:

1. Create a new iOS App project and name it WebKitApp.

2. Click the ContentView file in the Navigator pane.

3. Underneath the import SwiftUI line, add the following:

```
import WebKit
```

4. Create a structure and give it any name you wish:

```
struct WebView: UIViewRepresentable {

}
```

5. Inside the structure, add the following constant:

```
let url: URL
```

   To open a website, we'll need its URL address, which is a URL data type.

6. Add the following makeUIView function inside the structure:

```
func makeUIView(context: UIViewRepresentableContext<WebView>) ->
WKWebView {
    return WKWebView()
}
```

   WKWebView is a class defined in the WebKit framework
   (https://developer.apple.com/documentation/webkit).
   So this function needs to return a WKWebView. Notice that
   this function uses the structure name (WebView) to define the
   UIViewRepresentableContext like this:

```
UIViewRepresentableContext<WebView>)
```

7. Add the following updateUIView function inside the structure:

```
func updateUIView(_ webView: WKWebView, context: UIViewRepresentable
Context<WebView>) {
    let request = URLRequest(url: url)
    webView.load(request)
}
```

Notice that this function specifies the object that the makeUIView function returns:

```
_ uiView: WKWebView
```

In addition, this updateUIView function also uses the structure name (WebView) to define the UIViewRepresentableContext like this:

```
UIViewRepresentableContext<WebView>
```

8. Under the var body: some View line, add the following:

```
WebView(url: URL(string: "https://www.apple.com")!)
```

Notice that this is the name of the UIViewRepresentable structure and that it passes in a website address as a string ("https://www. apple.com"). Because the address may not be valid, the string is optional that must be unwrapped using the exclamation mark.

The entire ContentView file should look like this:

```
import SwiftUI
import WebKit

struct WebView: UIViewRepresentable {

    let url: URL

    func makeUIView(context: UIViewRepresentableContext<WebView>)
    -> WKWebView {
        return WKWebView()
    }
```

```swift
    func updateUIView(_ webView: WKWebView, context:
    UIViewRepresentableContext<WebView>) {
        let request = URLRequest(url: url)
        webView.load(request)
    }
}

struct ContentView: View {

    var body: some View {
        WebView(url: URL(string: "https://www.apple.com")!)
    }
}

struct ContentView_Previews: PreviewProvider {
    static var previews: some View {
        ContentView()
    }
}
```

9. Click the Live icon in the Canvas pane. The canvas pane displays
    the website specified by the string as shown in Figure 15-2. Click
    the different hyperlinks on the website, then change this string to
    another website address to display a different website.

Figure 15-2. *Displaying the Apple website within an app*

Integrating SwiftUI into Storyboard Projects

Because SwiftUI is so new, there are still many features that storyboards can access that
SwiftUI currently cannot. However, as SwiftUI matures over time, Apple will certainly
give SwiftUI more capabilities to equal and eventually surpass storyboards. That
means eventually you won't need to rely on integrating UIKit, WebKit, PDFKit, or other
frameworks into SwiftUI because SwiftUI will eventually support them.

What will likely become more common is that you'll need to modify existing projects created using storyboards and gradually add SwiftUI features. That means combining an existing storyboard project with SwiftUI views. That lets you create user interfaces quickly and easily using SwiftUI while using the time-tested code created and stored in a project created with storyboards.

To see how to integrate SwiftUI files into a storyboard project, follow these steps:

1. Create a new iOS App project, make sure it's a storyboard (not SwiftUI) as shown in Figure 15-3, and name it StoryboardApp.

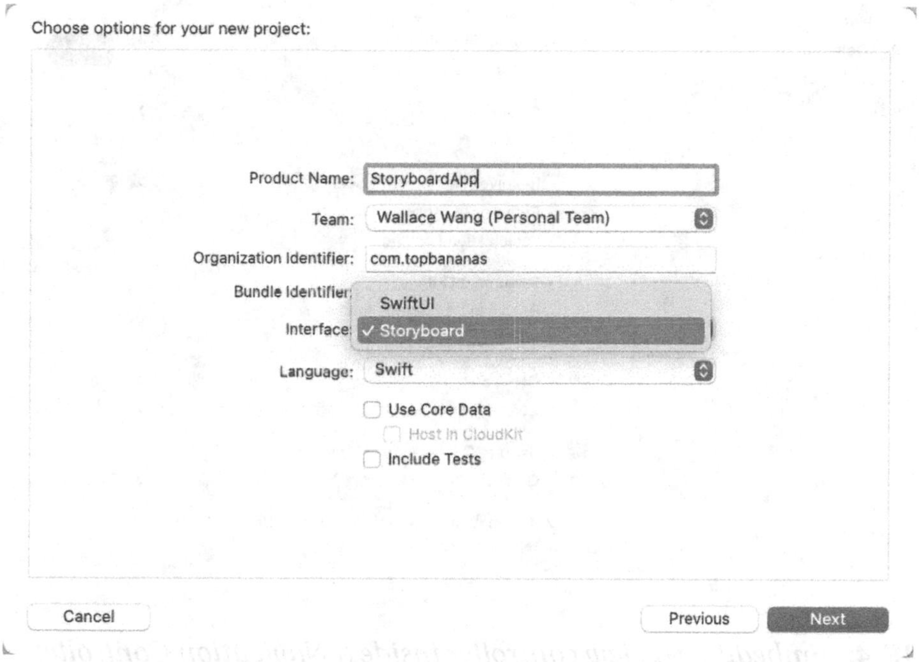

Figure 15-3. *Creating a Storyboard project*

2. Click Next, choose a folder to store your project, and click Create.

3. Click the Main file in the Navigator pane to see the storyboard that defines the user interface. Initially, the user interface consists of a single view controller that mimics an iPhone screen.

4. Click the View Controller (the iPhone screen) to select it.

287

5. Choose Editor ➤ Embed in ➤ Navigation Controller as shown in
    Figure 15-4. Xcode displays a Navigation Controller with an arrow
    pointing to the blank view controller (iPhone screen) as shown in
    Figure 15-5.

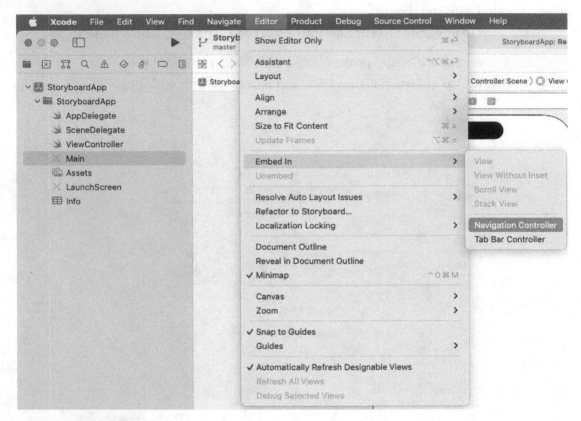

Figure 15-4. *Embedding a view controller inside a Navigation Controller*

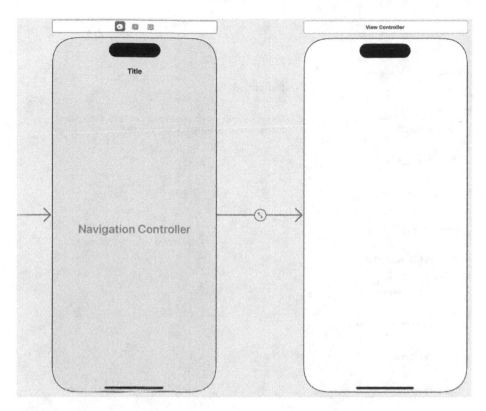

Figure 15-5. *A view controller inside a Navigation Controller*

6.   Click the Library icon (+ icon) in the upper-right corner to open
     the Library window as shown in Figure 15-6.

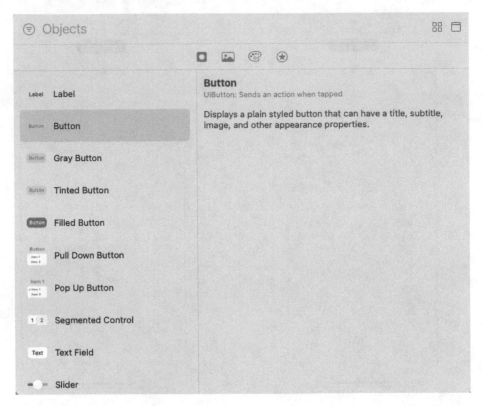

Figure 15-6. *Opening the Library window by clicking the Library icon (+)*

7. Drag and drop a Button on the view controller (white iPhone screen).

8. Choose Editor ➤ Resolve Autolayout Issues ➤ Reset to Suggested Constraints. Xcode adds constraints to keep the Button positioned a fixed distance from the top and left sides of the simulated iPhone screen.

9. Click the Library icon (+) and look for a Hosting View Controller as shown in Figure 15-7. A Hosting View Controller is a special controller that encloses a SwiftUI view so it can appear within a storyboard project.

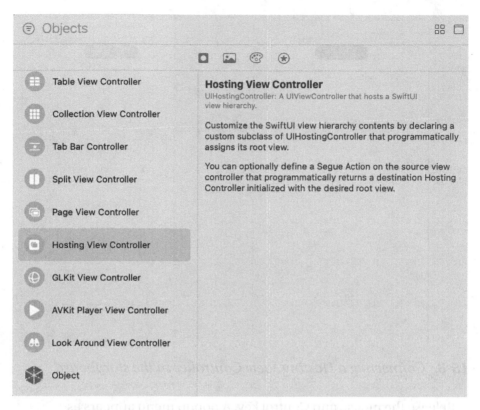

Figure 15-7. *The Hosting View Controller in the Library window*

10. Drag and drop a Hosting View Controller to the right of the existing view controller in the storyboard.

11. Click the Button on the view controller, hold down the Control key, hold down the left mouse button, and drag the mouse over the Hosting View Controller as shown Figure 15-8.

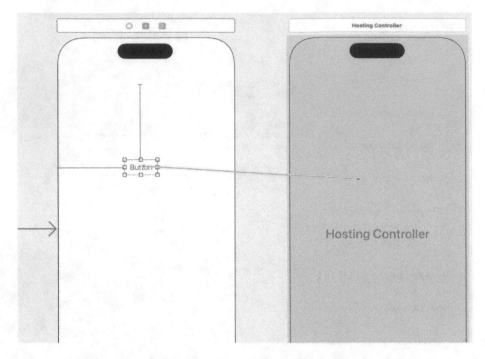

Figure 15-8. *Connecting a Hosting View Controller in the storyboard*

12. Release the mouse and Control key. A popup menu appears as shown in Figure 15-9.

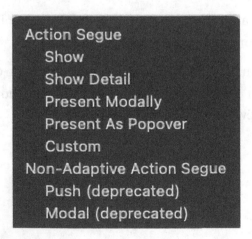

Figure 15-9. *A popup menu to define the type of connection between controllers*

13. Choose Show under the Action Segue category. Xcode draws
     a line, called a segue, that connects the view controller to the
     hosting controller as shown in Figure 15-10.

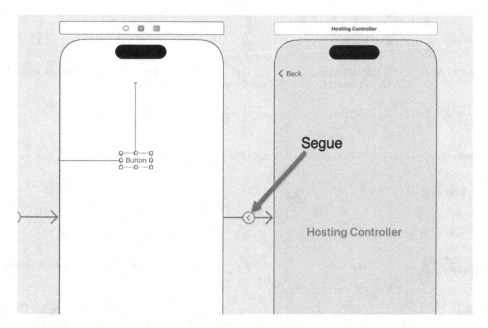

Figure 15-10. *A segue connects the view controller to the hosting controller*

14. Choose File ➤ New ➤ File and choose SwiftUI View as shown in
     Figure 15-11.

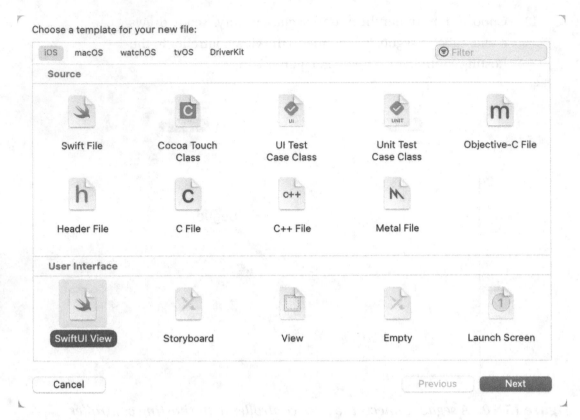

Choose a template for your new file:

iOS   macOS   watchOS   tvOS   DriverKit   ⊘ Filter

Source

Swift File   Cocoa Touch   UI Test   Unit Test   Objective-C File
               Class   Case Class   Case Class

Header File   C File   C++ File   Metal File

User Interface

SwiftUI View   Storyboard   View   Empty   Launch Screen

Cancel   Previous   Next

Figure 15-11.   Creating a SwiftUI View

15. Click Next. The default file name for the file will be SwiftUIView.

16. Click Create. Xcode adds a SwiftUIView file in the Navigator pane.

17. Click the SwiftUIView file and edit it so the entire file looks like this:

```
import SwiftUI

struct SwiftUIView: View {

    var name: String

    var body: some View {
        Text("Hello, \(name)")
    }
}
```

```
struct SwiftUIView_Previews: PreviewProvider {
    static var previews: some View {
        SwiftUIView(name: "Hanna")
    }
}
```

This SwiftUI view does nothing more than display a name in a Text view such as "Hello, Hanna". The "name" variable will let us pass a string into the SwiftUI view.

18. Click the Main file in the Navigator pane to view the entire storyboard.

19. Click the Add Editor on Right icon in the upper-right corner as shown in Figure 15-12. This splits the editor pane in half.

Figure 15-12. *The Add Editor on Right icon*

20. Click the right half of the editor pane and then click ViewController in the Navigator pane. Xcode displays the contents of the ViewController file in one of the editor panes and the contents of the Main file in the other editor pane.

21. Click in the editor pane that contains the Main storyboard file (it should look entirely gray). The Main storyboard should appear after you click in its editor pane.

22. Move the mouse pointer over the segue that connects to the Hosting Controller.

23. Hold down the Control key and the left mouse button, then drag the mouse above the last curly bracket at the bottom of the ViewController file as shown in Figure 15-13.

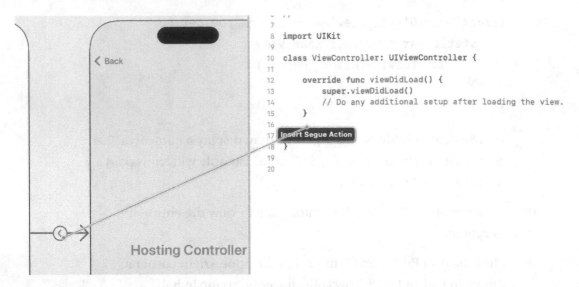

```
7    ''
8    import UIKit
9
10   class ViewController: UIViewController {
11
12       override func viewDidLoad() {
13           super.viewDidLoad()
14           // Do any additional setup after loading the view.
15       }
16
17   Insert Segue Action
18   }
19
20
```

< Back

Hosting Controller

Figure 15-13. Control-dragging from the segue to the ViewController file

24. Release the Control key and the left mouse button. A window appears as shown in Figure 15-14.

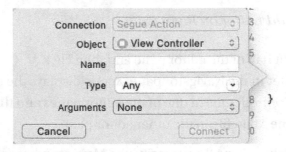

Connection	Segue Action
Object	◯ View Controller
Name	
Type	Any
Arguments	None

Cancel   Connect

Figure 15-14. Defining a Segue Action function

25. Click in the Name text field and type a name such as openSwiftUIView and click the Connect button. Xcode creates an @IBSegueAction function.

26. Edit the @IBSegueAction function as follows:

```
@IBSegueAction func openSwiftUIView(_ coder: NSCoder) ->
UIViewController? {
    return UIHostingController(coder: coder, rootView:
    SwiftUIView(name: "Nancy"))
}
```

The preceding code simply loads the SwiftUIView file and passes the "Nancy" string into the "name" parameter. Feel free to substitute "Nancy" with any name you wish. Notice that Xcode displays an error message.

27.   Add the following underneath the import UIKit line to eliminate the error message:

import SwiftUI

28.   Click the Run button or choose Product ➤ Run. The user interface appears in the Simulator displaying the Button.

29.   Click the Button. The SwiftUI view appears displaying "Hello, Nancy".

30.   Choose Simulator ➤ Quit Simulator.

Summary

SwiftUI is the future for creating user interfaces, but it still lacks many features that storyboards can provide. Fortunately, you can combine features from other frameworks such as UIKit, PDFKit, WebKit, and many others into a SwiftUI project. Eventually, Apple will provide SwiftUI support for all of its frameworks, but until that happens, you can still use Apple's various frameworks anyways.

While you can include storyboard features in SwiftUI, you can also add SwiftUI to existing storyboard-based projects. By giving you the ability to combine SwiftUI and storyboards in a single project, Xcode lets you get the best of both worlds.

CHAPTER 16

Accessing the Photos Library

One of the most useful accessories on every smartphone has been the camera. Each year, the iPhone camera improves to the point of capturing high-quality images with resolutions that rival professional cameras of just a few generations ago. Not surprisingly, the camera is one of the most popular hardware accessories for an app to access and control.

Once you capture pictures through the camera, the iPhone stores your pictures in the Photos Library. The simulated iOS device in the Canvas pane and the Simulator both contain sample pictures already stored in the Photos Library, so we can write code to access and display those images by importing the PhotosUI framework like this:

```
import PhotosUI
```

After adding the PhotosUI framework, we can then use the PhotosPicker to access images and videos stored in the Photos Library. The data type that represents pictures in the Photos Library is called PhotosPickerItem.

Using the PhotosPicker

The PhotosUI framework gives us access to the PhotosPicker, which serves two purposes. First, the PhotosPicker defines a view (such as a Text view) that users can select. Second, after users select the PhotosPicker, the PhotosPicker can access images in the Photos Library as shown in Figure 16-1.

© Wallace Wang 2023
W. Wang, *Pro iPhone Development with SwiftUI*, https://doi.org/10.1007/978-1-4842-9544-1_16

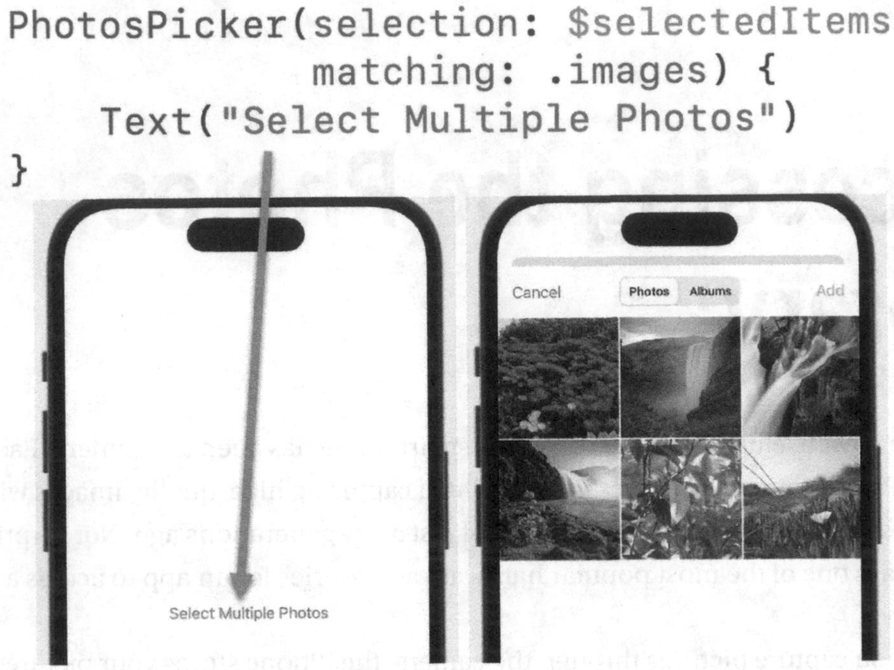

```
PhotosPicker(selection: $selectedItems,
             matching: .images) {
    Text("Select Multiple Photos")
}
```

Figure 16-1. *The PhotosPicker can act like a button to access the Photos Library*

To see how to access the Photos Library, follow these steps:

1. Create a new iOS App project and name it PhotoLibraryApp.

2. Click the ContentView file in the Navigator pane.

3. Add import PhotosUI under the import SwiftUI line like this:

   import PhotosUI

4. Add a State variable to define an array that can hold PhotosPickerItem values like this:

   @State **var** selectedItems: [PhotosPickerItem] = []

5. Add the following inside the var body: some View like this:

   ```
   PhotosPicker(selection: $selectedItems,
                maxSelectionCount: 2,
                matching: .images) {
       Text("Select Some Pictures")
   }
   ```

The Text view defines text that users can select to access the Photos Library. The selection parameter stores everything selected in the selectedItems array, which can hold PhotosPickerItem data. The maxSelectionCount is an option parameter that lets you define how many items the user can select. In this case, the maxSelectionCount limits the user to selecting a maximum of two items. The matching parameter filters the Photos Library to display only images.

The entire ContentView file should look like this:

```
import SwiftUI
import PhotosUI

struct ContentView: View {
    @State var selectedItems: [PhotosPickerItem] = []

    var body: some View {
        PhotosPicker(selection: $selectedItems,
                     maxSelectionCount: 2,
                     matching: .images) {
            Text("Select Some Pictures")
        }
    }
}

struct ContentView_Previews: PreviewProvider {
    static var previews: some View {
        ContentView()
    }
}
```

6. Click the Live icon on the Canvas pane.

7. Click the "Select Some Pictures" Text view displayed on the user interface. The default images stored in the Photos Library appear (see Figure 16-1).

8. Click two different images. A check mark appears in the bottom-right corner of each selected image, and a "Show Selected (2)" text appears at the bottom of the screen as shown in Figure 16-2. Notice that because the maxSelectionCount parameter is set to 2, you can only select a maximum of two items. If you want to select a different item, you must deselect a previously selected item first.

Figure 16-2. *The PhotosPicker showing two selected images*

9. Click "Show Selected (2)". The PhotosPicker shows the first selected image and the other selected image thumbnails at the bottom of the screen as shown in Figure 16-3.

Figure 16-3. *The PhotosPicker showing a selected image and thumbnails of other selected images*

10. Click Done. The Photos Library shows all images again.

11. Click the Albums tab at the top of the screen to view a list of photo albums.

12. Click Cancel. The app returns to showing the PhotosPicker's text displaying "Select Some Pictures".

Viewing Different Types of Images in the Photos Library

When using the PhotosPicker, you can define a matching parameter that determines which types of images to view. Some of the different options are

- .bursts – Multiple high-speed photos

- .cinematicVideos – Videos

- .depthEffectPhotos – Photos with depth information

- .images – Still images and Live Photos

- .livePhotos – Only Live Photos

- .panoramas – Panorama photos

- .screenRecordings – Videos of screen actions

- .screenshots – Still image screenshots

- .slomoVideos – Slow-motion videos

- .timelapseVideos – Time-lapse videos

- .videos – All types of videos

To choose any of these types of images or videos, define them in the matching parameter like this:

```
PhotosPicker(selection: $selectedItems,
            matching: .videos) {
    Text("Open the Photo Library")
}
```

If you want to choose two or more types of images or videos to display, you can define an array to list multiple options like this:

```
PhotosPicker(selection: $selectedItems,
            matching: .any(of: [.bursts, .livePhotos])) {
    Text("Open the Photo Library")
}
```

The preceding code would display only .bursts and .livePhotos stored in the Photos Library but nothing else. Rather than specifically defining which images to display, you can also specifically define which images not to display by using .not to specify what type of image or video not to display like this:

```
PhotosPicker(selection: $selectedItems,
             matching: .any(of: [.videos, .not(.cinematicVideos)])) {
    Text("Open the Photo Library")
}
```

To see how to select which items to view and which items to hide in the Photos Library, follow these steps:

1. Create a new iOS App project and name it FilterPhotoLibraryApp.

2. Click the ContentView file in the Navigator pane.

3. Add import PhotosUI under the import SwiftUI line like this:

```
import PhotosUI
```

4. Add the following State variables like this:

```
@State var selectedItems: [PhotosPickerItem] = []
@State var wantedAssets = PHPickerFilter.images
@State var notWantedAssets = PHPickerFilter.screenRecordings
```

5. Add the following inside the var body: some View like this:

```
VStack {
    PhotosPicker(selection: $selectedItems,
                 matching: .any(of: [wantedAssets,
                 .not(notWantedAssets)])) {
        Text("Open the Photo Library")
    }

    HStack {
        Text("Items to view")
        Picker(selection: $wantedAssets) {
            Text("Bursts").tag(PHPickerFilter.bursts)
            Text("Cinematic videos").tag(PHPickerFilter.
            cinematicVideos)
```

```
                    Text("Depth effects photos").tag(PHPickerFilter.
                    depthEffectPhotos)
                    Text("Images").tag(PHPickerFilter.images)
                    Text("Live photos").tag(PHPickerFilter.livePhotos)
                    Text("Screen recordings").tag(PHPickerFilter.
                    screenRecordings)
                    Text("Screenshots").tag(PHPickerFilter.screenshots)
                    Text("Slow motion videos").tag(PHPickerFilter.
                    slomoVideos)
                    Text("Time lapse videos").tag(PHPickerFilter.
                    timelapseVideos)
                    Text("Videos").tag(PHPickerFilter.videos)
                } label: {
                    Text("Viewable items")
                }
            }
            HStack {
                Text("Items to filter out")
                Picker(selection: $notWantedAssets) {
                    Text("Bursts").tag(PHPickerFilter.bursts)
                    Text("Cinematic videos").tag(PHPickerFilter.
                    cinematicVideos)
                    Text("Depth effects photos").tag(PHPickerFilter.
                    depthEffectPhotos)
                    Text("Images").tag(PHPickerFilter.images)
                    Text("Live photos").tag(PHPickerFilter.livePhotos)
                    Text("Screen recordings").tag(PHPickerFilter.
                    screenRecordings)
                    Text("Screenshots").tag(PHPickerFilter.screenshots)
                    Text("Slow motion videos").tag(PHPickerFilter.
                    slomoVideos)
                    Text("Time lapse videos").tag(PHPickerFilter.
                    timelapseVideos)
                    Text("Videos").tag(PHPickerFilter.videos)
```

```
        } label: {
            Text("Non-viewable items")
        }
    }

  }
}
```

The preceding code displays a PhotosPicker and two Picker views
as shown in Figure 16-4.

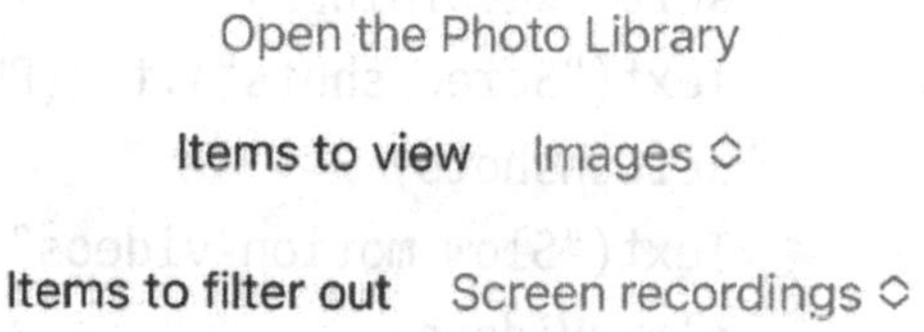

Open the Photo Library

Items to view   Images ◇

Items to filter out   Screen recordings ◇

Figure 16-4. *The PhotosPicker and two Picker views*

The entire ContentView file should look like this:

```
import SwiftUI
import PhotosUI

struct ContentView: View {
    @State var selectedItems: [PhotosPickerItem] = []
    @State var wantedAssets = PHPickerFilter.images
    @State var notWantedAssets = PHPickerFilter.screenRecordings
    var body: some View {
        VStack {
            PhotosPicker(selection: $selectedItems,
                        matching: .any(of: [wantedAssets,
                        .not(notWantedAssets)])) {
                Text("Open the Photo Library")
            }

            HStack {
                Text("Items to view")
                Picker(selection: $wantedAssets) {
```

```
                Text("Bursts").tag(PHPickerFilter.bursts)
                Text("Cinematic videos").tag(PHPickerFilter.
                cinematicVideos)
                Text("Depth effects photos").
                tag(PHPickerFilter.depthEffectPhotos)
                Text("Images").tag(PHPickerFilter.images)
                Text("Live photos").tag(PHPickerFilter.
                livePhotos)
                Text("Screen recordings").tag(PHPickerFilter.
                screenRecordings)
                Text("Screenshots").tag(PHPickerFilter.
                screenshots)
                Text("Slow motion videos").tag(PHPickerFilter.
                slomoVideos)
                Text("Time lapse videos").tag(PHPickerFilter.
                timelapseVideos)
                Text("Videos").tag(PHPickerFilter.videos)
            } label: {
                Text("Viewable items")
            }
        }
        HStack {
            Text("Items to filter out")
            Picker(selection: $notWantedAssets) {
                Text("Bursts").tag(PHPickerFilter.bursts)
                Text("Cinematic videos").tag(PHPickerFilter.
                cinematicVideos)
                Text("Depth effects photos").
                tag(PHPickerFilter.depthEffectPhotos)
                Text("Images").tag(PHPickerFilter.images)
                Text("Live photos").tag(PHPickerFilter.
                livePhotos)
                Text("Screen recordings").tag(PHPickerFilter.
                screenRecordings)
```

```
                    Text("Screenshots").tag(PHPickerFilter.
                    screenshots)
                    Text("Slow motion videos").tag(PHPickerFilter.
                    slomoVideos)
                    Text("Time lapse videos").tag(PHPickerFilter.
                    timelapseVideos)
                    Text("Videos").tag(PHPickerFilter.videos)
                } label: {
                    Text("Non-viewable items")
                }
            }
        }
    }
}

struct ContentView_Previews: PreviewProvider {
    static var previews: some View {
        ContentView()
    }
}
```

6. Connect your Macintosh to an iPhone or iPad using a USB cable.
    Use an iPhone or iPad that has multiple images and videos already
    stored in the Photos Library.

7. Choose your iOS device in the Xcode menu as shown in
    Figure 16-5.

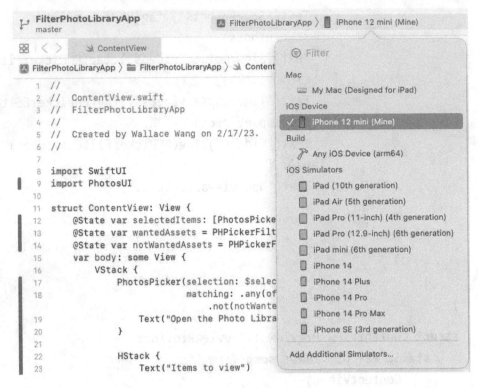

Figure 16-5. *Choosing an iOS device within Xcode*

8. Tap on the first Picker view to define the type of images/videos you want to see in the Photos Library.

9. Tap on the second Picker view to define the type of images/videos you do not want to see in the Photos Library.

10. Tap the "Open the Photos Library" PhotosPicker text to display the Photos Library. Notice that the Photos Library only shows the type of images/videos you defined and does not show the images/videos you specified you did not want to see.

11. Repeat steps 8–10 to experiment with viewing and hiding different types of images/videos.

12. Click the Stop icon (or choose Product ➤ Stop) in Xcode.

Summary

Many people capture still images and videos using the cameras on their iOS devices. By accessing the Photos Library, you can select one or more images/videos using the PhotosPicker. The PhotosPicker lets you define filters to choose only to view the type of images/videos you want and specify the type of images/videos you don't want. Accessing the Photos Library gives apps a way to retrieve previously saved images/videos.

CHAPTER 17

Using Machine Learning

Artificial intelligence (AI) has been around since the 1960s. In those early days, computer scientists dreamed of intelligent computers that could think, but the reality proved far less breathtaking. The biggest obstacle to AI was that computer scientists had to mimic intelligence by anticipating all situations. In limited domains like chess, this worked, but when dealing with large amounts of data, this primitive solution failed because it's impossible to anticipate all possible situations that might occur. That's why the latest developments in AI focus less on hand-coding all possibilities and focus more on machine learning.

Machine learning has proven valuable for creating "smarter" programs, especially when they must deal with previously unknown data. For example, credit card companies use machine learning to track your spending patterns. With so many customers, it's impossible for people to track each customer's spending patterns, so that's why they rely on machine learning instead.

Machine learning can analyze your spending patterns, and the moment it detects something unusual, such as a purchase in another country or a large, out-of-the-ordinary purchase, the machine learning program flags that as suspicious. Since your spending patterns may change subtly over time, the machine learning program can adjust and recognize valid purchases while spotting suspicious transactions. In this way, machine learning adapts to new situations and appears "smarter."

Machine learning is best used for dealing with data that can't be anticipated ahead of time although many programs can adapt machine learning to make the program easier to use. For example, when you type text to write an email or a note, the virtual keyboard displays words and phrases it thinks you're likely to write. By tapping on a word or phrase, you can type faster without writing out the entire word or phrase.

Machine learning can make apps more responsive and versatile. In this chapter, you'll learn how to incorporate machine learning in iOS apps.

© Wallace Wang 2023
W. Wang, *Pro iPhone Development with SwiftUI*, https://doi.org/10.1007/978-1-4842-9544-1_17

Understanding Machine Learning

The main idea behind machine learning is that computer scientists create generic algorithms that they train using large amounts of data. When the algorithm gets the problem right, it modifies its own code so it can identify similar types of problems in the future. When the algorithm gets the problem wrong, it also modifies its own code to reduce the chance of making the same mistake again. Such training and feedback creates a program that literally learns, hence the term machine learning. Best of all, the algorithm trains itself based on data it receives, so there's no need for a human programmer to modify the algorithm by hand, which would be tedious and inefficient.

Machine learning lets programs deal with situations it has never encountered before. One common machine learning problem involves image recognition. You can train an algorithm to recognize a dog or a boat in a picture, but that algorithm must eventually learn to recognize dogs or boats in pictures it has never seen before.

Most people may be familiar with an early form of machine learning that appeared in spam filters for email. It's impossible to identify all possible spam because spammers can simply modify their spam. As a result, spam filters use machine learning to identify possible spam. When you confirm that a message is spam, you're training the spam filter to recognize similar types of spam in the future. That's why over time, spam filters tend to get better simply because they keep getting trained by new data.

Machine learning involves three steps:

- Developing and writing algorithms

- Training the algorithm with large amounts of data

- Using the trained algorithm (called a machine learning model)

Creating algorithms can be difficult, and training algorithms can be time-consuming. In 2018, Apple introduced Create ML, which allows you to create your own machine learning models using Swift. This involves exposing the Create ML machine learning model to lots of data to gradually train it to recognize the data you want. Fortunately, if you don't have the time to design your own machine learning models, you can take trained machine learning models and simply use them without writing your own algorithms or training it with large amounts of data.

Note   Apple's Create ML framework is based on Turi Create, a machine learning company that Apple acquired in 2016. Turi Create was designed to let you create machine learning models using the Python programming language. Create ML is basically Turi Create redesigned for Apple's Swift programming language. You can learn more about Create ML from Apple's documentation (`https://developer.apple.com/documentation/createml`).

The advantage of simply using a trained machine learning model is that you can add artificial intelligence to your iOS apps quickly and easily. The drawback is that you need to find trained machine learning models that do what you need. In addition, you cannot increase the trained machine learning model's intelligence. You're essentially taking a fixed machine learning model that won't improve over time.

Since most people aren't able to write machine learning algorithms and train it with large amounts of data, they must rely on machine learning models that others have created. There are two sources of machine learning models:

- Core ML models

- Non-Core ML models

When you add a machine learning model to an iOS project, it must be stored in a file format known as Core ML (which stands for Core Machine Learning). Since Core ML is a new file format, most machine learning models are stored in different file formats. Fortunately, Apple has converted some popular machine learning models into the Core ML format. That means you can use these machine learning models in your iOS apps right away.

The main purpose for adding machine learning to your iOS apps is so your app can anticipate the user's needs. Essentially, machine learning lets your app become smarter. The smarter your app is able to respond to the user, the happier the user will be. Machine learning gives your app new capabilities without requiring you to exhaustively write instructions yourself.

Note   One huge problem with machine learning is that it's only as smart as the data it's trained on and the algorithms created by programmers who may have unknowingly added bias to their algorithms. Since facial recognition algorithms are typically written by men, many facial recognition systems have trouble recognizing minority women.

Likewise, if a machine learning model is trained with faulty data, it will never be accurate. Microsoft once created a chatbot nicknamed Tay, which learned from comments people typed in over the Internet. So people flooded Tay with sexist and racist comments. As a result, Tay gradually learned to use sexist and racist comments in all of its replies until Microsoft pulled the plug on Tay.

What this chapter will focus on is finding Core ML machine learning models, adding them to iOS projects, and using them in your iOS app.

Finding a Core ML Model

The simplest way to find a Core ML model to use is to visit Apple's machine learning developer's site at `https://developer.apple.com/machine-learning`. Apple provides a growing library of tested Core ML models that you can add to an iOS project. While this list may be relatively small, it will grow over time.

Besides Apple's site, you may also be able to find Core ML models on third-party sites where people have created or converted other machine learning model formats into Core ML. For the truly adventurous, you can find Core ML conversion tools on Apple's developer's site. By using these Core ML conversion tools, you can search for other machine learning models stored in different file formats and convert them into the Core ML format. This process of converting machine learning models into the Core ML format involves using the Python programming language and is beyond the scope of this chapter.

When evaluating different Core ML models to use, you need to look at what the machine learning model does and how large its file may be as shown in Figure 17-1.

SqueezeNet

Image Classification

A small Deep Neural Network architecture
that classifies the dominant object in a
camera frame or image.

View Models and Code Sample

Figure 17-1. *Core ML models briefly describe what the model does*

By clicking the button to view models, you can see more details about the
different variations available. Generally, the larger the Core ML model, the more
accurate it will be. Figure 17-2 shows the different variations of the SqueezeNet image
recognition model.

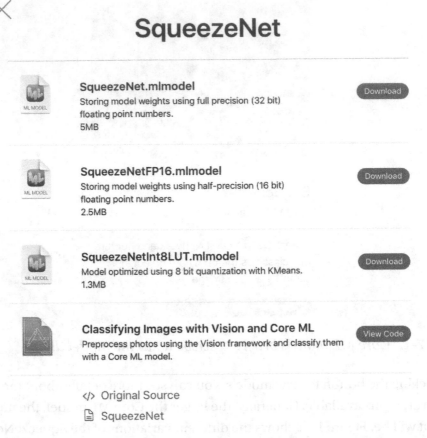

Figure 17-2. *Viewing details about Core ML models can define different file sizes*

Since the size of Core ML models can vary dramatically, you need to weigh the benefits of each model with its size. Adding 5 MB to the size of your iOS app may be reasonable, but adding 553.5 MB may not. There's often a trade-off between large file size and greater accuracy, but sometimes smaller models can outperform larger ones, so you may need to experiment with different models until you find the right one for your app that balances accuracy and file size.

Image Recognition

At the time of this writing, most of the Core ML models available on Apple's machine learning site focus on image recognition. This can work in two ways:

- Your app can load an image stored in the Photos app.

- Your app can view an item through the camera.

First, we'll start simple and add an image to an Xcode project. This will only allow us to recognize that single image hard-coded into the app, but it will let us focus on getting the Core ML model working within an app. Once we know the Core ML model works, we can focus on the nonmachine learning functions to retrieve an image from the Photos app or from the iPhone/iPad camera.

The first step is to download a Core ML model to your computer. Visit `https://developer.apple.com/machine-learning` and download the MobileNet and SqueezeNet models. Both models focus on image recognition, and both are fairly small in size. By experimenting with two different Core ML models, you can see how accurate both of them might be and how using any Core ML model works in similar ways.

The second step is to visit any search engine and look for images of any object such as a car, dog, computer, or bird. The exact image doesn't matter, but choose an image that has a blank background such as all white. By choosing an image that's isolated and not cluttered with other items, you'll improve the Core ML model's chance of recognizing it correctly.

Obviously, in real apps, you can't always choose pictures that are easiest for the Core ML model to identify, but for our purposes, we just want to get the Core ML model working to identify items in a picture. Once you have downloaded the Core ML models (SqueezeNet and MobileNet) and a single image of any object, you're ready to create the Xcode project to use machine learning.

To see how to use a Core ML file, follow these steps:

1. Create a new iOS App project and name it CoreMLImageApp.

2. Make sure you have downloaded the MobileNet and SqueezeNet models from Apple's website. Then drag and drop both of these models into the Navigator pane as shown in Figure 17-3. When a dialog appears, click the Finish button.

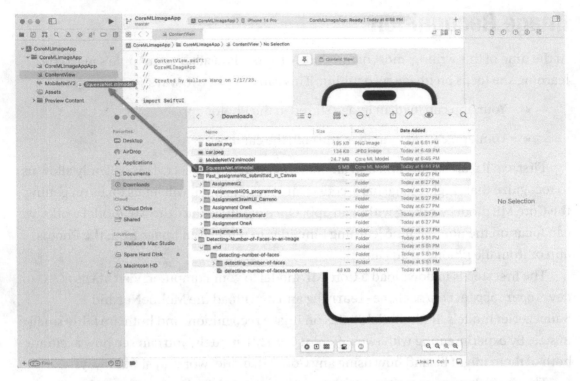

Figure 17-3. *Adding the MobileNet and SqueezeNet models to the Navigator pane*

3. Click the ContentView file in the Navigator pane.

4. Under the import UIKit line, add the following:

```
import CoreML
import Vision
```

The "import CoreML" line simply lets your project recognize
and use the Core ML model added to your project. The "import
Vision" line lets your project use the Vision framework for
recognizing items in an image.

5. Click the Assets folder.

6. Drag and drop several images into the Assets folder.

7. Drag and drop the same images into the Navigator pane, and when a dialog appears, click the Finish button. Make sure these image files have a descriptive name such as "cat.jpg" and that they have the same file extension such as .png or .jpg. Figure 17-4 shows several images stored in the Navigator pane.

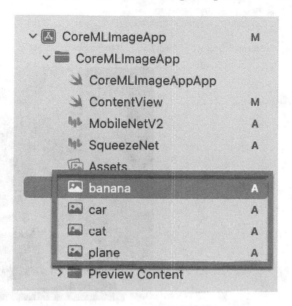

Figure 17-4. *Storing multiple images in the Navigator pane*

8. Click the MobileNetV2.mlmodel file in the Project navigator. The middle Xcode pane displays information about the machine learning model such as its authors and how it works.

9. Click the Preview tab. Xcode displays a box labeled Drag or Add Images to test the model's accuracy.

10. Drag and drop an image into the Drag or Add Images box. The Preview box displays the model's accuracy as shown in Figure 17-5.

Figure 17-5. *Previewing a model with an image*

11. Click the ContentView file in the Navigator pane.

12. Add the following State variables underneath the struct
    ContentView: View line:

```
@State var message = ""
@State var arrayIndex = 0
@State var image: UIImage = UIImage(named: "cat")!
```

The last State variable simply loads an image stored in the Assets folder, so make sure you replace "cat" with the name of an image you dragged and dropped into the Assets folder.

13. Add the following array underneath the State variables:

```
let photoArray = ["cat", "plane", "banana", "car"]
```

This array contains the names of all the images stored in the Assets folder. Make sure you change these names to the exact names of each image in the Assets folder.

Note   Your images must be referenced in three separate areas: in the Assets folder, in the Navigator pane, and by name in the photoArray.

---

14. Add a VStack with an Image, TextEditor, and Button inside like this:

```
VStack {
    Image(uiImage: image)
        .resizable()
        .aspectRatio(contentMode: .fit)
        .frame(width: 250, height: 250)
    TextEditor(text: $message)
        .padding()
    Button {
        useAI(sentImage: photoArray[arrayIndex])
    } label: {
        Text("Analyze Image")
    }.padding()
}
```

Notice that the Button calls a function called useAI, which we'll add later.

15. Underneath the Button, add an HStack with two Buttons like this:

```
HStack {
    Button {
        if arrayIndex == 0 {
            arrayIndex = photoArray.count - 1
        } else {
            arrayIndex -= 1
        }
        message = ""
        image = UIImage(named: photoArray[arrayIndex])!
    } label: {
        Image(systemName: "chevron.left.square.fill")
    }
    Button {
        if arrayIndex == photoArray.count - 1 {
            arrayIndex = 0
        } else {
            arrayIndex += 1
        }
        message = ""
        image = UIImage(named: photoArray[arrayIndex])!
    } label: {
        Image(systemName: "chevron.right.square.fill")
    }
}
```

These two Buttons display a left/right arrow that displays the previous or next item organized in photoArray. At this point, we've created the user interface. Now it's time to write Swift code. The machine learning model needs an image as input, so we need to identify the image file you added to your Xcode project. This involves two steps. First, you need to identify the file name, file extension of the image, and path of that image. Second, you need to store this information as a URL to give to the Core ML model.

To make the ModelNetV2 machine learning work, follow these steps:

1. Click the ContentView file in the Navigator pane.

2. Add the following function above the last curly bracket:

```
func useAI(sentImage: String) {

}
```

This function receives a string, which represents the name of the image to analyze.

3. Inside this useAI function, add the following:

```
guard let imagePath = Bundle.main.path(forResource: sentImage,
ofType: "jpg") else {
    message = "Image not found"
    return
}
let imageURL = NSURL.fileURL(withPath: imagePath)
```

This guard statement checks to make sure that the name of the image file sent to the function actually exists. Notice that this example checks for a .jpg file. If your images in the Assets folder are stored in the .png format, make sure you change "jpg" with "png".

If the guard statement determines that the image file exists, then it loads the location of that image file into the imageURL constant.

4. Add the following line under the previously added line in the function:

```
let modelFile = try? MobileNetV2(configuration:
MLModelConfiguration())
```

The "modelFile" constant can actually be any name you wish. MobileNetV2() identifies the MobileNetV2.mlmodel file added in your Xcode project. If you use a different Core ML model such as SqueezeNet.mlmodel, then you would replace "MobileNetV2" with "SqueezeNet".

Next, we need to tell your app to use the chosen Core ML model (identified by the "modelFile" constant) with the Vision framework. This means creating another constant with an arbitrary name (such as "model").

5. Add the following line under the previously added line in the function:

```
let model = try! VNCoreMLModel(for: modelFile.model)
```

Now the next step is to let the Core ML model examine the image. We already defined the image name, extension, and path in the "imageURL" constant, so we can use this to define an image request.

6. Add the following line under the previously added line in the viewDidLoad method:

```
let handler = VNImageRequestHandler(url: imageURL)
```

After requesting an image to examine, the next step is to request that your app actually use the Core ML model stored in the "model" constant. The Core ML model needs to examine the image and compare it to its trained data multiple times to maximize the chances of identifying it correctly. That means you need to request that the Core ML model run and provide it with a completion handler that defines what the Core ML model does when it identifies the image.

7. Add the following two lines under the previously added line in the viewDidLoad method:

```
let request = VNCoreMLRequest(model: model, completionHandler: findResults)
try! handler.perform([request])
```

The last step is to write the function for the completion handler, which is called "findResults".

8. Create a separate function in ContentView file as follows:

```swift
func findResults(request: VNRequest, error: Error?) {

}
```

This findResults function runs when the Core ML model examines an image. The first step for this findResults function is to make sure it can examine the image. If not, it needs to prevent the rest of its code from running. To check if the Core ML model can successfully examine an image, we can use a guard statement.

9. Add the following in the findResults function:

```swift
guard let results = request.results as?
[VNClassificationObservation] else {
    fatalError("Unable to get results")
}
```

Assuming that the Core ML model can examine the image, we need to keep track of its guesses with two variables that can be any arbitrary name.

10. Add the following in the findResults function:

```swift
var bestGuess = ""
var bestConfidence: VNConfidence = 0
```

The "bestGuess" variable will hold the Core ML model's current prediction of what it thinks the item in an image might be. The "bestConfidence" variable will hold the confidence level. Note that the "bestConfidence" variable must be defined as a VNConfidence data type, which holds a Float value.

Finally, we need a loop to exhaustively examine the image to determine the Core ML model's best guess of what that object might be. This loop assigns a confidence level and an identifier to the "bestConfidence" and "bestGuess" variables, respectively. Each time it comes across a prediction with a higher confidence level, it stores it in the "bestGuess" variable.

11.   Add the following in the findResults function:

```
for classification in results {
    if (classification.confidence > bestConfidence) {
        bestConfidence = classification.confidence
        bestGuess = classification.identifier
    }
}
```

Finally, after the loop has exhaustively searched through all possible predictions for what the item in the image might be, the loop stops and the "bestGuess" variable contains the guess, and the "bestConfidence" variable contains that confidence level. Now we need one last line of code to display this information in the label on the user interface.

12.   Add the following in the findResults function:

```
message = "Image is: \(bestGuess) with confidence \
(bestConfidence)) out of 1"
```

The entire ContentView file should look like this:

```
import SwiftUI
import CoreML
import Vision
struct ContentView: View {
    let photoArray = ["cat", "plane", "banana", "car"]
    @State var message = ""
    @State var arrayIndex = 0
    @State var image: UIImage = UIImage(named: "cat")!

    var body: some View {
        VStack {
            Image(uiImage: image)
                .resizable()
                .aspectRatio(contentMode: .fit)
                .frame(width: 250, height: 250)
            TextEditor(text: $message)
```

```
            .padding()
        Button {
            useAI(sentImage: photoArray[arrayIndex])
        } label: {
            Text("Analyze Image")
        }.padding()
        HStack {
            Button {
                if arrayIndex == 0 {
                    arrayIndex = photoArray.count - 1
                } else {
                    arrayIndex -= 1
                }
                message = ""
                image = UIImage(named: photoArray[arrayIndex])!
            } label: {
                Image(systemName: "chevron.left.square.fill")
            }
            Button {
                if arrayIndex == photoArray.count - 1 {
                    arrayIndex = 0
                } else {
                    arrayIndex += 1
                }
                message = ""
                image = UIImage(named: photoArray[arrayIndex])!
            } label: {
                Image(systemName: "chevron.right.square.fill")
            }
        }
    }
}
func useAI(sentImage: String) {
    guard let imagePath = Bundle.main.path(forResource:
    sentImage, ofType: "jpg") else {
        message = "Image not found"
```

```
            return
        }
        let imageURL = NSURL.fileURL(withPath: imagePath)

        let modelFile = try? MobileNetV2(configuration:
        MLModelConfiguration())
//      let modelFile = try? SqueezeNet(configuration:
        MLModelConfiguration())
        let model = try! VNCoreMLModel(for: modelFile!.model)
        let handler = VNImageRequestHandler(url: imageURL)

        let request = VNCoreMLRequest(model: model,
        completionHandler: findResults)
        try! handler.perform([request])
    }

    func findResults(request: VNRequest, error: Error?) {
        guard let results = request.results as?
        [VNClassificationObservation] else {
            fatalError("Unable to get results")
        }

        var bestGuess = ""
        var bestConfidence: VNConfidence = 0

        for classification in results {
            if (classification.confidence > bestConfidence) {
                bestConfidence = classification.confidence
                bestGuess = classification.identifier
            }
        }

        message = "Image is: \(bestGuess) with confidence \
        (bestConfidence)) out of 1"
    }

}
struct ContentView_Previews: PreviewProvider {
    static var previews: some View {
```

```
        ContentView()
    }
}
```

13. Click the Live icon on the Canvas pane. The simulated iOS screen appears, displaying the image you added to the image view along with the Core ML model's guess and confidence level of the image as shown in Figure 17-6.

Image is: tabby, tabby cat with confidence
0.40701234) out of 1

Analyze Image

Figure 17-6. *Recognizing an image using a Core ML model*

If you modify your project by adding a different Core ML model, you'll notice that each Core ML model identifies the same object in slightly different ways with different confidence levels. You can also try adding different images to the Assets folder and Navigator pane of your project such as images containing apples, trees, horses, or trains to see how accurately it identifies the displayed item. Machine learning models aren't perfect, but you can see that we've created an app that can identify items with very little coding. Instead, we've let a trained machine learning model do all the hard work of identifying items in an image.

Detecting Languages

While artificial intelligence often requires training a model and adding it to a project, Apple has provided various frameworks that offer artificial intelligence as well. One interesting framework is the NaturalLanguage framework (`https://developer.apple.com/documentation/naturallanguage`), which can identify languages based on examining one or more words. Rather than add a machine learning model to gain these features, we just need to import the NaturalLanguage framework into any project.

To see how to use the NaturalLanguage framework to detect languages, follow these steps:

1. Create a new iOS App project and name it LanguageApp.

2. Click the ContentView file in the Navigator pane.

3. Add the following underneath the import SwiftUI line:

   ```
   import NaturalLanguage
   ```

4. Add the following State variables underneath the struct ContentView: View line:

   ```
   @State var language = ""
   @State var message = ""
   ```

5. Add a VStack underneath the var body: some View line and add a TextField, Text, and Button like this:

```
VStack {
    TextField("Type foreign text here", text: $language)
        .disableAutocorrection(true)
        .padding()
    Text("Language = \(message)")
        .padding()
    Button {
        if let prediction = predictLanguage(text: language) {
            message = prediction
        }
    } label: {
        Text("Identify Language")
    }
}
```

Notice the .disableAutocorrect(true) modifier. We need to disable auto correction so we can type foreign words into the TextField without auto correct trying to change it.

6. Add the following function above the last curly bracket of the struct ContentView: View:

```
func predictLanguage(text: String) -> String? {
    let locale = Locale(identifier: "en")
    let recognizer = NLLanguageRecognizer()

    recognizer.processString(text)

    guard let language = recognizer.dominantLanguage else {
        return "Unknown language"
    }

    return locale.localizedString(forLanguageCode: language.
    rawValue)
}
```

This function accepts a string written in a specific language. Then we create an NLLanguageRecognizer object from the NaturalLanguage framework. This NLLanguageRecognizer uses the .processString(text) method to analyze the text, and then the guard statement uses the .dominantLanguage method to determine which language the user typed into the TextField. Finally, this function returns the actual language identified.

The entire ContentView file should look like this:

```swift
import SwiftUI
import NaturalLanguage

struct ContentView: View {
    @State var language = ""
    @State var message = ""
    var body: some View {
        VStack {
            TextField("Type foreign text here", text: $language)
                .disableAutocorrection(true)
                .padding()
            Text("Language = \(message)")
                .padding()
            Button {
                if let prediction = predictLanguage(text:
                language) {
                    message = prediction
                }
            } label: {
                Text("Identify Language")
            }
        }
    }
}
```

```
func predictLanguage(text: String) -> String? {
    let locale = Locale(identifier: "en")
    let recognizer = NLLanguageRecognizer()

    recognizer.processString(text)

    guard let language = recognizer.dominantLanguage else {
        return "Unknown language"
    }

    return locale.localizedString(forLanguageCode: language.
    rawValue)
    }
}

struct ContentView_Previews: PreviewProvider {
    static var previews: some View {
        ContentView()
    }
}
```

7. Click the Live icon in the Canvas pane.

8. Click in the TextField and type a word or sentence in another language. (You may want to use Google Translate to learn different types of words you can type in using another language.)

9. Click the Identify Language Button. The app displays the language it thinks you typed into the TextField as shown in Figure 17-7.

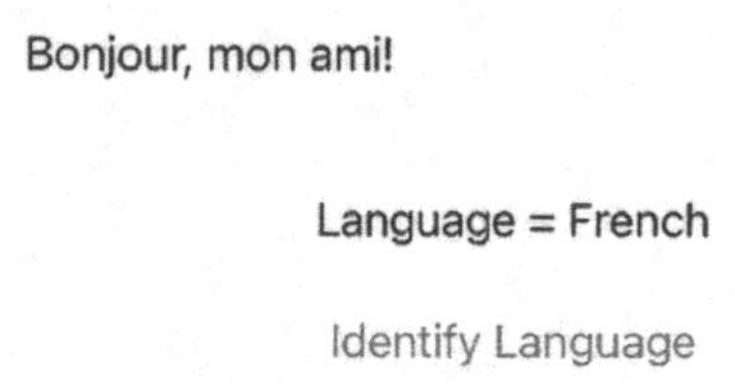

Bonjour, mon ami!

Language = French

Identify Language

Figure 17-7. *Identifying a language from typed text*

Summary

By adding artificial intelligence to your app, you can add additional features without writing a lot of code yourself. Core ML machine learning models can give your app the ability to recognize items in images, but they still have limitations in failing to recognize everything with perfect accuracy. Not all Core ML models are equal in accuracy or size, so you may need to experiment with different Core ML models until you find the one that works best with your app.

The main idea behind Core ML is that you can add the ability to deal with unknown data by simply using a trained machine learning model. Apple will continue adding new Core ML models that will likely offer different features beyond just image recognition. Over time, you'll be able to add these trained machine learning models to your apps and give your app artificial intelligence with little effort.

CHAPTER 18

Using Bottom Sheets

User interfaces need to present large amounts of information in a small amount of screen space. The most common solution is to divide a large user interface into multiple screens that can be linked together such as through a NavigationStack that lets users swipe between one screen to another or through a TabView that lets users jump from one screen to another by selecting an icon at the bottom of the screen.

One problem with both NavigationStacks and TabViews is that users can still only see one screen at a time. To get around this problem, SwiftUI offers bottom sheets that can appear at the bottom of a screen. Now the user has the option of either dismissing the bottom sheet altogether, viewing its information overlaid on top of another screen, or viewing the entire bottom sheet to fill up the entire screen as shown in Figure 18-1.

© Wallace Wang 2023
W. Wang, *Pro iPhone Development with SwiftUI*, https://doi.org/10.1007/978-1-4842-9544-1_18

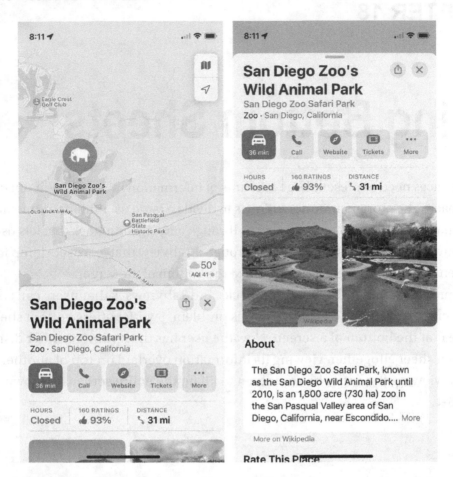

Figure 18-1. *Bottom sheets can appear partially on the screen or covering the entire screen*

In Figure 18-1, the bottom sheet partially covers the bottom of the screen. When pulled up to fill the entire screen, the bottom sheet provides more information. All of this information can then be pulled down completely to hide it from view.

Creating a Bottom Sheet

A bottom sheet can be any view from a simple Text or Image view to a complete user interface defined by a structure. To hide or display a bottom sheet, there must be a Boolean State variable that can toggle between true and false. When true, the bottom sheet appears. When false, the bottom sheet remains hidden.

Next, the bottom sheet must be attached to a view using the .sheet modifier like this:

```
.sheet(isPresented: $booleanStateVariable) {

}
```

The isPresented parameter uses a Boolean State variable to determine whether to display the bottom sheet (if the Boolean State variable is true) or to hide the bottom sheet (if the Boolean State variable is false).

The view that appears on the bottom sheet must be defined within the curly brackets of the .sheet modifier like this:

```
.sheet(isPresented: $booleanStateVariable) {
    Text("Just a Text view here")
        .presentationDetents([.medium, .large])
}
```

The .presentationDetents defines two ways the bottom sheet can appear. When first displayed, the first option (.medium in this example) defines how the bottom sheet first appears when its Boolean State variable is true. The second option (.large in this example) defines how the bottom sheet can appear next, where .large lets the bottom sheet fill the entire screen.

To see how to create a simple bottom sheet, follow these steps:

1. Create a new iOS App project and name it SimpleBottomSheetApp.

2. Click the ContentView file in the Navigator pane.

3. Add the following State variable underneath the struct ContentView like this:

    ```
    @State var flag = false
    ```

4. Modify the inside of the VStack like this:

    ```
    VStack {
        Toggle(isOn: $flag) {
            Text("Toggle me")
        }
    }.sheet(isPresented: $flag) {
    ```

```
Text("Just a Text view")
    .presentationDetents([.medium, .large])
}
```

The Toggle simply switches the Boolean State variable flag from true to false and vice versa. Then the .sheet modifier displays the bottom sheet when this Boolean State variable flag is true. The contents of the bottom sheet are defined by a single Text view ("Just a Text view").

Finally, the initial appearance of the bottom sheet is defined by .medium. Then its other appearance option is defined by .large, which allows the bottom sheet to expand to fill the entire screen. (If both options were identical such as [.medium, .medium], this would only display the bottom sheet to fill half the screen but would not allow the user to expand the bottom sheet to fill the entire screen.)

The entire ContentView file should look like this:

```
import SwiftUI

struct ContentView: View {
    @State var flag = false
    var body: some View {
        VStack {
            Toggle(isOn: $flag) {
                Text("Toggle me")
            }
        }.sheet(isPresented: $flag) {
            Text("Just a Text view")
                .presentationDetents([.medium, .large])
        }
    }
}

struct ContentView_Previews: PreviewProvider {
    static var previews: some View {
        ContentView()
    }
}
```

5. Click the Live icon in the Canvas pane. The bottom sheet remains hidden because the Boolean State variable flag is false.

6. Click the Toggle. The bottom sheet appears near the bottom, leaving part of the original screen visible as shown in Figure 18-2.

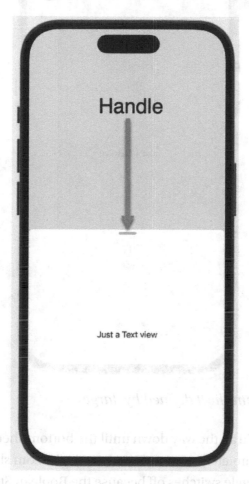

Figure 18-2. *The initial appearance of the bottom sheet defined by .medium*

7. Drag the handle in the top middle of the bottom sheet up. The bottom sheet expands to fill the entire screen as shown in Figure 18-3.

Just a Text view

Figure 18-3. *The bottom sheet defined by .large*

8. Drag the handle all the way down until the bottom sheet
    disappears completely. Notice that when the bottom sheet is
    hidden, the Toggle switches off because the Boolean State variable
    flag is now false.

Creating Custom-Sized Bottom Sheets

When you use the two defaults .medium and .large, the .medium option displays the
bottom sheet around half the height of the screen, while the .large option displays the
bottom sheet at the full height of the screen.

Since this choice between half height and full height might feel too restrictive, SwiftUI gives you three options for customizing the size of a bottom sheet:

- Fixed height

- Fraction of the screen height

- Custom height

Creating Fixed Height Bottom Sheets

A fixed height bottom sheet lets you define the height of the bottom sheet, measured in points. However, this means the bottom sheet always appears at this fixed height regardless of screen size. On a smaller iPhone SE screen, a fixed height might appear too tall, while on a much larger iPhone Pro Max screen, the same fixed height could appear too small.

To define a fixed height, simply replace .medium or .large with a .height followed by a numeric value measured in points such as

```
.height(175)
```

To see how to create a fixed height bottom sheet, follow these steps:

1. Create a new iOS App project and name it FixedHeightApp.

2. Click the ContentView file in the Navigator pane.

3. Add the following State variable underneath the struct ContentView like this:

   ```
   @State var flag = false
   ```

4. Modify the inside of the VStack like this:

   ```
   VStack {
       Toggle(isOn: $flag) {
           Text("Toggle me")
       }
   }.sheet(isPresented: $flag) {
       Text("Fixed height")
           .presentationDetents([.height(125), .height(455)])
   }
   ```

The entire ContentView file should look like this:

```
import SwiftUI

struct ContentView: View {
    @State var flag = false
    var body: some View {
        VStack {
            Toggle(isOn: $flag) {
                Text("Toggle me")
            }
        }.sheet(isPresented: $flag) {
            Text("Fixed height")
                .presentationDetents([.height(125), .height(455)])
        }
    }
}

struct ContentView_Previews: PreviewProvider {
    static var previews: some View {
        ContentView()
    }
}
```

5. Click the Live icon in the Canvas pane. The bottom sheet remains hidden because the Boolean State variable flag is false.

6. Click the Toggle. The bottom sheet appears near the bottom, defined by the fixed height of 125 points.

7. Drag the handle to expand the bottom sheet as high as it can go. Notice that this time the bottom sheet does not fill the entire screen because its height is fixed at 455 points.

Creating a Fractional Height Bottom Sheet

Rather than define a fixed height bottom sheet that may or may not look right on different screen sizes, SwiftUI also lets you define the height of the bottom sheet based on the fractional height of the screen size. By using a fractional height, the bottom sheet can adjust automatically based on the screen size of the iOS device that the app is running on.

To define a fractional height, simply replace .medium or .large with a .fraction followed by a numeric value measured in decimals that represents a percentage such as

```
.fraction(0.25)
```

The preceding code defines a fractional height of 25% of the screen height. By changing the numerical value, between 0 and 1, you can define different fractional heights.

To see how to create a fractional height bottom sheet, follow these steps:

1. Create a new iOS App project and name it FractionalHeightApp.

2. Click the ContentView file in the Navigator pane.

3. Add the following State variable underneath the struct ContentView like this:

    ```
    @State var flag = false
    ```

4. Modify the inside of the VStack like this:

    ```
    VStack {
        Toggle(isOn: $flag) {
            Text("Toggle me")
        }
    }.sheet(isPresented: $flag) {
        Text("Fractional height")
            .presentationDetents([.fraction(0.25), .fraction(0.85)])
    }
    ```

The entire ContentView file should look like this:

```swift
import SwiftUI

struct ContentView: View {
    @State var flag = false
    var body: some View {
        VStack {
            Toggle(isOn: $flag) {
                Text("Toggle me")
            }
        }.sheet(isPresented: $flag) {
            Text("Fractional height")
                .presentationDetents([.fraction(0.25),
                    .fraction(0.85)])
        }
    }
}

struct ContentView_Previews: PreviewProvider {
    static var previews: some View {
        ContentView()
    }
}
```

5. Click the Live icon in the Canvas pane. The bottom sheet remains hidden because the Boolean State variable flag is false.

6. Click the Toggle. The bottom sheet appears near the bottom, defined by the fractional height of 25% of the screen height.

7. Drag the handle to expand the bottom sheet as height as it can go. Notice that this time the bottom sheet does not fill the entire screen because its height is defined by the fractional height of 85% of the screen height.

Creating a Custom Height Bottom Sheet

Instead of defining a fixed height or a fractional height, a third option is to define custom heights where you can define two values:

- A minimum height

- A height based on a percentage of the screen height

By defining two values, SwiftUI will use the largest value. So if you define a minimum height of 400 and a 75% height of the screen, SwiftUI will compare which value is larger and then use that larger value. On some screens, the larger height might be 400 points, and on other screens, the 75% height might be the larger height.

To define a custom height, there are two steps. First, you must define a structure that conforms to CustomPresentationDetent. Within this structure, you define a minimum fixed height value and a percentage of the screen height:

```
struct InitialDetent: CustomPresentationDetent {
    static func height(in context: Context) -> CGFloat? {
        return max(20, context.maxDetentValue * 0.1)
    }
}
```

The preceding code defines a fixed minimum height of 20 points or a 10% height of the screen. Whichever value is larger will be the value used.

To see how to create a custom height bottom sheet, follow these steps:

1. Create a new iOS App project and name it CustomHeightApp.

2. Click the ContentView file in the Navigator pane.

3. Add the following State variable underneath the struct ContentView like this:

    ```
    @State var flag = false
    ```

4. Create the following two structures in between the struct ContentView and the struct ContentView_Previews structures like this:

    ```
    struct InitialDetent: CustomPresentationDetent {
        static func height(in context: Context) -> CGFloat? {
    ```

```
            return max(20, context.maxDetentValue * 0.1)
        }
    }

    struct ExpandedDetent: CustomPresentationDetent {
        static func height(in context: Context) -> CGFloat? {
            return max(70, context.maxDetentValue * 0.75)
        }
    }
```

The InitialDetent structure defines either a 20-point height or 10% screen height for the initial appearance of the bottom sheet. The ExpandedDetent structure defines either a 70-point or 75% screen height for the expanded appearance of the bottom sheet.

5. Modify the inside of the VStack like this:

```
VStack {
    Toggle(isOn: $flag) {
        Text("Toggle me")
    }
}.sheet(isPresented: $flag) {
    Text("Custom height")
        .presentationDetents([.custom(InitialDetent.self), .custom
        (ExpandedDetent.self)])
}
```

The entire ContentView file should look like this:

```
import SwiftUI

struct ContentView: View {
    @State var flag = false
    var body: some View {
        VStack {
            Toggle(isOn: $flag) {
                Text("Toggle me")
            }
        }.sheet(isPresented: $flag) {
```

```swift
        Text("Custom height")
            .presentationDetents([.custom(InitialDetent.self),
            .custom(ExpandedDetent.self)])
    }
    }
}

struct InitialDetent: CustomPresentationDetent {
    static func height(in context: Context) -> CGFloat? {
        return max(20, context.maxDetentValue * 0.1)
    }
}

struct ExpandedDetent: CustomPresentationDetent {
    static func height(in context: Context) -> CGFloat? {
        return max(70, context.maxDetentValue * 0.75)
    }
}

struct ContentView_Previews: PreviewProvider {
    static var previews: some View {
        ContentView()
    }
}
```

6. Click the Live icon in the Canvas pane. The bottom sheet remains hidden because the Boolean State variable flag is false.

7. Click the Toggle. The bottom sheet appears near the bottom, defined by either the fixed height of 20 points or 10% of the screen height.

8. Drag the handle to expand the bottom sheet as height as it can go. Notice that this time the bottom sheet does not fill the entire screen because its height is defined by either the fixed height of 70 points or 75% of the screen height. Experiment with different values and run the app on different iOS devices with smaller or larger screen sizes to see how the heights of the bottom sheets may change depending on the screen size.

Summary

Bottom sheets can be a handy way to provide additional information to the user. Although a bottom sheet can contain just a single view such as a Text view, it's far more common to display an entire structure containing multiple views such as text, images, and buttons (see Figure 18-1).

By default, the height of the bottom sheet appears about halfway up the screen and expands to fill the entire screen. You can define a fixed height for both values, a fractional height, or a custom height. You can even mix two different options such as a fixed height for the initial appearance of the bottom sheet and a fractional height for the expanded appearance of the bottom sheet.

Bottom sheets give apps another way to display information without forcing users to leave the current screen. By using bottom sheets, your app can provide useful information that's easy to display and hide at any time.

CHAPTER 19

Using ViewThatFits and AnyLayout

User interfaces need to adapt to different screen sizes and different orientations (landscape and portrait). SwiftUI can adapt easily to different screen sizes, but sometimes a user interface designed for portrait orientation looks odd when viewed in landscape orientation and vice versa.

Rather than compromise and try to design a less than optimal user interface that looks okay in both portrait and landscape orientations, it can be better to optimize two different user interfaces: one optimized for portrait orientation and one optimized for landscape orientation. While this can create extra work, it can also create a far better user interface experience for the user.

To help create the best user interface experience possible, SwiftUI offers two similar options called ViewThatFits and AnyLayout.

Using ViewThatFits

ViewThatFits is a new view that acts like a stack that can contain two different views. Based on the current orientation of an iOS device, ViewThatFits determines which view to display. That means you can create one view optimized for portrait (vertical) orientation and a second view optimized for landscape (horizontal) orientation.

ViewThatFits looks like this:

```
ViewThatFits {

}
```

© Wallace Wang 2023
W. Wang, *Pro iPhone Development with SwiftUI*, https://doi.org/10.1007/978-1-4842-9544-1_19

Within the ViewThatFits curly brackets, you can define two different views. The simplest views can be a single view like a Text view such as

```
ViewThatFits {
    Text ("Short text")
        .frame(width: 300, height: 500)

    Text ("This is a much longer example of text that fits in a
    longer amount of space.")
        .frame(width: 800, height: 500)
}
```

In portrait orientation, the preceding code would display the "Short text" Text view as shown in Figure 19-1.

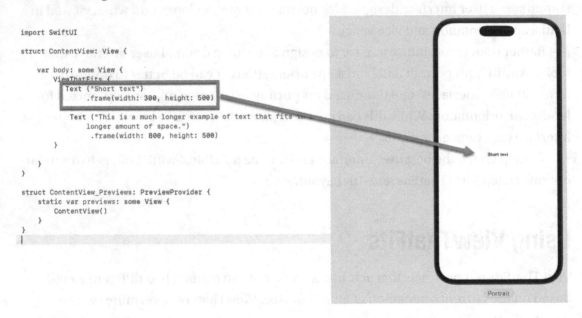

Figure 19-1. *ViewThatFits displays the short text in portrait orientation*

When the iOS device switches to landscape orientation, the ViewThatFits chooses the Text view displaying a large amount of text defined by a wider frame width (800) as shown in Figure 19-2.

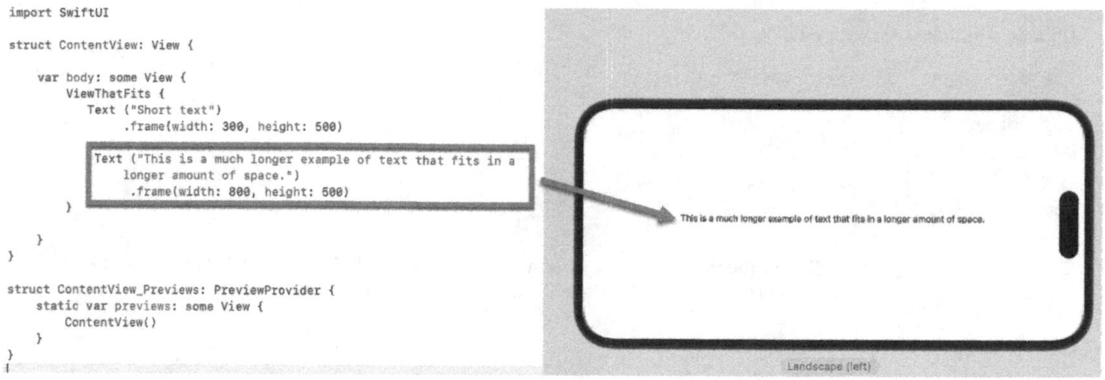

```
import SwiftUI

struct ContentView: View {

    var body: some View {
        ViewThatFits {
            Text ("Short text")
                .frame(width: 300, height: 500)

            Text ("This is a much longer example of text that fits in a
                longer amount of space.")
                .frame(width: 800, height: 500)
        }

    }
}

struct ContentView_Previews: PreviewProvider {
    static var previews: some View {
        ContentView()
    }
}
```

This is a much longer example of text that fits in a longer amount of space.

Landscape (left)

Figure 19-2. *ViewThatFits displays the wider Text view in landscape orientation*

To see how to use ViewThatFits to create custom portrait and landscape orientation user interfaces, follow these steps:

1. Create a new iOS App project and name it ViewThatFitsApp.

2. Click the ContentView file in the Navigator pane.

3. Edit the struct ContentView like this:

```
struct ContentView: View {
    var body: some View {
        ViewThatFits {
            VerticalView()
            HorizontalView()
        }
    }
}
```

This creates a ViewThatFits stack that contains two views called VerticalView and HorizontalView, which don't exist yet.

4. Choose File ➤ New ➤ File. A dialog appears as shown in Figure 19-3.

Figure 19-3.   *Choosing a SwiftUI View file*

5. Choose SwiftUI View and click Next. A dialog appears.

6. Type VerticalView for the file name and click Create.

7. Repeat steps 4–6 except name the SwiftUI View HorizontalView. You should have a VerticalView and HorizontalView files in the Navigator pane as shown in Figure 19-4.

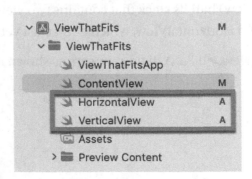

Figure 19-4.   *Displaying two SwiftUI Views in the Navigator pane*

8. Click the VerticalView file in the Navigator pane.

9. Edit the VerticalView file so the entire file looks like this:

```
import SwiftUI

struct VerticalView: View {
    var body: some View {
        VStack (spacing: 25){
            Rectangle()
                .frame(width: 250, height: 200)
                .foregroundColor(.red)

            Circle()
                .frame(width: 250, height: 200)
                .foregroundColor(.green)

            Capsule()
                .frame(width: 250, height: 200)
                .foregroundColor(.blue)

            Text("Vertical View")
                .font(.largeTitle)

        }.padding()
    }
}

struct VerticalView_Previews: PreviewProvider {
    static var previews: some View {
        VerticalView()
    }
}
```

This defines a vertically oriented user interface that displays a rectangle, a circle, a capsule, and a Text view stacked on top of each other as shown in Figure 19-5.

```
//

import SwiftUI

struct VerticalView: View {
    var body: some View {
        VStack (spacing: 25){
            Rectangle()
                .frame(width: 250, height: 200)
                .foregroundColor(.red)

            Circle()
                .frame(width: 250, height: 200)
                .foregroundColor(.green)

            Capsule()
                .frame(width: 250, height: 200)
                .foregroundColor(.blue)

            Text("Vertical View")
                .font(.largeTitle)

        }.padding()
    }
}

struct VerticalView_Previews: PreviewProvider {
    static var previews: some View {
        VerticalView()
    }
}
```

Figure 19-5. *The user interface defined by the VerticalView file*

10.   Click the HorizontalView file in the Navigator pane.

11.   Edit the HorizontalView file so the entire file looks like this:

```
import SwiftUI

struct HorizontalView: View {
    var body: some View {
        VStack {
            HStack (spacing: 25){
                Rectangle()
                    .frame(width: 250, height: 200)
                    .foregroundColor(.red)
```

```
        Circle()
            .frame(width: 250, height: 200)
            .foregroundColor(.green)

        Capsule()
            .frame(width: 250, height: 200)
            .foregroundColor(.blue)
    }.padding()

    Text("Horizontal View")
        .font(.largeTitle)
        }
    }
}

struct HorizontalView_Previews: PreviewProvider {
    static var previews: some View {
        HorizontalView()
    }
}
```

This defines a horizontally oriented user interface that displays
a rectangle, a circle, and a capsule side by side with a Text view
stacked underneath all of them as shown in Figure 19-6.

```
//

import SwiftUI

struct HorizontalView: View {
    var body: some View {
        VStack {
            HStack (spacing: 25){
                Rectangle()
                    .frame(width: 250, height: 200)
                    .foregroundColor(.red)

                Circle()
                    .frame(width: 250, height: 200)
                    .foregroundColor(.green)

                Capsule()
                    .frame(width: 250, height: 200)
                    .foregroundColor(.blue)
            }.padding()

            Text("Horizontal View")
                .font(.largeTitle)
        }
    }
}

struct HorizontalView_Previews: PreviewProvider {
    static var previews: some View {
        HorizontalView()
    }
}
```

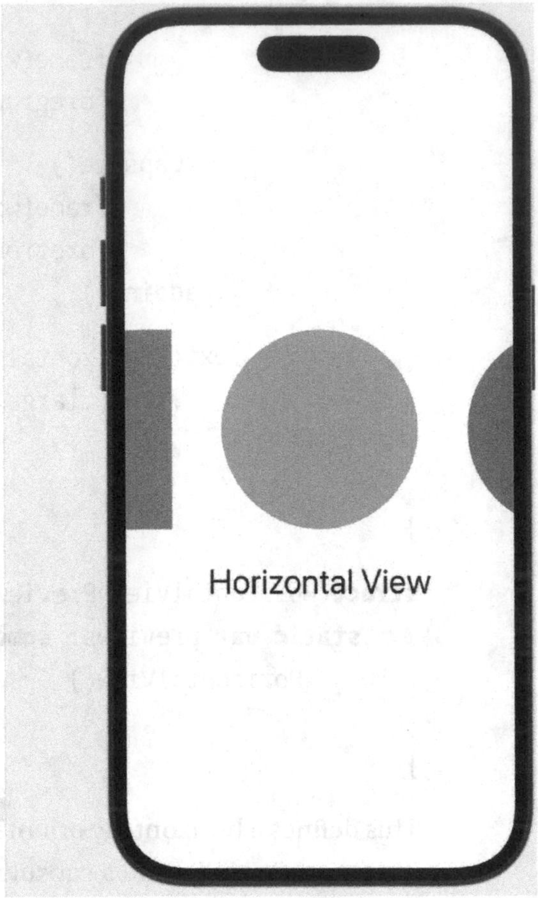

Horizontal View

Figure 19-6. *The user interface defined by the HorizontalView file*

Notice that the user interface defined by the HorizontalView file gets cut off on the left and right because it's not designed for portrait orientation.

12. Click the ContentView file in the Navigator pane.

13. Click the Live icon in the Canvas pane. Notice that in portrait orientation, the user interface displays the VerticalView as shown in Figure 19-7.

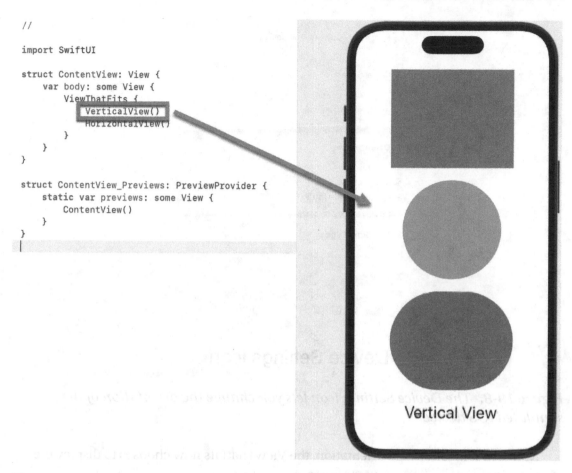

```
//

import SwiftUI

struct ContentView: View {
    var body: some View {
        ViewThatFits {
            VerticalView()
            HorizontalView()
        }
    }
}

struct ContentView_Previews: PreviewProvider {
    static var previews: some View {
        ContentView()
    }
}
```

Vertical View

Figure 19-7. *In portrait orientation, the ViewThatFits displays the VerticalView file*

14. Click the Device Settings icon and click the Orientation toggle to turn it on. Make sure one of the Landscape options' button is selected as shown in Figure 19-8.

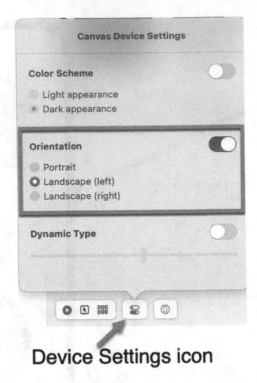

Device Settings icon

Figure 19-8. *The Device Settings icon lets you change the orientation of the simulated iOS device*

Notice that in landscape orientation, the ViewThatFits now chooses to display the HorizontalView file as shown in Figure 19-9.

```
import SwiftUI

struct ContentView: View {
    var body: some View {
        ViewThatFits {
            VerticalView()
            HorizontalView()
        }
    }
}

struct ContentView_Previews: PreviewProvider {
    static var previews: some View {
        ContentView()
    }
}
```

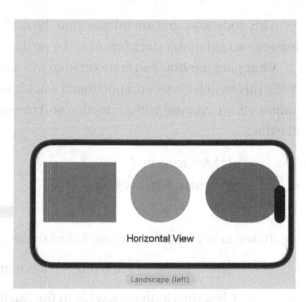

Figure 19-9. *The HorizontalView file appears in landscape orientation*

Using AnyLayout

AnyLayout lets you switch between a horizontal stack layout and a vertical stack layout. To use AnyLayout, you must first define a Boolean State variable like this:

```
@State var changeMe = false
```

Next, you must define an arbitrarily named constant that uses the Boolean State variable to switch between a horizontal stack and a vertical stack layout like this:

```
let myLayout = changeMe ? AnyLayout(HStackLayout()) :
AnyLayout(VStackLayout())
```

The preceding code says if the changeMe variable is true, use the HStackLayout. Otherwise, use the VStackLayout. Once we've defined this constant, we can use it within a VStack or an HStack like this:

```
VStack {
    myLayout {

    }
}.padding()
```

361

This code says that anything within the curly brackets of myLayout will change between a horizontal stack layout and a vertical stack layout.

Changing the Boolean State variable will automatically change the layout. To make this switch between a horizontal stack layout and a vertical stack layout appear animated, we can use withAnimation and change the Boolean State variable within like this:

```
withAnimation {
    changeMe.toggle()
}
```

To see how to use AnyLayout, follow these steps:

1. Create a new iOS App project and name it AnyLayoutApp.

2. Click the ContentView file in the Navigator pane.

3. Add the following State variable underneath the struct ContentView like this:

    ```
    @State var changeMe = false
    ```

4. Under the var body: some View line, define a horizontal stack layout and a vertical stack layout using AnyLayout like this:

    ```
    let myLayout = changeMe ? AnyLayout(HStackLayout()) :
    AnyLayout(VStackLayout())
    ```

5. Create a myLayout inside a VStack like this:

    ```
    VStack {
        myLayout {

        }
    }.padding()
    ```

6. Add a Button above the last curly bracket of the VStack but underneath the last curly bracket of myLayout like this:

    ```
    VStack {
        myLayout {

        }
    ```

```
Button("Change layout") {
    withAnimation {
        changeMe.toggle()
    }
}
}.padding()
```

This Button will change the changeMe Boolean State variable using withAnimation.

7. Add the following inside the myLayout curly brackets:

```
myLayout {
    Rectangle()
        .frame(width: changeMe ? 100 : 250, height: changeMe ?
        100 : 200)
        .foregroundColor(.red)

    Circle()
        .frame(width: changeMe ? 125 : 250, height: changeMe ?
        100 : 200)
        .foregroundColor(.green)

    Capsule()
        .frame(width: changeMe ? 125 : 250, height: changeMe ?
        100 : 200)
        .foregroundColor(.blue)
}
```

The entire ContentView file should look like this:

```
import SwiftUI

struct ContentView: View {
    @State var changeMe = false
    var body: some View {

        let myLayout = changeMe ? AnyLayout(HStackLayout()) :
        AnyLayout(VStackLayout())
```

```
        VStack {
            myLayout {
                Rectangle()
                    .frame(width: changeMe ? 100 : 250, height:
                    changeMe ? 100 : 200)
                    .foregroundColor(.red)

                Circle()
                    .frame(width: changeMe ? 125 : 250, height:
                    changeMe ? 100 : 200)
                    .foregroundColor(.green)

                Capsule()
                    .frame(width: changeMe ? 125 : 250, height:
                    changeMe ? 100 : 200)
                    .foregroundColor(.blue)
            }

            Button("Change layout") {
                withAnimation {
                    changeMe.toggle()
                }
            }
        }.padding()
    }
}

struct ContentView_Previews: PreviewProvider {
    static var previews: some View {
        ContentView()
    }
}
```

8. Click the Live icon on the Canvas pane. Because the Boolean
   State variable changeMe is initially set to false, the initial layout is
   VStackLayout. In addition, the width and height of the rectangle,
   circle, and capsule also use the second value listed within its
   .frame modifier. For example, the Capsule() uses a width of 250
   and a height of 200 as shown in Figure 19-10.

```
struct ContentView: View {
    @State var changeMe = false
    var body: some View {

        let myLayout = changeMe ? AnyLayout(HStackLayout()) :
            AnyLayout(VStackLayout())

        VStack {
            myLayout {
                Rectangle()
                    .frame(width: changeMe ? 100 : 250, height:
                        changeMe ? 100 : 200)
                    .foregroundColor(.red)

                Circle()
                    .frame(width: changeMe ? 125 : 250, height:
                        changeMe ? 100 : 200)
                    .foregroundColor(.green)

                Capsule()
                    .frame(width: changeMe ? 125 : 250, height:
                        changeMe ? 100 : 200)
                    .foregroundColor(.blue)
            }

            Button("Change layout") {
                withAnimation {
                    changeMe.toggle()
                }
            }
        }.padding()
    }
}

struct ContentView_Previews: PreviewProvider {
    static var previews: some View {
```

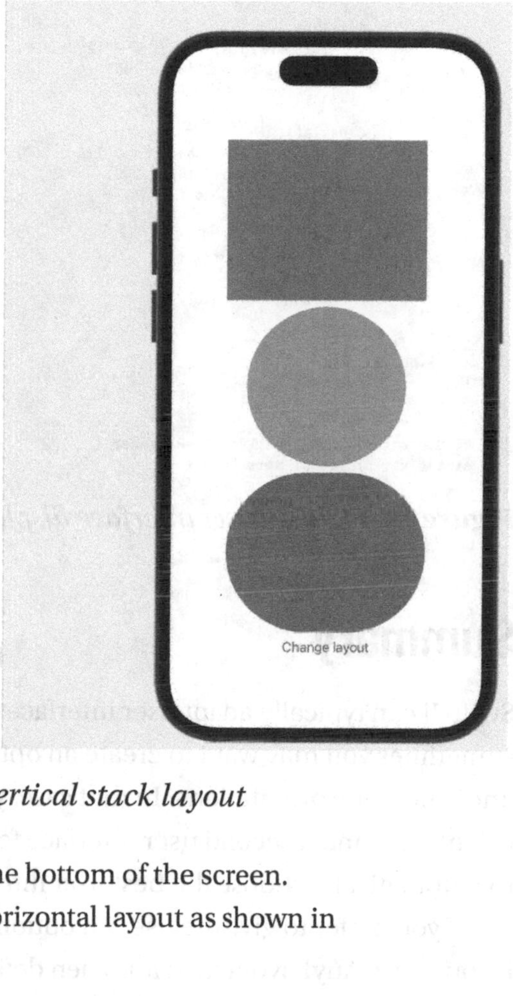

Change layout

Figure 19-10. *The initial appearance in a vertical stack layout*

9. Click the "Change layout" Button at the bottom of the screen.
   Notice that the layout switches to a horizontal layout as shown in
   Figure 19-11.

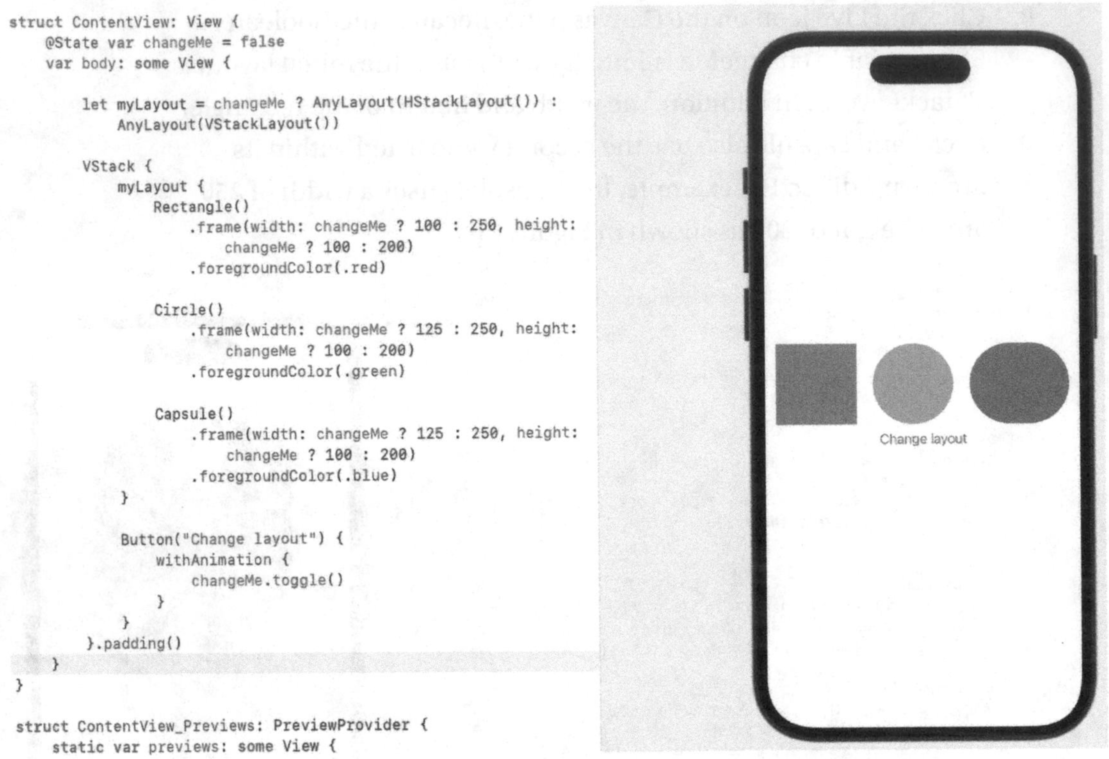

```
struct ContentView: View {
    @State var changeMe = false
    var body: some View {

        let myLayout = changeMe ? AnyLayout(HStackLayout()) :
            AnyLayout(VStackLayout())

        VStack {
            myLayout {
                Rectangle()
                    .frame(width: changeMe ? 100 : 250, height:
                        changeMe ? 100 : 200)
                    .foregroundColor(.red)

                Circle()
                    .frame(width: changeMe ? 125 : 250, height:
                        changeMe ? 100 : 200)
                    .foregroundColor(.green)

                Capsule()
                    .frame(width: changeMe ? 125 : 250, height:
                        changeMe ? 100 : 200)
                    .foregroundColor(.blue)
            }

            Button("Change layout") {
                withAnimation {
                    changeMe.toggle()
                }
            }
        }.padding()
    }
}

struct ContentView_Previews: PreviewProvider {
    static var previews: some View {
```

Figure 19-11. *The user interface displayed in a horizontal stack layout*

Summary

SwiftUI can typically adapt user interfaces to any screen size and orientation. However, sometimes you may want to create an optimized user interface for both portrait and landscape orientations. In that case, you can define a user interface for portrait orientation and a second user interface for landscape orientation and use ViewThatFits to automatically choose the best user interface for portrait or landscape orientation.

If you prefer to give the user an option to switch between vertical and horizontal layouts, use AnyLayout instead. Then define all the views that you want to alternate between vertical and horizontal layouts.

By using ViewThatFits and AnyLayout, you can create user interfaces that look best no matter what orientation of the iOS device the app runs on.

CHAPTER 20

Handling Errors

In a perfect world, you would write code, run it, and it would work exactly as you expected. Unfortunately, we don't live in a perfect world, and in our world, writing software is never simple and easy. In most cases, you'll write code that almost works, but not quite. Then the majority of your time will be spent trying to tweak your code to make it finally work the way you want.

When writing any type of software, always expect the unexpected. In other words, you can never anticipate all possible problems your program might face, but you have to plan for it anyway. Suppose your app needs to retrieve data from a server over the Internet. While your code may work perfectly well, there are so many unknown situations that are completely out of your control such as

- Is there even an Internet connection?

- Is the Internet connection reliable or does it lose data being sent and received?

- Is the server up and running that your app is trying to reach?

- Does the server have the data your app needs?

- Is the data in the right format that your app expects?

- What happens if the data takes too long to receive?

- Does your app knows how to accept and process data received from a server?

With so many unknowns to handle, you might write code that works perfectly well under ideal circumstances, but fails dramatically when one little thing goes wrong that's out of your control. Rather than let your app crash and frustrate the user, it's much better to write code that can handle all possible problems.

© Wallace Wang 2023
W. Wang, *Pro iPhone Development with SwiftUI*, https://doi.org/10.1007/978-1-4842-9544-1_20

Error handling doesn't necessarily mean that your code will be able to fix or avoid problems, but that your app won't crash or go haywire when an error does occur. Error handling lets your app deal with possible problems even though you may not even know what that problem might be. Essentially, error handling means your app will keep running and deal with errors gracefully.

Using the Guard Statement

Assume nothing will go right. Then write code from the perspective that every assumption you make will go wrong. By taking this mindset, you can write code that can anticipate possible problems and deal with them when (not if) they do occur.

Suppose your app needs to load an image to display on the user interface. The assumption is that the image will exist. If that assumption proves wrong, then your app will try to load a nonexistent image and wind up displaying nothing (at best) or crashing (at worse).

To check if something is true or not before continuing, Swift offers the guard statement, which is similar to an if-then statement. The purpose of a guard statement is to make it clear that your code is checking to make sure something is right before allowing the rest of your code to continue.

To see how to protect against errors, follow these steps:

1. Create a new iOS App project and name it GuardApp.

2. Click the ContentView file in the Navigator pane.

3. Drag and drop a picture into the Assets folder. In this example, the picture file is called "car.jpg" but you'll need to replace the code with the name of the picture file you added to the Assets folder.

4. Add the following State variable:

    ```
    @State var showImage: UIImage = UIImage(systemName: "photo")!
    ```

    This loads an SF Symbol image. Notice the exclamation mark at the end because the showImage variable is an optional variable since it's possible that it won't contain any image at all.

5. Add a VStack, Image, and Button underneath the var body: some
   View line like this:

```
VStack {
    Image(uiImage: showImage)
        .resizable()
        .scaledToFit()
        .frame(width: 300, height: 400)
    Button {
        getImage()
    } label: {
        Text("Add Picture")
    }
}
```

This displays an Image view to show pictures. When the user
clicks the Button, it calls a getImage function to retrieve an image.

6. Add the following function above the last curly bracket of the
   struct ContentView: View like this:

```
func getImage() {
    showImage = UIImage(named: "car")!
}
```

Notice that this function tries to load an image file stored in the
Assets folder called "car". The assumption is that the "car" image
file exists. The entire ContentView file should look like this:

```
import SwiftUI

struct ContentView: View {
    @State var showImage: UIImage = UIImage(systemName: "photo")!
    var body: some View {
        VStack {
            Image(uiImage: showImage)
                .resizable()
                .scaledToFit()
                .frame(width: 300, height: 400)
```

```
                    Button {
                        getImage()
                    } label: {
                        Text("Add Picture")
                    }
                }
            }
        func getImage() {
            showImage = UIImage(named: "car")!
        }
    }
}

struct ContentView_Previews: PreviewProvider {
    static var previews: some View {
        ContentView()
    }
}
```

7. Click the Live icon on the Canvas pane.

8. Click the Add Picture Button. Notice that the image you stored in
   the Assets folder appears on the user interface.

The last State variable simply loads an image stored in the Assets folder, so make
sure you replace "car" with the name of an image you dragged and dropped into the
Assets folder.

At this point, it's easy to assume your code works correctly, but the assumption is
that the proper image file exists. To see the problem with this assumption, change the
name of the image file to a nonexistent image file like this:

```
func getImage() {
    showImage = UIImage(named: "xyz")!
}
```

Click the Live icon on the Canvas pane and then click the Add Picture Button again.
Because the "xyz" image file does not exist, your app will crash as shown in Figure 20-1.

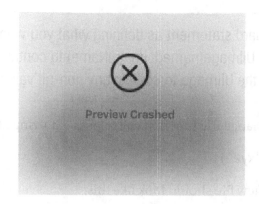

Figure 20-1. *An app will crash when it can't handle unexpected errors*

Ideally, your code should test if a particular image file exists before trying to load it. If it does not, then load a default image. Change the getImage function as follows:

```
func getImage() {
    if UIImage(named: "xyz") != nil {
        showImage = UIImage(named: "xyz")!
    } else {
        showImage = UIImage(systemName: "xmark.octagon.fill")!
    }
}
```

Although the preceding if-then statement works, it's not immediately obvious that this if-then statement is checking for possible problems. To make it clear that your code is checking or guarding against possible problems, it's better to use the guard statement instead.

The guard statement makes it blatantly obvious that it exists solely to guard against a possible error. Rewrite the getImage function as follows:

```
func getImage(imageName: String) {
    guard UIImage(named: imageName) != nil else {
        showImage = UIImage(systemName: "xmark.octagon.fill")!
        return
    }
    showImage = UIImage(named: imageName)!
}
```

> **Note**   Think of the guard statement as defining what you want. In the preceding example, we want the UIImage(named: imageName) to contain an actual file. In other words, we want the UIImage to contain any non-nil value.

You'll also need to change the function call to pass it a string like this:

```
getImage(imageName: "xyz")
```

The entire ContentView file should look like this:

```
import SwiftUI

struct ContentView: View {
    @State var showImage: UIImage = UIImage(systemName: "photo")!
    var body: some View {
        VStack {
            Image(uiImage: showImage)
                .resizable()
                .scaledToFit()
                .frame(width: 300, height: 400)
            Button {
                getImage(imageName: "xyz")
            } label: {
                Text("Add Picture")
            }
        }
    }

    func getImage(imageName: String) {
        guard UIImage(named: imageName) != nil else {
            showImage = UIImage(systemName: "xmark.octagon.fill")!
            return
        }
        showImage = UIImage(named: imageName)!
    }
}
```

```
struct ContentView_Previews: PreviewProvider {
    static var previews: some View {
        ContentView()
    }
}
```

Notice that the guard statement checks to see if it can load the image file or not. If not, then it loads the "xmark.octagon.fill" image instead and immediately stops the rest of the code in the function from running (return). However, if the image file does exist, the guard statement lets the rest of the code to run, which loads the image file to appear inside the Image view.

Guard statements are often used in the beginning of functions to check that the function received valid data before trying to run. By using guard statements to protect or guard against possible errors, you can reduce the chance that your app will crash when it doesn't receive expected data.

Using the Do-Try-Catch Statement

Another way to handle errors is to use a do-try-catch statement. Essentially, the do-try portion tries to run a command. If that command should fail for any reason, then one or more catch portions will handle the error. The simplest do-try-catch statement looks like this:

```
do {
    // try something here
} catch {
    // catch errors here
}
```

The try keyword calls a function defined with the throws keyword like this:

```
func someFunction() throws {

}
```

Once a function has been defined to throw an error, you can call that particular function using the try keyword like this:

```
try someFunction()
```

To catch errors, we need to create an enumeration that lists different types of problems that might occur. This enumeration must conform to the Error protocol so that it can return an error value from inside a function. A typical enumeration might look like this:

```
enum MajorProblems: Error {
    case divideByZero
    case noNegativeNumbersPlease
}
```

To see how to use the do-try-catch statement to catch possible errors, follow these steps:

1. Create a new iOS App project and name it ErrorApp.

2. Click the ContentView file in the Navigator pane.

3. Add the following State variables underneath the struct ContentView: View line:

```
@State var message = ""
@State var numeratorSlider: Float = 0.0
@State var denominatorSlider: Float = 0.0
```

   The last two State variables are Float data types because they represent the value of Sliders, which store values as Float data types.

4. Add a VStack underneath the var body: some View line and add two HStacks that contain a Text and a Slider view. Then add a Button and a Text view like this:

```
VStack {
    HStack {
        Text("Numerator = \(numeratorSlider)")
        Slider(value: $numeratorSlider, in: -20...20, step: 1.0)
    }
    HStack {
        Text("Denominator = \(denominatorSlider)")
        Slider(value: $denominatorSlider, in: -20...20, step: 1.0)
    }
```

```
Button {
    divideFunction(numerator: Double(numeratorSlider),
        denominator: Double(denominatorSlider))
} label: {
    Text("Divide")
}
Text(message)
}
```

The two HStacks display a Text view and a Slider side by side. Then the Button and Text view appear underneath as shown in Figure 20-2.

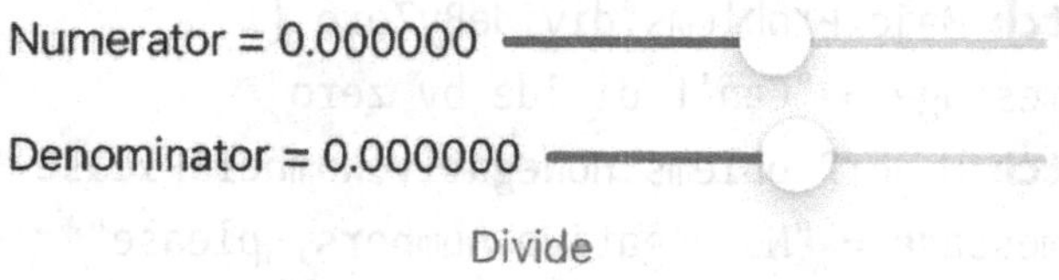

Numerator = 0.000000 ━━━━━━━⬤━━━━━

Denominator = 0.000000 ━━━━━━⬤━━━━━

Divide

Figure 20-2. *The user interface of the app*

5. Add the following function above the last curly bracket of the struct ContentView View.

```
func checkMe (top: Double, bottom: Double) throws {
    guard (bottom != 0) else {
        throw MajorProblems.divideByZero
    }

    guard (top > 0 && bottom > 0) else {
        throw MajorProblems.noNegativeNumbersPlease
    }
}
```

This function accepts two numbers (Double data types) and uses two guard statements. Notice that the function is defined by the throws keyword. That means to call this function, we'll need to use the try keyword. Inside this function are two guard statements.

The first guard statement checks to make sure the denominator (bottom) is not zero. If it is zero, then it throws the MajorProblems. divideByZero error. The second guard statement makes sure that both numbers are positive. If one or both are negative, then it throws the MajorProblems.noNegativeNumbersPlease error.

6. Add the following function above the last curly bracket of the struct ContentView: View:

```
func divideFunction (numerator: Double, denominator: Double) {
    do {
        try checkMe(top: numerator, bottom: denominator)
        message = "Answer = \(numerator / denominator)"
    } catch MajorProblems.divideByZero {
        message = "Can't divide by zero"
    } catch MajorProblems.noNegativeNumbersPlease {
        message = "No negative numbers, please"
    } catch {
        message = "Some other error occurred"
    }
}
```

This function uses the do-try-catch statement. The do portion contains two statements. The first uses the try keyword and calls the checkMe function, which is defined by the throws keyword. This checkMe function checks for possible errors. If it does not detect any errors, then it divides the two numbers (numerator and denominator) and stores the result in the message State variable.

Notice that there are multiple catch portions that catch all the errors defined by the MajorProblems enumeration. The catch MajorProblems.divideByZero looks for problems trying to divide by zero, while the catch MajorProblems. noNegativeNumbersPlease looks for negative numbers.

The last catch portion runs in case neither the division by zero nor negative number error runs. This catch portion will catch any problems that may not be foreseen ahead of time.

The entire ContentView file should look like this:

```swift
import SwiftUI

struct ContentView: View {

    @State var message = ""
    @State var numeratorSlider: Float = 0.0
    @State var denominatorSlider: Float = 0.0

    enum MajorProblems: Error {
        case divideByZero
        case noNegativeNumbersPlease
    }
    var body: some View {
        VStack {
            HStack {
                Text("Numerator = \(numeratorSlider)")
                Slider(value: $numeratorSlider, in: -20...20,
                    step: 1.0)
            }
            HStack {
                Text("Denominator = \(denominatorSlider)")
                Slider(value: $denominatorSlider, in: -20...20,
                    step: 1.0)
            }
            Button {
                divideFunction(numerator: Double(numeratorSlider),
                    denominator: Double(denominatorSlider))
            } label: {
                Text("Divide")
            }
            Text(message)
        }
    }
```

```swift
    func checkMe (top: Double, bottom: Double) throws {
        guard (bottom != 0) else {
            throw MajorProblems.divideByZero
        }

        guard (top > 0 && bottom > 0) else {
            throw MajorProblems.noNegativeNumbersPlease
        }
    }

    func divideFunction (numerator: Double, denominator: Double) {
        do {
            try checkMe(top: numerator, bottom: denominator)
            message = "Answer = \(numerator / denominator)"
        } catch MajorProblems.divideByZero {
            message = "Can't divide by zero"
        } catch MajorProblems.noNegativeNumbersPlease {
            message = "No negative numbers, please"
        } catch {
            message = "Some other error occurred"
        }
    }
}

struct ContentView_Previews: PreviewProvider {
    static var previews: some View {
        ContentView()
    }
}
```

7. Click the Live icon in the Canvas pane.

8. Drag the top slider (numerator) to a positive number.

9. Click the Divide Button. Notice that the message "Can't divide by zero" appears. That's because the MajorProblems.divideByZero error has been thrown by the checkMe function.

10. Drag the bottom slider (denominator) to a negative number and click the Divide Button. Notice that the message "No negative numbers, please" appears. That's because the MajorProblems. noNegativeNumbersPlease error has been thrown by the checkMe function.

11. Drag the two Sliders so they both represent a positive number and then click the Divide Button. Notice that the division now works as expected.

Using try? and try!

The try keyword is used to call a function within a do-catch statement. However, to simplify matters, you can eliminate the do-catch statement and call a function defined with the throws keyword by using the try? keyword instead.

The main difference is that the try? returns an optional value. Rather than use the clumsy do-try-catch statement, we can simplify the calling function like this:

```
func divideFunction (numerator: Double, denominator: Double) {
    if let answer = try? checkMe2(top: numerator, bottom:
    denominator) {
        message = "Answer = \(answer)"
    } else {
        message = "Error occurred"
    }
}
```

The preceding if let statement checks if the try? checkMe2 function returns a value. If so, then store that answer in the message State variable. If the checkMe2 function returns an optional, then display "Error occurred". To use the preceding code, the checkMe2 function needs to look like this:

```
func checkMe2 (top: Double, bottom: Double) throws -> Double {
    guard (bottom != 0) else {
        throw MajorProblems.errorOccurred
    }
```

```
    guard (top > 0 && bottom > 0) else {
        throw MajorProblems.errorOccurred
    }

    return top / bottom
}
```

Notice that the .errorOccurred is stored in the MajorProblems enum, which is now defined like this:

```
enum MajorProblems: Error {
    case errorOccurred
}
```

To see how to use the try? keyword, follow these steps:

1. Create a new iOS App project and name it TryApp.

2. Click the ContentView file in the Navigator pane.

3. Edit the ContentView file so it looks like this:

```
import SwiftUI

struct ContentView: View {

    @State var message = ""
    @State var numeratorSlider: Float = 0.0
    @State var denominatorSlider: Float = 0.0

    enum MajorProblems: Error {
        case errorOccurred
    }

    var body: some View {
        VStack {
            HStack {
                Text("Numerator = \(numeratorSlider)")
                Slider(value: $numeratorSlider, in: -20...20,
                step: 1.0)
            }
```

```
        HStack {
            Text("Denominator = \(denominatorSlider)")
            Slider(value: $denominatorSlider, in: -20...20,
            step: 1.0)
        }
        Button {
            divideFunction(numerator: Double(numeratorSlider),
            denominator: Double(denominatorSlider))
        } label: {
            Text("Divide")
        }
        Text(message)
    }
}

func checkMe2 (top: Double, bottom: Double) throws -> Double {
    guard (bottom != 0) else {
        throw MajorProblems.errorOccurred
    }

    guard (top > 0 && bottom > 0) else {
        throw MajorProblems.errorOccurred
    }

    return top / bottom
}

func divideFunction (numerator: Double, denominator: Double) {
    if let answer = try? checkMe2(top: numerator, bottom:
    denominator) {
        message = "Answer = \(answer)"
    } else {
        message = "Error occurred"
    }
}

}
```

```
struct ContentView_Previews: PreviewProvider {
    static var previews: some View {
        ContentView()
    }
}
```

4. Click the Live icon in the Canvas pane.

5. Drag the top slider (numerator) to a positive number.

6. Click the Divide Button. Notice that the message "Error occurred" appears. That's because the MajorProblems.divideByZero error has been thrown by the checkMe function.

7. Drag the bottom slider (denominator) to a negative number and click the Divide Button. Notice that the message "Error occurred" appears. That's because the MajorProblems. noNegativeNumbersPlease error has been thrown by the checkMe function.

8. Drag the two Sliders so they both represent a positive number and then click the Divide Button. Notice that the division now works as expected.

The try keyword must call a function within a do-catch statement. The try? keyword returns an optional variable. The third variation is the try! keyword.

Like try?, the try! keyword also returns an optional variable. However, the try! keyword unwraps that optional value without checking if it's nil or not. If it is a nil value, then the app will crash (see Figure 20-1). To see how the try! keyword works, edit the TryApp project with the following divideFunction:

```
func divideFunction (numerator: Double, denominator: Double) {
    let answer = try! checkMe2(top: numerator, bottom: denominator)
    message = "Answer = \(String(describing: answer))"
}
```

The preceding function will work as long as the denominator is not zero or both the numerator and denominator are positive. Otherwise, the try! keyword will crash if there's an error.

Since the try! keyword can be so dangerous, use it only if you're positive that there's no possibility of an error. Otherwise, use the try keyword within a do-try-catch statement, or use the try? keyword and check for an optional value.

Summary

Never assume that your program will receive the data it needs. Instead, always assume that you need to check for valid data at all times. By constantly checking to verify that your program receives the data it expects, you can minimize the chances that your app won't crash.

The simplest way to verify data is correct is to use an if-then statement. To make it clear that you're verifying data, it's better to use a guard statement, which works much like an if-then statement. With a guard statement, you define what type of data you want. If the guard statement fails, then it exits out of a function without running the rest of the function's code. This prevents possible crashes by trying to manipulate invalid data.

Yet another error handling method is to use the try keyword to call a function defined by the throws keyword. When calling a function that can throw an error, you must call that function within a do-try-catch statement where the catch portion can trap one or more possible errors.

To avoid using the do-try-catch statement, you can also use the try? keyword. If the try? keyword calls a function that throws an error, the try? keyword will retrieve an optional variable, which could be a nil value. Both the try and try? keywords help catch possible errors that could crash your app.

The try! keyword unwraps any optional variables, which could be dangerous if the optional value is nil. For that reason, use the try! keyword sparingly and rely on the try or try? keywords instead.

CHAPTER 21

Odds and Ends

The main purpose of writing a program in any language is to make the computer do something useful whether it's to retrieve data, calculate complex mathematical formulas, or just play a game. However, programming is more than just writing commands in a particular language syntax. Programming is really about thinking and problem solving.

When you write any program, you're revealing how you solve problems. There's generally a trade-off between clarity and efficiency. When you write clear, understandable code, it may take longer to type and take up more space. When you write efficient code, it's faster to type and takes up less space, but may not be as easy to understand.

As a general rule, strive for clarity first and efficiency second. That's because most programs are not just written once but modified multiple times often by different people. The easier your code is to understand, the easier it will be for someone else to modify or debug it.

Creating a Launch Screen

When many apps start, they can take a while to load. Rather than appear unresponsive, it's better to display a launch screen, which is often a short advertisement for the app by displaying the app's name, the developer's name, and graphic images that visually describe what the app does.

In SwiftUI, you can create a launch screen by following these steps:

- Add a Launch Screen file to your project.

- Define that file as the Launch Screen File.

- Modify that file to display what you want to appear.

© Wallace Wang 2023
W. Wang, *Pro iPhone Development with SwiftUI*, https://doi.org/10.1007/978-1-4842-9544-1_21

Note   You can only preview your app's launch screen by running it on the Simulator or on an actual iOS device. You cannot preview a launch screen in the Canvas pane.

A Launch Screen file is a storyboard file that lets you place items like text, images, and shapes on specific locations on an iOS screen. Since your app may appear on different size iPhone and iPad screens, the Launch Screen file uses something called constraints that align text (stored in a label) in the center of the screen. That way, no matter what iOS screen size your app runs on, it will always appear centered.

To see how to create a launch screen, follow these steps:

1. Create a new iOS App project and name it LaunchScreenApp.

2. Choose File ➤ New ➤ File. A dialog appears.

3. Choose Launch Screen under the User Interface category as shown in Figure 21-1.

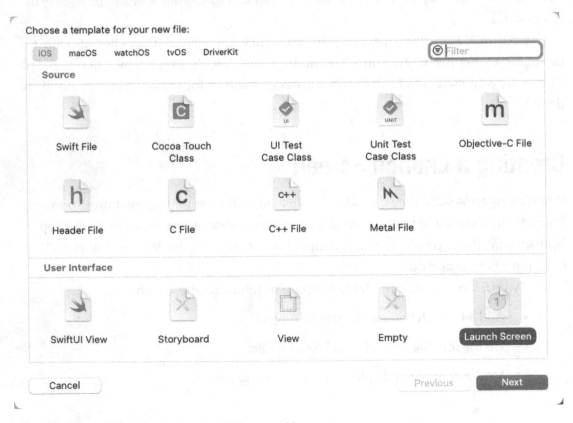

Figure 21-1. Creating a Launch Screen file

4.   Click Next. Another dialog appears letting you choose a name for your Launch Screen file and a location to save it.

5.   Keep the default name "Launch Screen" and click Create. Xcode adds your LaunchScreen storyboard file to the Navigator pane as shown in Figure 21-2.

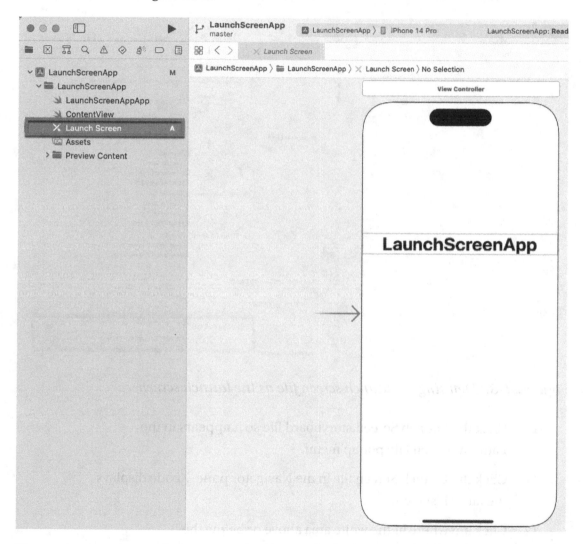

Figure 21-2.   *A Launch Screen file's appearance in the editor pane*

6.   Click the project name (LaunchScreenApp) at the top of the Navigator pane.

7.   Click the General tab.

8. Scroll down to the App Icons and Launch Screen category.

9. Click the Launch Screen File popup menu. A popup menu appears, listing all the valid launch screen files in your project, including the Launch Screen file you just created as shown in Figure 21-3.

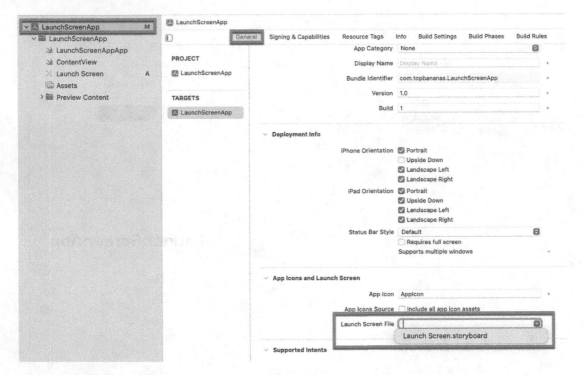

Figure 21-3. *Defining the launch screen file as the launch screen*

10. Click the Launch Screen.storyboard file so it appears in the Launch Screen File popup menu.

11. Click the Launch Screen file in the Navigator pane. Xcode displays the launch screen.

12. Click anywhere in the white area above or below the LaunchScreenApp text. An Inspector pane appears in the right side of the Xcode window as shown in Figure 21-4.

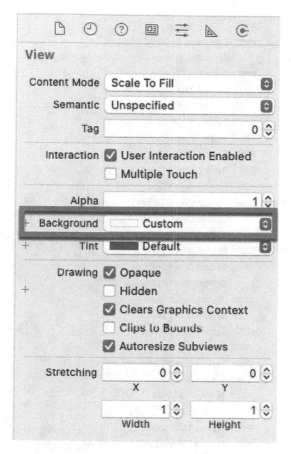

Figure 21-4. *The Inspector pane*

13. Click the Background popup menu. A popup menu of different colors appears as shown in Figure 21-5.

Figure 21-5. *The Background color popup menu*

14. Choose a distinctive color. Notice that the entire Launch Screen background changes to the color you selected.

15. Click the Run button or choose Product ➤ Run to run the app in the Simulator, or connect an iPhone or iPad to your Macintosh through its USB cable and make sure you choose your iPhone or iPad at the top of the Xcode window. The launch screen appears briefly before disappearing and displaying the ContentView.

Animating SF Symbol Icons with Color

Apple provides the free SF Symbols program (`https://developer.apple.com/sf-symbols/`) that provides hundreds of icons you can use in your SwiftUI projects. Besides displaying icons in your app, you can also animate them with colors. These simple animations just gradually color an icon from bottom to top, which can provide another way to show progress of a task.

To see how to animate an SF Symbol icon with color, follow these steps:

1. Make sure you have loaded the LaunchScreenApp in Xcode from the previous section.

2. Click the ContentView file in the Navigator pane.

3. Add the following State variable underneath the struct ContentView: View line:

   ```
   @State var value = 0.0
   ```

4. Modify the VStack to include an Image and a Slider like this:

```
VStack {
    Image(systemName: "wifi", variableValue: value)
        .font(.custom("", size: 125))
        .foregroundColor(.red)

    Slider(value: $value) {
    }
}
.font(.largeTitle)
```

The entire ContentView file should look like this:

```
import SwiftUI

struct ContentView : View{
    @State var value = 0.0
    var body: some View {
        VStack {
            Image(systemName: "wifi", variableValue: value)
                .font(.custom("", size: 125))
                .foregroundColor(.red)

            Slider(value: $value) {
            }
        }
        .font(.largeTitle)
    }
}

struct ContentView_Previews: PreviewProvider {
    static var previews: some View {
        ContentView()
    }
}
```

5. Click the Live icon in the Canvas pane.

6. Drag the Slider to the right. Notice that as you drag the Slider to the right (increasing the value that the Slider represents), the WiFi SF Symbol icon keeps highlighting in color as shown in Figure 21-6.

Figure 21-6. *Gradually changing the color of an SF Symbol icon*

Summary

A launch screen can help define your app's name, logo, and visual style as soon as the user starts it. Some developers like using launch screens to customize the appearance of their app, while others prefer not to use a launch screen, so decide what's best for your project.

SF Symbol icons can be handy to use to create standard icons without the need to create and design them yourself. By coloring an SF Symbol icon gradually, you can show progress. Such a minor change can make your app look distinctive and playful, which can increase a user's enjoyment.

Ultimately, the purpose of any app is to solve a problem, but subtle touches like gradually colored SF Symbol icons can make any app's user interface more enjoyable to use on a consistent basis.

Index

A

AnyLayout
ContentView file, 363, 364
horizontal/vertical stack layout, 361,
362, 366
steps, 362
vertical stack layout, 365
VStack, 361
Artificial intelligence (AI), 313, 315,
332, 336
Audio/video files
AVFoundation project, 242
ContentView file, 246
file formats, 241
navigator pane, 245
PlaySound file, 244
steps, 243
Swift file, 243
videos (*see* Video files)
web sites, 242

B

Bottom sheets
ContentView file, 340
custom heights, 347–349
customizing process, 343
fractional height, 345, 346
entire screen, 337, 338, 341, 342
fixed height sheet, 343, 344
NavigationStacks/TabViews, 337
screen view, 341

sheet modifier, 339
steps, 339
VStack file, 339

C

Closures
data, 54–56
func keyword, 49, 50
parameter, 52, 53
process information, 49
run option, 51
source code, 51
steps, 50
trailing data
advantages, 56–58
pass parameters, 58, 59
return values, 59, 60
value capturing, 54
Concurrency
asynchronous function, 84–88
await keyword, 86, 87
completion handlers, 85
processing information, 84
sequential processing risks, 83
time-consuming tasks, 83
user interface, 88–95
Core Data model
data model file, 108–113
definition, 107
entities/attributes, 107
existing project

© Wallace Wang 2023
W. Wang, *Pro iPhone Development with SwiftUI*, https://doi.org/10.1007/978-1-4842-9544-1

G

H, I, J, K

L

W, X, Y, Z

Printed in the United States
by Baker & Taylor Publisher Services